D0539434

Africa
Dances

GEOFFREY GORER

ELAND
London

First published by Faber and Faber in 1935
This edition first published by Eland,
61 Exmouth Market, London ECIR 4QL in 2003

© 1962 Geoffrey Gorer

ISBN 090787118 6

Cover designed by Robert Dalrymple
Cover photograph © Andy Gall

Text set in Great Britain by Antony Gray
Printed in Spain by GraphyCems, Navarra

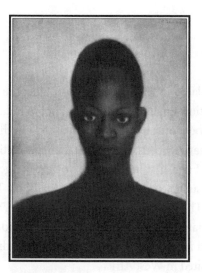

This book is dedicated
to
FÉRAL BENGA
before, during, and after,
to
FODÉ SANGHOR AND ALIOUNE DIOUF
companions on the journey,
to
KING ELY MANEL FALL
chef de canton de M'Bayar and
PRINCE JUSTIN AHO
chef de canton d'Oumbégamé,
and all the other people, both negro and European,
to whose help and kindness I hope the
following pages testify

Note

I have spelt the names of places in French possession after the local fashion, and not in the tradition English way: Ouidah, not Whidah (or Fida, as Bosman writes it); Abengourou, not Abenguru, etc. On the few occasions where I have used native words, I have spelt them phonetically, giving the consonants their English value and the vowels the general Italian value. In Book One such words are in Wolof, in Book Three in Ffon, or its derivatives. The one or two other words are Dioula (Sudanese). On occasion I have written about 'Africa' or 'negroes' to avoid clumsiness, but I do not intend any remarks to refer to any district or race except those that I visited in West Africa.

Contents

ITINERARY ONE

Introductory

M Y FRIEND PAVEL TCHELITCHEW had introduced himself to Féral
Benga after the latter's dance recital at the Théâtre des Champs
Elysées in the autumn of 1933. Benga had already made a reputation for
himself as a dancer at the Folies Bergères, a reputation that was enhanced
by the 'mystery' surrounding his private life – which being translated
into English from the Parisian meant that if he had love affairs they were
not known about and he was practically never seen in fashionable
houses or night clubs. On this negative foundation were built the most
fantastic legends; he was reputed to be extremely rich and impossible to
meet, either on account of his mythical vices – at one moment or
another every possible combination had been attributed to him – or of
the jealousy of whichever keeper rumour gave him at the moment.
Actually he was very shy, much distressed by the fact that because he was
a negro and a dancer everybody considered that they had a right, if not a
duty, to make sexual advances to him, and so poor that after the failure
of his dance recital he had barely enough to live on. For although his
dances in the recital had had enormous success, and the critics had been
uniformly and superlatively eulogistic, his associates had been laughed
off the stage and had refused to continue with the recitals projected for
the future; Benga had no money to continue alone.

Tchelitchew's enthusiasm for the dances had made him go and
congratulate Benga after the recital; but a certain courage was necessary –
for he believed implicitly in the legend – to invite him to visit him some
days later. However they got to know one another quite well and
Tchelitchew painted several portraits of him.

I was stopping for a few days in Paris on my way back from Morocco
in March, 1934, and Tchelitchew asked me if I would care to meet Benga.

11

I said I would very much like to, for though I had only seen him dance in the revues which did not give him sufficient scope I had much admired the verve and subtle pantomime of his performances; moreover I had never met a negro more than casually. In company with several others we had dinner and spent the evening together. Rather late in the evening Benga announced that he was shortly leaving for West Africa to study the native dances and if possible bring back a black ballet.

'How wonderful,' I said conversationally. 'I wish I could come too.'

'Well, why don't you?'

'I haven't the money.'

'It's going to cost practically nothing, beyond the fare out. Z, whom I'm going with, is working for the paper *Paris-Dakar*, and also for an advertising agency to link up the colonies and Paris; besides he's got all sorts of connections with the ministry of the colonies, so that the expedition will be officially sponsored.'

'What could I do in an expedition like that?'

'You'd be very useful as interpreter for the English colonies. Neither the editor of *Paris-Dakar* nor Z speak English, and they want to organise an exchange of articles with the English colonial papers. There would be plenty of room for you; where there's room for three there's room for four.'

I don't think anything more was said that night, nor did I take what had been said seriously. Things said at two o'clock in the morning are not meant to be taken that way. But when I met Benga a couple of days later, and in the afternoon, he took up the subject again. He had been serious.

The idea of the journey attracted me enormously, romantically. I knew nothing whatsoever about West Africa, beyond the fact that the English colonies were habitually referred to as 'white man's graves'; I had to consult an atlas to find out what countries could be so described, and even to find out the position of Dakar, the unavoidable port of arrival, and Benga's native town. My only palliation of this ignorance was a slight knowledge of, and great admiration for negro carvings, many of which I knew came from the Ivory Coast; some very fine and exciting photographs of negro dances and enthralled accounts of the private performances of West African dances that had been given at the French Colonial Exhibition in 1931 were an added inducement; otherwise my ideas of the region had been chiefly formed by films like *Trader Horn*. Of course I realised that there could not be quite such a profusion of the larger mammals and reptiles, but I should have been surprised if I had been told that I should travel about seven thousand miles without seeing any live wild animal larger than an antelope; I certainly expected the natives to be nearly if not quite naked.

I had travelled fairly extensively in Europe and in the countries bordering the Mediterranean – Palestine, Tunis, Algiers, Morocco – but I had never been anywhere where there wasn't some sort of hotel and my communication with and knowledge of the natives had therefore been slight and impersonal. I thought that travelling in the wilds in the company of natives would be novel, exhilarating, informative and good for me; 'roughing it' seemed to have some mysterious cathartic virtue, difficult to put into words but nevertheless definite. All the best authorities were agreed on that point. Actually I cannot see that three months of doing my own cooking and sleeping on a rug or a camp bed in insect-ridden huts has had in my case, or is likely to have in any case, much effect. But that is what 'roughing it' comes to. Except that most roughers don't do their own cooking.

The most attractive part of the whole scheme however to my mind was the idea of travelling with negroes; I hoped thereby to be able to see and learn many things which European travellers could not usually do, even, it was hoped, to penetrate into a convent of fetish worshippers which, it was said, no European had done. It was this idea which encouraged me in the face of numerous setbacks and disappointments, and eventually I did get into the convent; how much else I saw and did which Europeans usually do not do I cannot tell for I have read no books on the subject, either before or since, which would enable me to judge. I expected some awkwardness in the British colonies would result from my travelling with natives, an obvious lowering of prestige; but in the French colonies, in which most of our route was planned, I expected none; I believed that the French boast of treating natives and Europeans alike and the vaunted citizenship they had granted to the natives counted for something.

I did not immediately consciously decide to go, but spent much time discussing the project, firstly in Paris, and then, when I found hotel life too expensive, at home in London. Benga accepted my invitation with many qualms, for his position in Paris was rather like that of the fashionable divorceé in the nineteenth century: a person whom it was chic to be seen with in the right places, but whom one did not invite to the house; a person moreover whom one did not always recognise in public, should it be compromising to one's companions. I was not conscious of this at the time, for I found him an agreeable and amusing companion, and very quickly forgot that he was coloured, forgot to such an extent that I did not even consider the possibility of prejudice in others. I had no previous experience of negroes which could have guided me, and beyond the difficulty of age I have no automatic feeling about differences of race or class. We talked French.

Whatever the faults of Englishmen may be they are as a race polite. My family, my friends, and even the servants treated Benga as they would have any other guest of mine; he was not overtly stared at in the streets, or in any way distinguished or slighted in hotels or theatres; even the village children in Somerset kept their curiosity within reasonable bounds. Benga was delighted and astounded at such an experience, quite unparalleled during the ten years of his life in Europe. During his stay with me I had an attack of flu, and his behaviour while I was laid up convinced me that he would be a very good travelling companion. Z wrote that the editor of *Paris-Dakar* was delighted that I should be accompanying them, and that all land expenses were already guaranteed. So when he returned to Paris I arranged to follow a fortnight later, with the intention of staying there a couple of days before taking the boat. In the interval I would make my preparations.

These were unexpectedly painful. My brother who was working at the Lister Institute arranged for me to be immunised against typhoid, paratyphoid, plague, cholera, and yellow fever. The last operation was performed by Dr Finlay of the Welcome Institute; the method is a new one and still in the experimental stage; if it is successful, and all the indications seem to point that way, probably the greatest danger of life in the tropics is removed. The result of these various injections was that I felt permanently ill during the whole fortnight, and bought clothes with even less enthusiasm than usual. These consisted chiefly of short-sleeved shirts, riding breeches and Newmarket boots 'to guard against the bites of snakes'. For all the snakes I saw I might as well have worn iron anklets. I had been lent Paul Morand's extremely misleading *Paris Timbuctoo*, and following his advice I bought a chemical ice-making machine, which was never used for its proper purpose, and a large selection of objects from Woolworth's, believing his assertion (completely incorrect, as far as my experience goes) that they were necessary as money had no value in the interior. Despite the advice of most of my friends I did not get any firearms, chiefly because I did not know how to use them, and thought that they would disconcert me far more than any hostile person or animal, and also to avoid difficulties at the customs. I also bought a camera.

This was for me an almost revolutionary act. I have never owned nor wanted to own one. When I have been in the company of photographers I have always considered them social nuisances. It has been an axiom of mine that nine out of ten subjects photographed have already been better reproduced by professional postcard makers. The souvenir snapshot I detest. I have a good visual memory and prefer the distortions my mind may produce to the flat and colourless memory-joggers of the camera. I do not like living in my own past, however pleasant it may once have been; the snows of yesteryear are where they belong. In short I do not like cameras.

But now the case was different. I owed it to myself, to friends, to bring back some records of so strange an adventure (I was still thinking in terms of *Trader Horn*). I was taking my typewriter and intended to keep a very full diary – indeed I did do so, writing every day, sometimes two or three times a day. But I have never been good at descriptive writing, and for such subjects as dancing, ritual and landscape a photographic record would be far more vivid than any painfully written description. So I explained my requirements to an expert, and shortly found myself the embarrassed possessor of a second-hand reflex Mentor camera, six double-dark slides for holding the plates – I had been told to get plates as the tropical heat destroyed films. I afterwards found that everyone in West Africa used film cameras – a changing bag, and about a hundred-weight of plates in little tin boxes. The apparatus was said to be as good as anyone could wish. The timing and focusing were controlled by four nasty little knobs.

This instrument, with its adjuncts, became the curse of my life from the moment I acquired it. It was abominably heavy and awkward to cart around; it was so big that it was impossible to disguise, and therefore useless on the many occasions when photos needed to be taken secretly. It went wrong twice and had to be costlily and amateurishly repaired. Every dozen photographs meant half an hour of exquisite discomfort, sitting with my hands encased in the changing bag, my wrists cut with the elastic, my hands getting continually stickier and clumsier as I fumbled with the plates (only to be held by the edges), the slides and the packing. In hot places my hands seemed to become deliquescent blocks of sweat before the operation was through. The plates were so heavy that they nearly broke the luggage carrier of the car, as well as the backs of the unfortunate people who had to carry the trunk they were in. I had to pay heavy duty for taking them into the French colonies, which is perhaps understandable, but I also had to pay duty for bringing them back into England to be developed, although I had taken all precautions against such a possibility; to the mind of an English custom official a plate which has been exposed to the light for a fraction of a second is thereby completely altered, becomes a new article on which a 25 per cent *ad valorem* duty must be charged. When the plates were developed I was told that a number of them had been affected by the heat; films would have been more suitable.

The camera was not altogether without its uses. Negroes loved look-ing into the reflex mirror, especially when I altered the focus, and it proved a very useful method of getting acquainted and gaining their confidence. I used to explain to one of the people by me, usually the village chief, how to look into the reflex; after a moment of puzzled wonder he would see clearly and laugh – laughter is used by the negro to express surprise, wonder, embarrassment and even discomfiture; it is not necessarily, or even often, a sign of amusement; the significance given to 'black laughter' is due to the mistake of supposing that similar symbols have identical meanings – and then explain what he had seen to those around him. At which there would immediately be such a crowd round me that I could barely keep my balance and no one could see anything at all; after I had pushed them about and sorted them out so that each could see properly from behind (many would stand in front of the lens and peer down) we had been in much too close contact to be strangers any longer. As I would not let them handle the camera they would often throw an arm round my neck and push their skull into my chin in an effort to burrow more deeply into the instrument. I rather enjoyed it.

It is always said that negroes smell unpleasantly. When they sweat they undoubtedly do emit a rather pungent catlike smell, but I cannot see that it is essentially more disagreeable than the acrid sour-milk sweat of Europeans. To my nose a cup-final crowd smells both nastier and stronger than any crowd of negroes with which I have been in contact. This is probably due to the sanitation of the houses from which the football enthusiasts come, and the expense and labour of washing clothes. Except in places where water is short all the negroes I came in contact with bathed two or three times daily and washed their clothes, if they wore them, frequently. The chief exceptions to this rule were missionary converts who wore shoddy European clothes, not strong enough to stand the pounding on rocks which is the principal part of negro laundry. The Cabrai, the only race I met which goes completely naked, anoint themselves with palm oil after every bathe.

The camera was also useful for bribing. I would promise the chiefs that if they did what I wanted – arranged a dance or a ritual – I would present them with a framed enlargement of themselves or any other subject they would choose. A number of them wished to have their caparisoned horse photographed; a few a favourite wife.

I also used it to create a false impression. It looked so extremely professional that I was able to persuade obstreperous administrators and chiefs that I was preparing a film scenario. Fodé, one of the chauffeurs, caught on to this story and used to explain that I was going back to Paris and would return in a few months with a large film unit that would come and stop for several days and spend a lot of money in the village, if what they had to show was worthwhile. I don't know if he believed this story himself but it was very successful.

Despite these accidental uses the camera was the most constantly unpleasant aspect of the journey. I had not the strength of mind to throw it away, or even to pack it in the luggage; conscientiously and miserably I would change plates daily, sometimes two or three times a day.

With all this impedimenta I left for Paris, expecting that everything would be so far advanced that I would just have time to get the camping equipment in Paris – it was cheaper there, and Benga, being Parisian, naturally knew how to get a reduction; no self-respecting Frenchman ever pays the proper price for anything – before the next boat left in three days. I was surprised to find that nothing definite had been done at all. Z it was true had seen lots of people; the most admirable schemes were on the point of realisation; not only was the journey being paid for, we would even gain money; the contract was going to be signed tomorrow. Or perhaps the day after.

As far as I know no contract ever was actually signed. When Z had written that all land expenses were guaranteed they had been, nearly; it was so certain to be true before the letter arrived that it had not been worthwhile making any proviso. He had been dealing with people for many months, one scheme after another being developed; and although each had fallen through at the last moment the next would surely be successful. Neither I nor Benga knew this at the time.

Z's story is a fairly good and typical example of the life of the Europeanised negro. He was the son of respectable petit-bourgeois negro parents and was born at Grand Popo, on the coast of Dahomey. He was educated by Catholic missionaries and after doing very well at his school he studied law for a little and became clerk of the court, or some equivalent post, at the assizes at Cotonou. After some years he left this and got a post in the Dahomey bank; when this bank opened an office in Paris he was transferred there. He spoke and wrote perfectly correct but very florid French. From the bank's proximity to and connection with the Bourse he was able to get some good tips and during the French currency fluctuations amassed about a million francs. With this capital he retired and lived for a while in great style. He returned to Africa and bought a banana plantation in Guinea; but as he did not wish to forgo the delights of Europe he entrusted its administration to an unknown European, with the result that both the plantation and the capital disappeared in six months. He did not revisit his home or family. The charitable explanation given by his parents for this was that he had had the clan marks – three small parallel scars on each cheek – removed, and was ashamed to appear home in such a condition. Certainly the marks were very faint. On his return he lived a life of leisured luxury until his capital was nearly gone, when in partnership with another European he formed a company for the exploitation of a toothpaste which incorporated the astringent juices of the twigs which the negroes chew constantly as a method of keeping their teeth white. They had not sufficient capital to make a success of this. Then Z took up freelance journalism, doing fairly well, for he had an extensive and influential collection of acquaintances; but he got constantly poorer, for when he had money he spent it on anything which would make a splash; he was chronically unpunctual, so that he often missed appointments and opportunities; and he was constantly spending time elaborating various get-rich-quick schemes, of which some may have been practical, but which none of them came to anything. The last of these was the Franco-colonial advertising agency in which we were involved. During the winter of 1933–4 he had been practically without money and without possessions. This did not seem to distress him, however, for he was living quite happily on his friends and acquaintances, wearing Benga's clothes and doing well on a hard-luck story. At the time of his affluence he had become engaged to a respectable young French girl, and though with changed circumstances both he and the girl's parents would have liked the match broken up, the girl insisted on its continuance. This always shocked Benga who disapproved of mixed marriages.

Africa Dances

I have not gone into so much detail entirely out of malice. In several points the story is representative of the evolution of many Europeanised Africans; distrusting and despising their own race is very general, as also is ostentatious extravagance and a rather exaggerated parody of European behaviour; the egocentricity, the lack of time sense, and the blind belief that something is bound to turn up are practically universal among negroes whose traditional way of life has been destroyed. The sexual success with white women is in Europe as far as I know practically confined to France, or rather Paris; in the rest of Europe it is considered at any rate eccentric for a woman to have a negro lover; in certain circles in Paris it is definitely chic. This, a successful negro explained to me, was due to their reputed greater development, and also to the fact that a negro, when not stimulated can continue almost indefinitely. The same informant told me that white women were not exciting, they were amorously so incompetent. He should know what he was talking about for he earned his living by exploiting his talents. He preferred it to clerking, but not much.

When I realised that neither Z nor the editor of *Paris-Dakar* – a young man playing so frantically at big business that he was almost permanently in an aeroplane going somewhere else – were to be depended on, I was faced with the choice of returning home, or of continuing by my own efforts. I decided against the former course on several grounds, of which perhaps the chief was the notion that I would look extremely silly in such a situation; I was also influenced by the fact that I had already spent considerable time and money which, should I return, would be completely wasted; moreover there were considerable hopes of help in Dakar; Benga knew a number of people in the administration, and his prospective brother-in-law owned a small lorry in which we could probably travel very cheaply.

Thus resolved, we purchased the minimum of equipment – camp beds with mosquito nets, folding chairs and table, cooking utensils and a lamp and stove which burned petrol – and took third-class tickets on the *Mendoza*, a French boat on the South American line which called at Dakar. As a matter of fact the class in which we travelled was called 'Deuxième Economique'. But that was merely done to comfort us.

Introductory

The ship was small and old-fashioned, in its upper classes nearly empty. In the second class were a number of nuns and priests on their way to a eucharistic congress at Buenos Aires. In our class there were to start with only three other passengers: a non-commissioned officer returning to his work in the topographical section of the Sudanese army, a young Brazilian student who had been studying for the Church at Lausanne, but who had later decided that he had not really a vocation, though profoundly religious, and had then proceeded to pick up inadequate smatterings of various knowledge, and lastly a middle-aged woman of uncertain nationality – she claimed at different times to be French, Spanish, half Martiniquais and Jewish – and doubtful profession. She had only one subject of thought or conversation and was extremely out-spoken; our single sitting- and dining-room in the evenings took on more and more the atmosphere of the anteroom of a brothel; Mrs Warren, as I had possibly rather maliciously nicknamed her, felt thoroughly at home. She used to tease the young Brazilian outrageously, but he did not understand her very much. After the boat had stopped at Barcelona she explained with great glee and fulsome detail how a taxi chauffeur had taken her to an extremely louche cabaret. I asked her if she had merely said 'Home, James' to the chauffeur. She was not offended. The young Brazilian spent most of his time with the priests in the second class. He was able to assist daily in the celebration of mass, so he had his fun.

After Barcelona we had several more passengers. A fat Spanish musician and his very thin French wife were returning to the colonies. Between them they played on a very large number of instruments, and earned their living by acting as orchestra in the principal cafés of the smaller capitals of the French colonies. They had been doing this for a number of years and intended to continue doing so. As representatives of the arts they felt themselves a cut above the rest of us and kept themselves as far as possible to themselves. There arrived also a Polish Jewess and a French-woman with three small children from the steerage.

In so far as the line was a paying proposition it was on account of the emigrants. Nearly two hundred of these wretched creatures had come on board at Genoa, chiefly Poles, Germans and Italians, setting out for the various South American states in the hope of finding work. During the month's journey they were herded between decks, their allotted space separated from the holds and the more select parts of the same deck by long wooden rails, crowded by day and night, and fed like prisoners. On their arrival at Rio or Buenos Aires they would be housed in the Immigrant hostels; if by the end of a month they had not found work – and unemployment was very severe in the Argentine and Brazil – they would be repatriated. They seemed to me very tragic; they had so little hope. But the young people were sure that they at any rate would find something; they had friends, letters of introduction; things were bound to be better than at home. The numerous children played and screamed all day long; the old people sat about looking at nothing. There were several complete families, with three generations represented; they were mostly Poles. The Italians formed a group apart, doubtless on account of the difficulty of communication, for few of them knew German which was the commonest language; I learned from one of them that they are forced to join the local fascio of the country in which they settle, or otherwise they would be prevented from keeping any work, if worse did not happen to them.

The Polish Jewess got into our class by complaining to the interpreter who was responsible for good order among the emigrants that people were trying to rape her. She was then given a cabin with three other women and complained that their filthy conversation and habits prevented her sleeping or working. She was then given a cabin alone and complained that people spied on her through the wire grating which ran along the top. I imagine that before the journey was over she was in the first class. The girl was completely obsessed by sex, doing her utmost to provoke every man on board, getting indignant if they responded to her allurements and furious if they did not. She had been trained as a dispensing chemist and was going to take up a post in Brazil; she was slightly educated and musical and was very superior about the other passengers. She succeeded in getting the good opinion of the Brazilian, but he was far too respectful for her tastes. She spent a great deal of time changing her clothes and making up her face, but the result was always spoilt by an excess of superfluous hair. The soldier, a pleasant and generous man from the Franco-German frontier, who was dying to go to bed with anyone, made the mistake of offering her a hundred francs in front of witnesses. We were very nasty to her, making remarks about her in front of her face in French, which she didn't understand.

The Frenchwoman with the three little children had paid the difference in fare because she couldn't stand the life in the immigrant class. She was returning in complete despair to rejoin her husband at Saint Louis. The husband was a lorry driver and had been doing quite well until the slump; even then he had carried on for a time with a government mail-delivering contract. This contract was withdrawn before its completion on some minor technical point, and the man was left to scrape up what work he could in the colony. There are a great number of these 'poor whites' in the whole of French West Africa, doing what odd jobs come their way, often taking work which a negro could do more expeditiously and economically. But they are rightly uncertain of getting any work at all if they return to France, and will not willingly give up the delicious superiority their pigmentation endows them with, whatever may be their habits and style of living. The prestige of the European, never as high as the Europeans imagine, falls to nothing when the negroes see whites living under conditions they themselves would never support. The negroes however are very charitable; Benga's half-sister practically kept in food her two white tenants who quite unsuccessfully tried to get a living with a broken-down lorry. They owed about two years' rent.

The cause of her husband losing his contract, the wife declared, was the Freemasons. He wasn't one, he wouldn't deign to be, but the person who had got the job instead was, so was the person who gave the contract, the judge before whom the case came up, counsel on both sides, the governor – in fact everyone with any position. She knew this was so, for they signed their letters with three dots at the end of their signatures, and when they greeted one another in the street they described triangles with their raised helmets.

It is difficult enough in France to discuss any subject without free-masonry being dragged in, but in the colonies it is an obsession which almost amounts to paranoia. Everything, from the slump to the flavour of the local brewed beer, is due to the wicked self-seeking machinations of the freemasons. Anyone who considers himself ill-treated – and there are few Frenchmen who do not – will tell you so. Every high government official is a mason, all contracts are given by masons to fellow masons, usually with a bit of dirty work thrown in, the only people who don't complain are masons themselves, and they are making a dishonest fortune. This persecution mania is one of the staple subjects of French colonial conversation.

It seems undoubtedly true that a majority of the higher-placed officials are masons, and as such inclined to be anti-clerical and upholders of the existing constitution. (One mason when he was drunk informed me that the 'trois pointes' which masons sign after their name stand for Liberty, Equality and Fraternity.) It is also probable that a certain amount of mutual aid takes place; indeed I had always understood that that was the chief object of masonry in England. But to deduce from those facts a gigantic and nefarious conspiracy which is destroying the existing order of society for its own criminal ends seems to me a long step. But I never found a Frenchman or an educated negro to agree with me.

The mother had been to France with her three children, on account of the latter's health. Although creoles they could not stand the West African climate without a break; they all looked very poorly and were quite unmanageable. The mother was a very beautiful ox-like woman, tall and fair, with the statuesque stupidity of a Greco-Roman Juno. She had been a saleswoman at the Trois Quartiers and had there, she said, missed many advantageous marriages because she wanted to be treated respectfully. She still clung to her virtue and would not consent to the methods by which so many women in the colonies procured their husbands' advancement. Besides the anxiety as to where and how she and her children would live, was the added dread that her husband would again get her with child. He was a very passionate lover (Mrs Warren's mouth literally watered when this passionateness was described in detail) and would take no precautions himself. I gave her plenty of good advice but the most effective preparations are apparently illegal in French possessions. She was a very unhappy and very plucky woman, victimised by a selfish and stupid husband.

Benga was immediately accepted by our fellow passengers, even the old colonials. I did not realise at the time how extraordinary this was. In the small Spanish towns however he created a furore. The boat stopped at Barcelona, Tarragona, Malaga, and Cadiz. At Barcelona we were ignored – there was an interprovincial 'futbol' match in progress – but in the small towns we were stared at as though we were a portent and followed everywhere by large crowds of children. They were perfectly friendly; they guided us everywhere chattering all the while; they insisted that Benga must be a 'boxeador', nor would they believe his denials. I did not mind this but Benga was much distressed; he had been a 'phenomenon' for ten years and hated it more bitterly all the time. Otherwise he found Spain more sympathetic than any other European country he knew; the life of the streets, the movement and the predominance of youth in the population were less foreign to him than life in Northern Europe.

After Cadiz we went due south for four days. Every day it got colder and greyer; every night the sun set earlier. After we entered the tropics the weather became like a calm but not particularly warm November; when we arrived at Dakar it felt as though it were going to snow. Sun helmets seemed a horrible mockery.

BOOK ONE

Senegalese

1. Dakar

UNTIL THE BEGINNING of this century Dakar was a large negro village, with few European buildings – missions and churches, a few traders, small government offices. The land belonged almost entirely to the natives, who were chiefly engaged in fishing and commerce. The island of Gorée which stands off Dakar had been in the hands of Europeans for centuries, first the Portuguese and later the French. Saint Louis had been colonised since the end of the seventeenth century, and many of its buildings date from the eighteenth century, two-storeyed wooden houses with large verandahs; the town is built on a narrow strip of land and has a homogeneous and rather charming architectural appearance which is completely lacking in all other French colonial towns. When the agreements were reached with the various kinglets of Senegal – for the colony was never conquered – Saint Louis became the administrative capital, which indeed for the colony of Senegal it still remains. But after the imperial division of Africa in the second half of the nineteenth century France found herself mistress of the whole of the north-western portion of the continent, from the Mediterranean to below the equator, save for some relatively small portions on the coast, which were owned by the other imperialist powers. This enormous chunk of land was divided administratively into five groups: Morocco, Tunis, Algeria, French West Africa (AOF) and French Equatorial Africa (AEF). In 1904 Dakar was made the administrative capital of AOF.

The reason for this choice was probably the excellent natural port, which has indeed been since so developed that all ships can come alongside the quay, the only port in AOF where this is possible; the enormous possibilities of the lagoon at Abidjan have not been exploited. Another probable reason for the choice was the mildness of the climate, which is somewhat similar to that of Marseilles. From the geographical aspect it would have been hard to choose a more unsuitable spot. Dakar is situated at the end of a cape some twenty miles long; communications with the interior are difficult – a train runs to Bamako once a week and the road is execrable – and neither climatically nor culturally is Dakar comparable to the mainland. The greater part of the government workers never leave the town, and contact with the areas administered is slight. Every decision of even minor importance is referred back to Dakar, and from there very often to Paris; consequently the time-lag is terrific.

There is no evidence to show that the modern Dakar was town-planned. The centre of the town is the Place Protet, a small ornamental garden, flanked on three sides by government buildings and on the fourth by cafés; there is a taxi-rank close by, which serves as a gossip centre for the negroes, as the café terraces do for the Europeans. From the Place streets go wandering off in every direction.

Dakar is a town of bureaucrats. Besides the Governor-General there are four other governors in the town, each with an enormous palace and a huge staff. There are also the usual ministries. The greater part of the public buildings look as if they had been made after models confected by a pastrycook on one of the luxury Italian boats who had paid a hurried visit to the French Colonial Exhibition. But even that won't explain the new cathedral.

There is perpetual war between the administration and the traders. The administrators, quite justifiably, suspect the traders of trying to exploit the natives. The traders, equally justifiably, accuse the administration of running the colony for their own profit and convenience, and of exploiting the natives already as much as they can. In this battle the administrators are the winners, possibly through force of numbers; there was hardly a European firm in Dakar in 1934 which was not on the verge of bankruptcy; many were already bankrupt, some of the more important being kept going by government subsidies granted at the last minute.

All the small trade is in the hands of the Syrians, or, as they prefer to describe themselves, Libanese. They are able to stand the climate, they are able and willing to live under worse conditions than the negroes, they are very hard-working, and thoroughly dishonest and unscrupulous. With such advantages they are able to undercut both Europeans and negroes; the intercolonial trade is almost entirely in their hands; the greater number of stores in the interior are owned and run by them; they are continually branching out into new lines. The Syrians have a very great feeling of race and family solidarity and co-operate very successfully; even a bankruptcy can be made to pay when six or seven join together. They know so well the limits of the law that it is extremely risky to have any dealings with them. Nevertheless the ordinary man should be grateful to them; they have reduced the cost of living by nearly forty per cent.

When they are poor they live as the natives do; a good deal of the native quarter in Dakar is inhabited and owned by them. As they get richer they come into the more select parts of the town, dress too smartly and desire to be treated as Europeans. They never are.

A whole quarter of Dakar is inhabited by Moroccans; some streets have all the appearance of souks. They keep themselves fairly much to themselves.

The policemen, guards, attendants in the government buildings, all the men in any subordinate position, are Bambara, brought down from the Sudan; they are strongly disciplined, good soldiers, very loyal, and detest the Senegalese.

The Senegalese? Oh, they are the original inhabitants of the country. They are French citizens.

2. The Wolof

The Senegalese, or rather the Wolof, for the racial and present administrative boundaries do not coincide, have been longer and more continuously in contact with European civilisation than any other negro race. For nearly three centuries they have been in contact with white men, but until very recently they had preserved their language, their customs and their race practically intact. This is doubtless largely due to the negative and conservative attitude of Mohammedanism, which till the advent of missionaries was the universal, and still is by far the most popular religion. As will be seen later, however, this Mohammedanism, though not schismatic, shows very great differences from the Arabian version. From the time of Louis XIV there have been Catholic missionaries in Senegal, and they have made many converts, especially in the bigger towns and fishing villages: the great stumbling-block to conversion is monogamy which is economically unsuitable to peasants. Religious animosity was at one moment fairly strong, but on the whole Catholics and Mohammedans live peaceably together, the feeling for the unity of the race overcoming the difference in creed.

The Wolof are remarkably race-proud, practically never mating with people of any other stock; as they have never been very numerous they are nearly all slightly interrelated; they all know their exact degree of kinship with their fellows. The physical type is very pronounced and it is nearly always easy to distinguish a Wolof among other negroes. They are among the most handsome of the negro races, tall with regular features and very round heads; they vary very considerably in colour, from a comparatively light coffee brown – they call this colour 'red' or 'blond' and it is considered by them, as by all other negroes, a desirable quality – to a black so black as to appear purple. Both sexes are narrow-waisted; the men are broad-shouldered, the women deep-bosomed. Albinism, whether red or white, is uncommon.

Actual slavery appears to have been introduced with the Europeans, and the richer negroes also acquired slaves at the same epoch. The slaves of Europeans considered themselves vastly superior to the slaves of negroes, and this feeling is still strong among their descendants today; the descendant of a European's slave will not easily marry one whose ancestors were owned by natives; genealogies are scrupulously kept. Conditions in the interior resembled slavery in most points, save that it was not considered so by the people; nearly all the land was owned by the chief or kinglet, for whom the rest of the population worked; in return he kept them, housed them and married them off. Thus the greater part of the population may have seemed like slaves, for they owned little or no property and had very limited freedom of action. This form of civilisation, in practice a sort of primitive communism, still exists today in those parts of the colony which are away from the rail and roads.

Very few Wolof were exported as slaves to the New World, but in the eighteenth century a considerable number were taken to Europe as pages and servants. The negro who added the exotic touch to the rococo boudoir was nine times out of ten from Senegal.

The Wolof have always been patriarchal, inasmuch as the head of the family is always a male, and succession goes from father to eldest son. But the milk tie is far more important than the blood tie, and foster children of the same mother are considered as closer relations than children of the same parents suckled by different women. The ideal marriage is that of the child with his father's nephews and nieces; the most abhorred with the mother's. This prohibition is extended to several generations; the descendants of children who have suckled the same breast must never marry.

With the exception of this one-sided cross-cousin marriage, exogamy was the rule; the feudal state of the land, when each kingdom was one large family, made this inevitable. The first and chief wife should always be of the same status as her husband. All subsequent wives owe respect and service to the chief wife, and unless she is divorced she is always counted as the equal and partner of her husband. When a man wishes to marry a second wife he asks the chief wife how much time she will allow him with the second wife; after this period, which is strictly adhered to, the two wives take it in turn to provide his food and share his bed. The same procedure is followed with each subsequent wife; but when they become numerous the chief wife does not work any more. It often happens that the chief wife will choose later wives for her husband, especially if she is getting old or is childless. When there are two wives only, relations are usually strained, but when they are numerous they get on well enough together. When a man is old and has taken several wives he has the right to marry a griote* and a slave-girl (two castes which are

---

* This term is explained on pp. 51–52.

otherwise quite untouchable and can only marry among themselves); if children should result from these matches, however, they are not considered legitimate and have no rights at all. It is only very rich men who are able to afford more than one or two wives. Goldsmiths can only contract alliances within their own guild, or with weavers and cobblers.

In customary law women have the same rights as men; they can be property owners and inherit property. But although women often bring a marriage portion, marriage is essentially contracted by purchase; the marriage money, or rather the equivalent, is paid to the bride herself, and not, as is usually the case elsewhere, to her family. These marriage gifts are known as 'the recompense for the pains of childbirth'; among Mohammedans a woman who is divorced and is childless has to return the gifts; if she has borne children she keeps them.

For a man to be acceptable as a husband he must be able to place at his wife's disposal a furnished room which she will not have to share with any other woman and he should provide her with a trousseau which should consist of three trunks full of clothes and at least one full set of gold ornaments – bracelets, a necklace with a heavy pendant, two large pin brooches, large hanging ear-rings and sets of small gold rings to be placed all round the outside of the ear. The thinner ornaments should be furnished with gold coins. The brooches and pendants often measure as much as four inches across; they are very elaborately and beautifully worked. The bridegroom should also provide a week's feasting for all the members of the two families.

With the ever increasing pauperisation and proletarianisation of the Wolof these conditions are becoming more and more neglected; very often the girl's family will help with the trousseau and for the gold ornaments will be substituted ornaments in baser metal cunningly gilded. Nevertheless, marriage still remains extremely expensive, at the cheapest about two thousand francs, especially for Catholics who are used to European furniture; consequently the average age of marriage has risen very considerably; it is very seldom that a man can afford to marry before he is twenty-five. One of the direct results of this state of affairs is a large increase in the number of illegitimate children. These

children suffer under some legal disadvantages in the matter of inheritance, but otherwise neither they nor their mother are under any slur –
indeed, since it proves the mother's fertility it is rather to her credit. It is
very seldom that the paternity is doubtful, for the Wolof are not by nature
promiscuous; very often the parents subsequently marry; when they do
not the child is nearly always accepted by the girl's future husband.
Occasionally the father adopts the child.

The Wolof have strict standards of sexual morality. Until recently
males were not circumcised until the age of eighteen or nineteen, in some
cases even later, and until that operation was performed they were not
considered to be men; even should they go against custom and try to have
sexual intercourse it would be very doubtful if they would find a woman of
their own race to accept them. Nowadays the operation is performed
shortly after puberty. Until modern times they were married almost as
soon as they were healed. Until modern times also women remained
virgin until married. Adultery was not, and is not, common; flirtatious
intrigues, gallantries not brought to their logical conclusion, are. The
women's behaviour is continually provocative; their movements, their
glances, their sighs, their manner of speaking are all, almost unconsciously, alluring. They are nevertheless generally virtuous; moreover,
they do not tolerate perversions, or even alterations in customary sexual
behaviour (different for Catholics and Mohammedans).

There are, however, among the Wolof a number of courtesans in the
grand style. Their houses are the most cultured in Senegal; the best
musicians and poetry can be heard there, the finest stuffs and jewels can
be found. They are prized as much for their wit as their beauty. They are
seldom kept by a man; they will from caprice, or because a man has been
exceptionally generous, retain him when the other guests leave; but men
can, and often do, ruin themselves for such women without receiving any
recompense; it is always the women who remain in the superior position.
If a courtesan happens to fall in love she will marry, and retire into private
life. Only men of their own race are received by them.

A Wolof marriage is a long and complicated ceremony. For weeks
beforehand all the female relations of the bride arrive from all over the

Africa Dances

country with gifts to get the house and the wedding feast ready. The
bride's mother does not help in this, and the groom's family rarely. The
griots and griotes gather for the ceremony, where they will chant the
praises of the two families and receive presents. During the whole of the
ceremony the children of the sisters of the bride and groom have
complete licence; they can dress up in clothes of the opposite sex and can
take whatever they can lay hands on. (This is probably a vestige of
the matriarchal inheritance laws, which still survive in some distant
provinces.) On the day of the marriage the legal and religious ceremonies are performed as early as possible, and the day given up to feasting;
it is the great time for the griots. Late in the evening the eldest female
relations of the bride – the grandmother, the great-aunts and so on –
take the bride to the marriage chamber, prepare the bed and address a
number of moral reflections to the girl, giving her advice and foretelling
the disgrace which will fall on the family if she is not proved a virgin. This
usually reduces the girl to tears. They then undress her, lay her on the
bed, summon the husband and wait in an adjoining room. As soon as
the girl screams they all rush in, and the husband shortly retires. The girl
is meant to faint – if she doesn't she pretends to – and the old ladies
revive her, take away the marriage sheet, remake the bed and the
husband returns. Early the next morning the sheet is exhibited to the
guests who have passed the night dancing and feasting (they do not eat
together but are divided into different groups according to their importance and their relation to the married couple and are mortally offended
if the proper order is not adhered to), and if it is in a satisfactory state
there is wild rejoicing and the bride is smothered with gifts; the husband
usually hides his under the pillow. The bride's mother, who has up till
then had no part in the proceedings, is congratulated and praised by
everyone. For a week the bride does not go out of the house or do any
work; dressed in all her finery, which should be changed every day, she
presides over the feasting and receives her guests; the week passed, she
goes out to pay visits for a month, still, if the marriage is a proper one,
with new clothes every day; it is only at the close of that period that she
settles down to domestic life.

When a girl reaches puberty – contrary to general belief this does not take place earlier than with Europeans: it is generally between the ages of thirteen and fourteen – her mother sits her on the three stones which usually hold the cooking pot, and explains her condition to her, and tells her what her future conduct must be. Menstruating women are unclean and must never touch water; if they come into contact with certain grigris (magical charms) they destroy their efficacy. Till this time the girl's head has been shaved, but now the hair is allowed to grow for a year; at the end of that period her hair is dressed, and if she has been promised in marriage the future husband must send head-cloths. When a boy – formerly a young man – is circumcised, he stays away from houses and people, wears a special costume and lives in special huts till he is healed. He is accompanied by magicians who are fire-eaters and fire-dancers, and in the evenings these tricks are performed to the accompaniment of special songs. The chief magician – not the man who performs the operation but the leader of the band – whips the young men and makes them undergo various unpleasant ordeals to prove their bravery and manhood. Before the operation the candidates, 'ahrt', are dressed practically like women, with shells and jewels in their long hair; they are not considered to be men and an animal killed by them is unclean. The topknots are cut off at the same time as the foreskin; it is an occasion for rejoicing. Circumcision usually takes place after the harvesting. Once the young man is healed he returns to his family, when a feast is held and he is given a magical potion called 'toulh' which renders his body immune to all knife blows. The circumcision rites are to a man what marriage is to a woman.

I never heard of a Wolof prostitute; and they are very seldom mistresses to Europeans. The State-countenanced brothels (negroes admitted at the side door) are filled with Frenchwomen; the few street-walkers are mostly Bambara, the mistresses, who seldom live with their lovers, mostly negresses from Portuguese Guinea. One of these last was for many years a tenant of Benga's stepfather and her most constant client was a Catholic priest; she did not speak French and the only phrase she learned from him and which she turned into a catchword was

'Frottez plus fort!' It is, however, chiefly the Syrians who patronise the negresses; such Frenchmen as do not keep to their own race usually prefer boys.

It is said that homosexuality is recent among the Wolof, at any rate in any frequency; but it now receives, and has for some years received, such extremely august and almost publicly exhibited patronage, that pathics are a common sight. They are called in Wolof men-women, gor-digen, and do their best to deserve the epithet by their mannerisms, their dress and their make-up; some even dress their hair like women. They do not suffer in any way socially, though the Mohammedans refuse them religious burial; on the contrary, they are sought after as the best conversationalists and the best dancers. This phase is usually transitory, finishing with the departure of the European who has been keeping the boy; but a certain number from taste, interest, or for economic reasons continue their practices and there is now quite a large pederastic society. If I am right in ascribing the increase in European homosexuality to a neurotic fear of life and responsibility, the conditions of urban life in Africa lead to the prognosis that this society will greatly increase. My informants on this subject had not heard of lesbianism.

Many Catholics and a few Mohammedans wear European dress, sometimes as a sign of evolution but more frequently from economy. The native dress is splendid but very expensive. The men wear white pantaloons to below the knee, very full – in times of prosperity as much as twenty yards of stuff will go to a single pair – and a boubou, or sleeveless shirt, going down to the ground. This is either white or dark blue, and is elaborately embroidered by hand; it opens on the chest and has pockets inside. Moroccan sandals (usually white) and a black tarboosh are worn by the more prosperous. The women's dresses are very full in the skirt, and it is a sign of smartness and wealth to wear several dresses one on top of the other, each a little shorter than the one below it. This gives them a voluminous appearance. The dresses are in various colours, though white and black and blue patterns predominate. They also wear a large shawl, by means of which a small baby can be tied against the back. Unmarried women are meant to wear their head bare, and also to have longer dresses; married women all wear wigs made out of sisal of stylised and unrealistic fashion and over them brightly coloured silk handkerchiefs or head-cloths, tied into a knot behind. The fashion in head-cloths changes very frequently; when I was there all the better-dressed women wore glacé silk, though a few had still the now demoded flowered foulards. They always wear a number of gold ornaments, and on festive occasions they are smothered with them; they used to wear heavy silver anklets, but a tax was put on them some years ago and they have now quite disappeared. Women have their lower lip, and both sexes very often their gums, tattooed indigo. This is very becoming. Some people have also a thin line of blue tattooed on the lower eyelid directly under the lashes, which effectually makes the eyes appear larger. Black dye for the eyelashes is common. The Wolof, especially the women, have invented an appearance quite as artificial and quite as decorative as the polite European eighteenth century, with its wigs, power and hoops. The gestures and language of polite intercourse are stylised and graceful; a greeting is a formal litany of question and answer embracing everyone and everything connected with the two people meeting (the questions are merely formal and a dying person is stated to be in good health so as not to break the rhythm of the responses) and continuing for several minutes; women accompany it with a swaying movement of the body; with people to whom special deference is due the formula is resumed several times during conversation; saying goodbye is equally elaborate. Verbal wit, to which the language is well suited, is the most highly prized of the lesser social qualities, and intellectual attainments, especially those acknowledged by diplomas, of the greater. This veneration for intellectuality is carried to ridiculous lengths; there are comparatively few openings in the administration, medicine and law, which are the only 'respectable' methods of earning a living, and old-fashioned Wolof will rather live in poverty than soil their hands with commerce, with the result that now most branches of commerce are closed to them. One reason for this is that all traditional crafts belonged exclusively to certain families; a goldsmith or a weaver is born, not made. The more elegant speak French among themselves.

The most marked moral characteristic of the Wolof is pride, or dignity; even their appearance is redolent of it. This sense of personal dignity is almost universal from the richest to the poorest – there is as yet no feeling of class difference founded on wealth – and is universally respected by the Wolof. From the point of view of social intercourse this trait is most engaging, especially in West Africa, where from both Europeans and negroes you get either cringing or bullying; but from the point of view of social survival it is deplorable. It makes them bad servants and subordinates, for though their pride will drive them to kill themselves rather than renounce anything they have undertaken to do (a not uncommon occurrence) they are continually on the lookout for slights and extremely impatient of them; if they think they are being treated wrongly they will at once withdraw. They do not respect force or violence and it has the minimum of effect on them; they are morally almost morbidly sensitive. If you treat them properly it is impossible to have more loyal and willing friends and helpers, as I found out; but most Europeans are unable or unwilling to understand their psychology and prefer to employ negroes of other races; they give the Wolof a very bad character. This is not true of all Europeans; I know of a few who excite general admiration; and these men can get whatever they wish out of the Wolof. There is one man who is notorious for not paying his servants' wages, but there is hardly a Wolof who would not enter his service tomorrow. (Nobody in Dakar can hope that anything about him will remain unknown; it is all discussed in the Place Protet.) This man is not familiar with the negroes, nor does he allow the negroes to be familiar with him; he treats them as social equals, though not as intimates, using the formal courtesy they prize in all his dealings with them and thereby gets far more out of them than either bullying or money could do.

The Wolof are much preoccupied with money; it is one of the most constant words in their conversation. They do not value it for its own sake, however; as soon as they have paid their taxes and their debts they will employ whatever money they possess in gifts and in ostentation. When the groundnut cultivators were making a great deal of money they would as soon as they were paid ransack the shops for the most expensive perfumes, clothes, cigars; they would flaunt these till they had been seen by everyone and then discard them, and wait in comparative poverty till the next harvest. The idea of hoarding or saving is quite alien to them.

They have very high traditions of generosity and hospitality. When they are cooking they always prepare far more than is necessary so as to be able to give to strangers and the poor. Amongst Mohammedans this is particularly strong; and if a stranger comes up to one and says 'There is only you and Allah' he must house him and feed him and share with him all that he has. Alioune, one of my chauffeurs, a very pious Mohammedan, was supporting no less than ten strangers or distant relations when he went away with me. (That was the chief reason for his readiness to come.) When in work he earned about five hundred francs a month. I paid him a hundred and fifty and his keep, and at the end of the journey he tried to refuse the money because he knew I was rather hard up; we nearly quarrelled for the first time before he would take it. When he finally accepted it he went to pay his taxes, sent a third to his family, and went and bought himself an outfit of the greatest splendour. I doubt if he had ten francs in the world when, the cynosure of every eye, he accompanied me to the ship. Most of his compatriots would have behaved in exactly the same way.

The Wolof have a great admiration for cunning. Many of their anecdotes – and their conversation takes largely that form – are concerned with successful tricks. It is usually the story of how a cripple – particularly blind men, who are credited with great sharpness – a poor man or a weak man gets the better of his stronger and richer neighbours. No moral judgement is implied in these tales of sharp practice but merely admiration for uncommon wit. It is a state of mind similar to that which was able to admire unreservedly the wily Odysseus, or to that of the boastful American business man. They are also very fond of conundrums, of which they have a large repertoire, and of fables. These fables about anthropomorphic animals have all the charm and variety of Aesop or *Reynard*;*

* The relative positions of the rabbit (the hero) and the hyena (the fool) make me think that they may be the originals of *Brer Rabbit*.

unfortunately they have not been written down – it would never occur to a negro to do so – and I did not have the time to make a collection of them. The Wolof are nearly all literate; the Catholics go to the missions and the Mohammedans to the Koranic schools; but they learn to write in a foreign language, either French or Arabic; it is an alien accomplishment and reserved for alien work.

Thus most Wolof are bilingual from childhood; and they mostly learn foreign languages easily and quickly. Fodé, my chauffeur-interpreter, spoke six unrelated negro languages fluently and Arabic and French very competently. They generally adapt themselves very well to changed conditions, and nearly all positions which require intellectual training and independence – such as auxiliary doctors, midwives, clerks to the administration, storekeepers – are filled by Wolof in French Guinea, French Sudan and the Ivory Coast. Farther east they are filled by Dahomeyans. The very qualities which make them bad subordinates and difficult to employ in their own country render them particularly suitable for responsible work abroad. Even when they spend their lives in foreign countries they do not marry with the people among whom they live but have wives chosen by their family sent out to them.

The Wolof are, as far as my experience goes, unique among negro races in having evolved a civilisation which can be stated in terms of our own. The Dahomeyans and, I am told, the Ashanti had their own civilisations before they were conquered, but in each case they were impregnated with a completely alien religion which so thoroughly per-meated their modes of thought and action as to render them nearly impossible to translate into European terms; moreover they were both civilisations founded on and dependent on war and conquest. Although they are said to make good soldiers war has little part in Wolof history or tradition. There have always been buffer races between them and the predatory Moors to the north and east.

The Senegalese were given French citizenship in the nineteenth century. I do not know the historical reasons for this gift, but it was probably a recompense either for accepting French protection or for the military help given in the conquest of other African races. The chief positive advantage of this citizenship is that the Senegalese have only to do one year's military service instead of the three of other negroes. It also gives them theoretical equality in law courts (actual outside Africa) and the right to elect a member to represent them in the French House of Commons. Elections are much enjoyed for the vote buying and free entertainment which accompany them; very strong feelings are roused between the partisans of the different candidates and an election is seldom brought to a close without casualties, never without bloodshed. The negro votes are confined to the male inhabitants of the four principal cities; all Europeans with the proper qualifications vote at the same elections. For the sake of propaganda a negro or mulatto is always returned, but care is taken that the successful candidate should be one who will not be inconvenient to the authorities; if necessary dead registers are used, or the results simply faked.* Until his death in 1934 Blaise Diagne had represented Senegal continuously for twenty years; it is said that when he started his career he worked for the interests of his compatriots; but he was easily bought or won over and worked entirely in the interests of the administration. All his money and property were in Paris. He used his considerable influence to find or create good positions for his relations and European partisans, regardless of the suitability of the man for the work. Corruption and intrigue filled the civil services, with results that are deplored by white and negro equally. He continually used the services of fetishers and amulet makers. He was (inevitably) reputed to be a freemason. When he died a mulatto was elected in his place, pledged to reverse the policy of Diagne: the negro youth were united to return him and a number of devices to fake the result were exposed.

An indirect result of this citizenship is to fortify the Wolof's pride and independence. Consequently colonial administrators, especially outside Senegal, declaim against it loudly and constantly.

* *See* Michel Leiris: *L'Afrique Fantôme*, p. 150.

3. Religion

The Mohammedan proselytisers reached the coasts of Senegal in the eleventh century. This turned out to be the southern limit of the movement. To the north and west, in what are now Mauretania, French Sudan, the French colony of the Niger and Northern Nigeria, the greater part of the population was converted to Islam, but the inhabitants of the countries south and east of Senegal continued to practise their own religions for some centuries longer. Christian missionaries arrived in the second half of the seventeenth century, originally sent there by Louis XIV, or more probably Madame de Maintenon; for some time the Roman Catholics and the Dutch Protestants had the field more or less to themselves, but from the nineteenth century onwards the land was open to all comers, and there is now no sect, however obscure it may be or however extravagant its doctrines, which has not its representatives in West Africa. The French admit into their colonies only Catholics, Methodists and the Reformed Church; but in the countries under mandate, through the conditions imposed by President Wilson, and in the British colonies every shade of Christianity can be found. The regions in which the original African religions are openly practised and professed are getting fewer daily; the Christians are pressing in from the coast; Islam, though it now makes comparatively few converts, has very few apostates; so that it is only in a band roughly a hundred miles wide, starting about fifty miles from the coast, that the old religions can be found. The missionaries are constantly gaining ground and are continually making converts among the more primitive races; it is only in the old kingdom of Dahomey that anything like a solid front is presented against their inroads; the forest dwellers of the Ivory Coast are succumbing piecemeal.

The Wolof are nominally divided into Mohammedans and Catholics, in about the proportion of six to one; in point of fact a belief in magic and sorcery unites them far more than sectarianism divides them. The daily ritual prayers and Ramadan are observed more or less exactly by the Mohammedans; a few make the pilgrimage to Mecca; they all abstain religiously from forbidden foods, and the greater part from alcohol (this is one of the many reasons which make Mohammedan servants preferable to Catholics); the most severe do not smoke. Their women are not veiled or in any way secluded. Prayers and the Koran are said in Arabic, and are to many meaningless parrot noises; they are often much distorted.

One of the chief peculiarities of negro Mohammedanism is the system of marabouts, or holy men, or rather the elaboration it has received. These marabouts, often indicated by their miracle-working propensities, are objects of particular veneration; the most revered indeed are considered to hold the keys of heaven and hell in their hands. The chief marabout of Diourbel, Serine Bamba, was for many years the richest and most influential man in the interior of Senegal. So influential was he that he was exiled by the administration several times. He did not present the outward marks of holiness, for he lived in the greatest luxury in the midst of a large harem. But he was believed to have particular influence with Allah, and young men from all over the country would come to offer him a year's labour, either working on his land, which was considerable, for nothing, or hiring themselves out and paying over their entire wages to him. During this year of service they would eat the minimum necessary for the preservation of life; they would lie on the bare ground, and would not even pay to have their heads shaved, with the result that they became verminous; this was indeed a sign of devotion. In 1917 the French were having great difficulty in recruiting negro soldiers to fight in France; Blaise Diagne approached the marabout, who announced that 'all who believe in me and Allah will go and enlist'. From the day he made that announcement till the signing of the armistice not a man of military age could be found in the country; those who were rejected by the recruiting officers presented themselves again and again; many tried bribery to be allowed to enlist; if that failed they begged that at least they might be allowed to wear uniform and be stationed somewhere away from home. Otherwise they would lose their right to heaven. This marabout built a most splendid mosque out of his own money; at his death in 1925 he left several million francs. No one has since reached his pre-eminent position; there are several rivals contending for his influence, but allegiance is still divided.

Catholicism has developed on fairly orthodox lines, except that the magical properties of holy water, crosses, medallions and so forth are much emphasised. I witnessed, however, a pretty little piece of religious-financial racketeering. There is a small village some sixty miles from Dakar called Popenguine, where a church has been built to Notre Dame de la Délivrance; there was formerly a seminary there, but it has since been removed. The priests have organised a pilgrimage there on every Whit Monday; dispensations are granted for a mass said there. More important, the insignia of various Catholic orders of merit, such as the ribbon of the Enfants de Marie (which carry with them certain privileges), are only handed over there, so that by one means and another the greater part of the Catholic community is induced to make the pilgrimage. To convey the faithful thither all available lorries and buses are hired by the clergy and a place in one is sold for twenty francs. The pilgrims are packed as tightly as possible; the roads are very jolty; and as they have to make the journey fasting to be able to communicate on arrival a great number vomit *en route*. A considerable sum must be netted by the transport; candles and relics are also sold *in situ* at very high prices. When I arrived there at midday the religious celebrations were finished and people were eating the lunches they had brought with them. Most of the women had taken off their outer dresses – it was excessively hot – and were in their shifts, which were more or less white and extremely modest in cut, but which gave a look of dingy debauchery to the scene which was further enhanced by the fact that the greater number were fairly tipsy and a few roaring drunk; the more drunk they were the louder they sang hymns and canticles in Wolof, horribly out of tune. Almost as many were sick on the return journey as on the outward one. There seems to be no *raison d'être* other than financial for the pilgrimage; the image of Mary is modern and of no special sanctity, and although visions have been reported a couple of times they have never been given official recognition.

The great majority of both Catholics and Mohammedans believe in the efficacy of amulets or grigris, the existence of sorcerers and demons, and in soothsaying and magic. The wearing of unsanctified amulets is officially frowned on by the Catholic Church and some priests refuse to minister to people wearing them. So the Catholics leave them at home during church services.

The greater number of Wolof amulets consist of a piece of paper covered with Arabic signs and writing and enclosed in leather dyed either black or red. These grigris are worn as bracelets, as necklaces attached round the neck with a thin cord or they are tied on to the body with slings. A certain number of empty cases are worn, especially the most prominent, so that if an enemy tries to disarm you he will fail. Some of the bulkier grigris contain a selection of objects, such as special pebbles and bones, herbs and animal skins. These are more truly magical and are therefore specific and limited in their action* and generally require some ritual or prayer before they function. The paper charms are more general in their application and roughly correspond in their functions to the Jewish phylactery. The quantity of these grigris worn by the Wolof is extraordinary: those of the chauffeur Alioune made a bulky packet weighing about two pounds, and some of the wrestlers wore so many that you could barely see their bodies or arms. A few amulets are put on children as soon as they are born, and the quantity is increased to meet every new crisis or danger.

The belief in sorcerers is common to negroes throughout Africa. Sorcerers are pre-eminently antisocial, evil and dangerous: they *eat people's souls*. It is possible for a man to be a sorcerer, as among the Italians for a man to have the evil eye, involuntarily. Indeed, sorcery is a sex-linked malady, being inevitably imbibed with the mother's milk. All the children of a sorceress are certain to be sorcerers; the children of a sorcerer by a normal woman will be clairvoyant, but will neither be able to eat people's souls nor suck their blood. Except possibly in the case of the leopard men of Liberia and other secret societies, they work privately

---

* A detailed discussion of magic will be more apposite in the description of the Fetishist or Voodoo religion of Dahomey in Book III.

and as individuals, though a sorcerer who has got a victim may invite others to share his feast and assist him in his necromantic practices; they are the greatest menace to the community. The only thing the Wolof fear as much as sorcerers is spoken praise, which, especially when addressed to children, will inevitably bring disaster. There is no hidden 'true' name* among the Wolof, but it is most important never to mention the day or hour of your birth, which would give great power to your enemies. (It is quite legitimate to make magic to hurt and destroy your enemies and rivals, and there are canonical methods of doing this.) The sorcerers' power is confined exclusively to killing people and eating their souls; they are able to transform themselves into wind to do this and a 'dust devil' is the sign of a sorcerer. The usual blasting powers of witches – sterility, crop failure – belong to the canonical magicians. It is not easy to recognise a sorcerer, for they do not use apparatus by the possession of which they can be known; they are sometimes caught through the possession of their victims' remains which are difficult to dispose of. Contrary to most magic, a sorcerer's power is greatly diminished if he is recognised for what he is. Then his victims can take precautions against him; the effects of sorcery can only be undone when it is known who has caused them. A revealed sorcerer is practically powerless. He can only be truly recognised by people in trance.

The people, nearly always women, who have the faculty of going into a clairvoyant trance are known among the Wolof as m'Deup; the dances during which these revelations are obtained have the same name. Men are occasionally m'Deup, but they are looked down on as debauchees and effeminate. The m'Deup dances are started when a woman has spontaneously fallen into catalepsy and are continued until she speaks. There are special m'Deup songs and also special drums; these occasionally consist of a small calabash floating upside-down in a large calabash filled with water. These are only used for m'Deup whose guardian spirits live in the water; for all other spirits the drum is used.

* It is general for primitive people to have one 'true' name which is never mentioned.

46

When the dances start the woman in trance and the bystanders dance as they feel moved, sometimes with the same movements as the ordinary dances which are done for pleasure, more often with extravagant gestures and grimaces, rolling on the ground and eating earth. Usually a number of the bystanders also fall in fits. People dance singly and spasmodically, starting and stopping as they feel inclined. The true m'Deup cannot hear the rhythm without dancing till they have got out of range.

When a m'Deup is going into trance she goes through a curious pantomime, acting as if she had just been awakened from sleep, stretching her arms and staring about. She will open her eyes with her forefingers, and touch her ears, nose and mouth. Then, with her eyes no longer focused on anything, she will start to dance. If she is not removed by force – she can no longer hear or see ordinary people – she will go on dancing for an indefinite period which may extend to several days without rest or food, until the crisis comes and she falls to the ground with only the whites of her eyes showing. In this state she will prophesy and name sorcerers. If by any chance there is a sorcerer in the near neighbourhood she will get up from the ground, her eyes still reversed, and fall on the guilty man, clawing and wounding him until she is dragged off. When a sorcerer has been pointed out in this fashion denial is useless; they will indeed very often confess to get the m'Deup removed. Life for a known sorcerer becomes very difficult and they usually leave the country. In earlier times, and even now in out-of-the-way communities, they would be killed. With slight variants this type of sorcerer-finding dance exists in all the portion of West Africa I visited. The women in trance are usually forcibly removed as soon as their state is clear; this type of catalepsy is apparently general and not uncommon. It sometimes happens that magicians can make sorcerers confess, and they sometimes confess spontaneously because one of their victims has been too powerful for them.

I have no evidence of any value either way concerning the powers of sorcerers. No one will ever admit to being a sorcerer, much less give an exhibition of sorcery. On the other hand, the belief in them is universal in Africa amongst all negroes in every stage of culture, and this belief always contains the strange conditions that the sorcerer must be unknown to be powerful. It is the generally accepted theory of magic that the victim must know he is being bewitched, and that this knowledge and the conviction of ineluctability are the real reasons for the bewitched person's illness or death. But with the sorcerer the case is reversed, and the only hope for the victim consists in finding out who is bewitching him, after which cure is comparatively simple; whence the witch-finding dances, or in cases of urgency the ordeal by poison. Of course any number of rationalistic explanations can be found; in primitive cultures disease and death are never natural and the sorcerer may be merely the innocent scapegoat. Pending conclusive evidence I think I am open minded on the subject; but I should try to avoid the society of a person who was reputed to have the evil eye.

About devils I have even less evidence, though I have heard a great number of stories about them. 'Devils' is perhaps the wrong word; inhuman and generally malevolent spirits would be a better description. There are many varieties of these spirits, but I didn't hear of any which could not be paralleled in European folklore or legend. Stories are told about poltergeists, trolls, goblins, incubi, vampires and vaguer harmful spirits which fly in the night similar to lamias and the ogres which used to frighten the Romans. These evils spirits have all their own names and strictly defined powers; it needs a powerful magician (a man with magical powers which are publicly avowed and keep within the limits of accepted religion) to exorcise them. Possibly the 'little people' come under a different category. In places as far apart as Diourbel in Senegal, Axim in the Gold Coast and Dassa Zoumé in Dahomey I heard tales of little people about four feet high who live among the rocks; they have not any special powers, but only certain people, usually fetishists, can communicate with them. The accounts of them seem very similar to Miss Murray's fairies in Western Europe.* Pygmies have not been found outside Equatorial Africa.

* See *The God of the Witches*, by Margaret Murray.

I do not intend to say anything more in this place about magic. Fortune-telling and soothsaying are much practised by the Wolof after the Arabian fashion, with sand. It would be ungracious of me to criticise this in any way, for I did a great deal of fortune-telling myself in Africa. I have a curious and, as far as I am concerned, unexplained knack of being able to reconstruct people's character and past life by holding their hands. I do not follow any system or pay much attention to skin markings; I am not always successful, and very rarely with people I know; but with strangers I am in many cases surprisingly accurate. I also tell the future by this means. I have no great belief in this talent which I do not like exercising; it is something of a strain, and since I do not remember what I tell I get very little kick out of it. But among the negroes it was a godsend; in a couple of critical cases I hit on surprising truth with the result that the fetishists accepted me as a confrère, explaining that a spirit of some dead fetishist had taken up his abode in my body; in consequence they were, I think, more open with me than they would otherwise have been and told me and showed me many things. On a couple of occasions I acceded to the request to make grigris; I do not think pentagrams and cabalistic signs on pieces of typing paper can have done any harm, but I was not very happy about it. I also told lies about the wonders I could have worked if I had had the apparatus with me, but the fetishists did the same, so no harm was done by that.

There is a curious relic of totemism among the Wolof. Nearly all family names are the names of animals (m'Benga is the name of the jackal, Diagne of the snake), and the animal whose name a man bears is taboo to him; if he eats its flesh he will be very ill, and should he merely touch it his skin will break out in a rash and blisters. Both Benga and Fodé are Large Green Lizard on their mothers' side, and on different occasions each told me that whenever there was a birth or death in the family a large green lizard would appear in the room. A saucer of milk would be given it, and after drinking it the animal would go away. They both declared they had witnessed this. Fodé once handled the corpse of one of these lizards and immediately developed very bad skin rash. This vestigial totemism has no longer any religious significance; the sympathetic connection between men and animals of the same name is taken for granted. The urticaria resulting from contact with the forbidden animal is a constant feature of fetishist belief. Ashes can sometimes avert this.

Another curious fact which is not given any supernatural explanation is the power of certain fishermen or 'mol' to stay under water almost indefinitely. This power is confined to a few members of certain families; the greater number live near Saint Louis. I was sceptical of this claim and one of these divers offered to demonstrate. I chose the place where he was to dive, the water being particularly limpid, and asked him to stop at the bottom for twenty minutes. He stopped there for three quarters of an hour; I had him continuously in view and he had no apparatus of any kind; occasionally he would send an air bubble to the surface. At the end of the period he came up to ask if he had stayed down long enough. To all my inquiries as to how he did it he replied that 'he breathed like a fish', which didn't advance matters much. No importance is attached to this hereditary gift; it needs training to be developed. I only heard of these people by chance; for the Wolof they are completely ordinary.

No matter what the religion of the negro, whether Christian, Mohammedan or fetishist, they are fanatical in their belief in a future life. I have heard it many times said that the European is superior here; this world belongs to him; the negro is here in purgatory and all the misfortunes which fall on him are the will of God against which it would be impious to protest; they are punishments for former or future sins. In the next world the position will be reversed. This belief explains a great deal of the negro's passivity and fatalism.

4. Wrestling

Amateur wrestling is by far the most popular, indeed almost the only West African sport. (I do not count the organised games which have been introduced into the English colonies.) It has been developed to an extent which makes it comparable with the Olympic games. The title of champion wrestler of the AOF is very highly esteemed, and the holder of it brings great glory to his village. Eliminating bouts are held locally throughout the year and the championship is fought for at Dakar throughout the month of January. Any young man who wishes is allowed to compete, but until recently it was an essential condition that the challenger of the champion should be uncircumcised, that is, a virgin; it was only after victory or withdrawal that the operation could be performed and the distinguishing tuft of hair, rather like a bullfighter's plait, could be cut. This condition is still fulfilled in some of the outlying fishing villages, from which the best wrestlers come. (The physical development of fishermen, whether on the coast or the big rivers, is remarkable; they have strength and beauty which contrast strangely with the puny ugliness of the greater part of the races of the forest and the savannah.) As the young men often reach the early twenties before they stop competing a great number of emotional complications arise; underhand intrigues are made almost impossible by the presence of the griot, who never leaves alone the wrestler he is attached to.

The griot is one of the most extraordinary Wolof institutions (he exists with his functions somewhat modified among the neighbouring races) and the most difficult to explain. The griots form a special caste and never by any chance marry with anyone except another griot. They are outcasts from all religions and can never be buried in consecrated ground. The position is a hereditary one, and unless the child of a griot emigrates he can find no other occupation. They are looked down upon by the rest of the population as slightly untouchable; at the same time they have a great importance and often become very rich. They are the only musicians and no one who was not a griot would condescend, or be able, to play the tomtom, the balafron (a kind of xylophone), the cora (a kind of guitar) or any of the other instruments which are necessary for dancing or singing. Most Europeans writing about West Africa seem to consider that that is their only function, and use the word 'griot' as a synonym for musician. This is partially correct for Senegal and the neighbouring countries (West French Guinea and Southern French Sudan), but outside that limited area the term is meaningless; instruments can elsewhere be played by anybody; and even in Senegal it is only one of their functions. Griots are by tradition attached to families; they are family jesters and buffoons with unlimited licence, whose duty it is to keep the company amused; they are the family bards, who learn and recite the family and national history (unless a griot can recite your family history for seven generations he is not paid) and the traditional stories and fables; they are the channel by which all gossip and rumour passes, for it is part of their duty to go daily to the marketplace and collect and bring back all the latest news; they are family magicians, who must be present at all ceremonies and whose advice must be taken; they are the first to hold the newborn baby and the last to touch the corpse; they are the actual recipients of most gifts given to their patrons; they are the spiritual mentors and guides of the young (griots are of both sexes); they are the women's hairdressers; they console the mourner and comfort the downcast with music and song; they are the family's official boasters, singing their merits, triumph and wealth on public occasions; they are lower than the meanest servant and often richer and more powerful than the master.

If a young man wishes to enter for the wrestling championship he will be accompanied everywhere by his griot, who will look after his comfort and morals, help him with his grigris, act as his boaster in the arena, play the drum which will announce his entrance and collect the greater part of the money and gifts, which, should he be successful or popular, will be showered on him. The preliminary bouts take several months; each village champion goes about to the neighbouring villages and if successful there farther and farther afield; only those who have become champions of a considerable area go to the finals at Dakar.

I was not in Africa at the time of the real championships, but on Whit Monday I was present at some semi-professional wrestling, at which the actual holder defended his title against a local champion who had been unable to fight at the proper time, and I was told that except for the size of the crowd – entrance had to be paid for; the real championship is in the open – almost everything was the same as at the real championships. But if the crowd was, comparatively, small, it had all the keenness of real aficionados. Another difference from the real championships was the small number of women present; usually there is a solid phalanx of them, singing and ululating, egging the fighters on and taunting them if they do badly; if the fighters delay too long they challenge them themselves, or take off their dresses and tell the men to put them on while they wrestle. I saw the wrestling in company with a young goldsmith who followed all the fights. His family were goldsmiths to Benga's family; goldsmiths are a separate caste and the trade is hereditary; they are attached to certain families, and the making and placing of the first tiny bracelet on the newborn baby has a symbolical and ritualistic meaning.

The preliminaries to the wrestling are more entertaining than the actual fights. The fighters enter the arena in order of merit at about ten-minute intervals – there are several smaller fights as well as the championship, and popular favourites make an appearance without the intention of fighting to gratify their fans – dressed in wrestling costume, a full dhoti-like loincloth in bright patterned materials, arranged so that a tail, sometimes in a different and contrasting material, falls behind. Their bodies and arms are smothered in grigris. They are preceded by the griots with drums, and followed by a group of supporters and sparring partners dressed in the same fashion. The griots take up their position in a corner of the arena, playing for their patron regardless of the rival griots by them, shouting their patron's glory, occasionally turning somersaults and handsprings to make people laugh, and before the fight doing the necessary grigri with their patrons (this usually consists of praying to the objects, which must be hidden from the crowd, generally in a hat) and making spells to avert ill luck. Meanwhile the champions swagger round the ring with a curious syncopated walk – a pause after every second step – walking on the balls of their feet with the shoulders slightly forward and the body swinging. They are followed by the crowd of their supporters. As they walk round the arena they chant the stories of their past victories: 'I am the man who threw Babakar Dy, I am the man who threw the champion of Joal . . . ' accompanying their boasts with the most dramatic gestures and with grimaces which are meant to be ferocious but are usually grotesque; occasionally they do various difficult gymnastic movements to show their strength. From time to time one fighter challenges another by lifting both hands; a corresponding movement from the other means that the challenge is accepted. If the wrestler is popular he will be given all sorts of gifts by the spectators, money, walking-sticks, even the clothes they are wearing. Open generosity always seems to excite a sort of mad rivalry among the Wolof; if one gives his coat the next will give his coat and vest also; the most popular notoriety is to be pointed out as the man who gave a thousand francs to the griot.

The afternoon I was present a young local fighter roused the popular enthusiasm and received showers of gifts. Intoxicated with his success he challenged Babakar Thiaw, the aspirant to the championship (the champion had not arrived), and probably piqued by the other's popular success Thiaw accepted. This astounded everyone, for the young man was in no way qualified to fight Thiaw, and all the spectators poured into the arena. The young man's family and backers were in a terrible position, for if the young man should fight and be beaten, as he was sure to be, he would have to withdraw definitely from the ring, and all their hopes would be dashed, whereas if he worked his way up gradually there was a great chance of his one day becoming champion. After long argument, in which everyone joined, his griot withdrew the challenge and the young man left the arena in tears, vowing that if he was not allowed to fight Babakar Thiaw on the next possible occasion he would give up wrestling; the crowd pursued him with hoots and catcalls. Babakar Thiaw was now as popular as the other had been, and he in turn was smothered in gifts which he handed to his griot; he seemed much more detached than the other fighters, and did not boast or do anything to attract the populace. Amongst many handsome people he was out-standingly beautiful, with a very refined and mobile face, so expressive that it was unnecessary to know the language to understand what he was saying, and a slim and elegantly proportioned body. About an hour and a half late the champion Massamba Déguène arrived, a great butchery gladiator of a man, with an absolutely enormous retinue of griots, dancers and followers who filled the arena and accompanied his dancing and boasting. Babakar Thiaw stood aside till Massamba should have played up to the public sufficiently, then challenged him and was accepted, and both wrestlers stripped for the fight – that is they took off their innumerable bracelets and amulets. The actual wrestling is similar to all-in wrestling, except that blows are not allowed, and once a man is thrown he is beaten. The fighters crouch opposite one another and rub their hands in the dust to get a good grip and start clawing at one another, with movements that are somewhat feline and animal, and yet so stylised as to resemble dancing. The fight is usually quite short, for a throw often follows from the first clinch. The finer points are as difficult for a novice to see as the work of a bullfighter; but in both cases the aficionados recognise and applaud them. Apparently the fight between Babakar Thiaw and Massamba Déguène made wrestling history; it lasted far longer than any other I had seen, and the grips were continually changed. After a very even fight Massamba was thrown and to the general delight Babakar Thiaw was acclaimed champion. He was smothered in gifts – men took off their belts and women their shawls and head-cloths and gave them to him – and was escorted in triumph through the town to some patron's house where he would be offered a great feast. The griot was staggering under the gifts.

My companion told me that the standard of wrestling had fallen terribly in recent years. Young men have to do their military service at a critical point in their training and they do not get enough to eat to develop properly. Moreover, they learn to drink alcohol.

5. Food

The foundation of African food is the absence of wheat. The substitute staple food depends on the climatic conditions of the region; the most general is millet, and after that maize and rice, the farinaceous roots of manioc and yam, and in the forest regions the unsweetened banana or plantain. All these grains and roots have to be ground to flour by hand, and the commonest sight in West African villages is women stripped to the waist, their breasts which they crush as early as possible to give the appearance of fertility hanging forward, and usually a small baby spread-eagled against their back, standing and pounding grain in a two-foot-high wooden mortar with a four-foot wooden pestle; the pestle is occasionally topped with a stone. This pounding is a laborious business and a great deal has to be done every day, for the resulting cake with a sauce is practically their only food. The time which must be taken in preparing food is one of the chief reasons against monogamy in the country; a good tip for missionaries who want to increase their flock would be to install a mill. Most Negroes eat, when they can, two solid meals a day; in the places which have goats or cattle they usually start the day with curdled milk. Such meat, fish or vegetables (chiefly okra, like cucumber) as they can get is made into a sauce into which portions of the warm cake can be dipped; the sauce is cooked on a foundation of oil (either groundnut, palm, or shea butter: this last stinks abominably) and very liberally flavoured with peppers, to an extent which makes it almost intolerable to a European palate; the peppers are used medicinally as a diaphoretic and febrifuge; a couple of old colonials told me that when they ran out of quinine they found peppers an adequate substitute. The food is prepared in two bowls and the eaters squat round on their heels, take a lump of the cake, knead it into a ball and dip it into the sauce. The first time I ate in this manner I committed the grave social error of feeding myself with the left hand – I am somewhat ambidextrous; this was not only a breach of good manners but was likely to bring bad luck. No food is ever eaten without the person who has cooked it eating a little in front of the diners; the fear of poisoning is, justifiably, very strong. A sort of beer, *dolo*, is prepared from millet; it is sweetish and very heady, not unpleasant. Another intoxicant, *raffia*, is produced from the sap of the palm tree; according to its freshness and manner of preparation it varies very considerably in its alcoholic content. I was several times offered and drank these liquors, and indeed they formed an accompaniment of some of my most enjoyable experiences; but I still think it was the most dangerous thing I did in Africa, for the drink is served in large calabashes (dried half gourds) and passed from mouth to mouth. I didn't catch anything.

Among the Wolof cooking is much more elaborate and varied. The ordinary diet is curdled milk in the morning, rice at midday and millet in the evening, but any excuse which can possibly be made is used for a feast and the most complicated dishes are prepared. Every sort of delicious sea fish is caught near Dakar and the Senegalese fish rice is noted throughout the colony; it is prepared in the following manner. Groundnut oil is heated in a dish; when it is hot onions and tomatoes are sliced into it and pieces of every sort of crustacean and sea fish are put into it, with small cabbages, okra, manioc and yam, spices, small peppers and seasoning. This is covered with water and cooked slowly for about an hour, when the fish and big vegetables are taken out and put on one side; rice pounded small is then put into the liquor and cooked slowly till all the liquid is absorbed, when it is served with the fish and vegetables warmed through. This dish is absolutely delicious. Senegalese couscous is also much appreciated; it is a foundation to a dish rather than a dish itself, for a variety of sauces can be served with it. Pounded millet is worked by hand till it is as fine as sand; it is then thoroughly steamed. Then dried and powdered baobab leaves are mixed with it and the whole is steamed again till the leaves have quite disappeared, leaving only their perfume and a slightly glutinous feeling to the sandy millet. It is now ready to serve as a foundation to a number of piquant meat and vegetable stews. It takes two days to prepare. A number of good dishes are made with maize flour, and several with groundnuts; I did not like these latter much owing to the burnt flavour of the nuts. Senegal is very rich in fruits: delicious, but unfortunately green-skinned oranges, the mango like a large plum with a slightly terebinthine flavour, the paw-paw, a tree fruit which resembles a melon, save that it is softer in texture and more perfumed; the corossol, another tree fruit with a pith that looks and feels rather like cotton wool but which is full of a juice with the flavour of pineapple sorbet; the darkassou, a plum-like fruit in which the stone is outside the pulp, full of an astringent but very refreshing juice which stains materials indelibly; small sweet lemons and many more whose names I did not learn.

I have always maintained that a varied cuisine with its resulting appreciation of subtle flavours is one of the certain signs of a refined civilisation.

6. Personal Histories

Benga's paternal grandfather was *receveur de l'enregistrement* and *commissaire priseur* at Dakar. These functions have no exact English equivalent and can best be translated as public notary and auctioneer. They were important key posts and all public business passed through his hands; the older colonial administrators all knew him and many welcomed Benga for his sake. He was one of the richest property owners in Dakar, to which he had moved when the administrative service had been removed from the island of Gorée. He built the first two-storeyed stone house in Dakar, and also owned a number of important sites. He was a strict Catholic and his children were given their primary education by the missionaries (there was no lay education at the time), and his sons were then sent to complete their education at Montpellier in France. The younger son studied law, was articled to a solicitor in Paris, married a Frenchwoman and set up as barrister in a French provincial town, very successfully. He has only paid one short visit to Africa since his childhood, and has refused the numerous invitations which have been made to him to stand for parliament in Senegal. The elder son, Benga's father, returned to Dakar and took a position in his father's office, subsequently holding various posts in the administration. As a child he had been very fond of a distant cousin of his and had been engaged to her; but she died and he did not wish to marry her elder sister, as both families desired, since he had fallen in love with a young girl named Marie Loum. This match was bitterly opposed by his father, who did not consider the alliance good enough. Marie Loum's father came from the Saloum, one of the provinces of Senegal; he was occupied with intercolonial commerce and was also well known as a healer. He had 'magical' powers and some very powerful grigris by which he made many famous cures. His daughter helped him a great deal in this and had considerable knowledge herself, though less than she imagined; after the death of her father a near relation was involved in a criminal case and was condemned to five years' penal servitude; to prevent him being transported, as would normally be the case, she went to Guinea to fetch a very powerful grigri called Nya Nya; the desired result was obtained, the condemned man being singled out at the moment of embarking to take a clerical post in the prison; but she was not able to control the forces she had invoked and her bodily and mental ruin and her death resulted before the grigri could be properly returned; since no one can now cope with it, it remains hidden in the unfortunate and unhappy house.

These two young people were so desperately in love that they hoped to force his parents' consent by presenting them with a *fait accompli*; but when the girl was big with child a terrific scandal ensued and the man denied his paternity. Loum for a time turned his daughter away, but they were reconciled before the baby was born. The newly born child so strongly resembled its father that old Benga, when he saw it, accused his son of lying, and the special Wolof ceremonies attending the birth of a child and his first being taken out of the house, normally performed by the husband, were performed by the husband's sister, who was the oldest member of the second generation. After the baby was born old Benga wished the marriage to take place, but Loum, whose pride had been insulted, absolutely refused his consent. So Benga, piqued and wearied, finally married the cousin, as his parents had wished; the same week Marie Loum was married, to demonstrate to the world that she was not a woman who could be abandoned. It did not need a fortune-teller to predict that neither marriage would be happy. Moreover, Marie Loum had cursed Benga's wife with sterility, and for very many years she had no children, to her husband's great grief; several years after the marriage a curious circumstance raised the curse for a moment and she bore a girl. When Benga saw that his wife was not going to produce an heir he claimed, recognised and adopted the child of Marie Loum, who was now given his name and known as François Benga. But the father was a man of strong and uncontrolled emotions, and his love for the child was often replaced by anger for all the disappointments in his own life that the child represented. Moreover, his wife hated the child, and was said by the neighbours to make magic to antagonise the father. Her life was very unhappy, for her husband brought mistresses to live in the same house and gave the housekeeping, which was properly her business, into the hands of his son.

Marie Loum had had three children, two girls and a boy, but she always considered little François her child. She was as capable as she was beautiful and managed efficiently her vacillating husband's business.

Young François passed an unhappy life between the two houses, neither of which he could call home. He received what education he could, where he could; when he was with his mother, with the missionaries who had their establishment opposite the house – he was a choirboy for a certain time; when he was with his father, at the lay schools and for a short time at a boarding school. Old Benga, in an effort to repair the evil he had done the child, had paid down money to the school at Montpellier so that he should receive a thorough education; but his father's spite prevented his availing himself of this. The father treated his son with a mixture of affection and gross brutality, at one time cozening him and at another using him as a servant, making him clean the shoes and wait at table, particularly when Europeans were present, and rewarding any lapse with blows. The father was very extravagant and dissipated the greater part of the family fortune. He used to make frequent trips to Europe for the greater diversity of pleasures to be found there, and on one of these he took François, now aged seventeen. François saved up a few francs and took the opportunity to run away. He took what work he could find to get a living in Paris (there is no sort of hostel for West African negroes in Paris) until an acquaintance told him that negroes were wanted to walk on at the Folies Bergères. He applied for and got the job, was noticed by the producer dancing during rehearsals – he had always had a passion for dancing, which was so much his natural mode of expression that without any specialised training he could do the most difficult technical feats – was given a little business to do by himself, and within a few years became one of the star attractions of the establishment. His father and mother both died while he was in Paris, and though his chief grief at his father's death – the man had died very young – was that it had come before he could revenge himself, he was much distressed at the death of his mother and returned to Dakar for her funeral. His mother's family had always seemed more his own. He returned to Paris for seven years more, during which time his reputation as a serious artist greatly improved though his financial position did not, and then returned with me in 1934.

His formerly rich family were now mostly poor, much of the money dissipated, more gone in death duties and taxes. The famous stone house was now a café, the greater part of the rest of the property either sold or falling into ruins. His mother's family welcomed him; his elder sister with the most admirable devotion had managed the household since she was twelve, when her mother had raised the grigri, looking after her young sister and her hypochondriac bedridden father and bringing up another orphan on a minute allowance of money (her brother had died young). She is one of the kindest, tenderest-hearted and most practical women I have ever had the good fortune to meet, and I sincerely hope her marriage will be a success. His father's family – chiefly aunts – on the other hand received him with contumely. How dared he, they asked, disgrace the family's name by flaunting it on the music-hall? Was he not ashamed of earning so disgraceful a living? None of them could actually be said to be doing anything very spectacular; the man who had the best job was driving a steamroller – but in the government's service! A position far more honourable than any independent work. They were very proud, very white-Russian, living in the memories of the glorious past, willing to let the present fall to pieces, while they might carry on a dead ceremonial and tradition and dream of what once had been.

Fodé Sanghor was born in the fishing village of Joal, some seventy miles from Dakar. The village is extremely picturesquely situated on the edge of the sea, with opposite it an island inhabited by fishermen. On this island the people live practically naked, and all their water is so salt that they have to come to the mainland in pirogues – hollowed-out tree trunks – to fetch drinking water. The country is extremely fertile and all the varieties of palm grow near it. There are several seminaries in the neighbourhood and the population is predominantly Catholic. Fodé's family was mostly Catholic, but his father was a Mohammedan, and when Fodé was seven years old he was given in the charge of a wandering marabout, whom he accompanied for seven years over most of the region, learning the Koran and incidentally picking up half a dozen native languages. At the death of the marabout Fodé returned home, but was so harshly received by his family that he left for Dakar to strike out for himself. He apprenticed himself to a chauffeur in whose house he lived many years, working for his keep and learning the business. When he knew the trade sufficiently he became a taxi chauffeur. There is no taxi-owning company in Dakar, but various Europeans and Syrians buy one or two cars for which they get a taxi licence and which they let out on hire. The cars are not fitted with taximeters; they are hired either by the journey or by the hour. The chauffeur gets a retaining fee and a percentage of the gross takings – it speaks well for the honesty of the Wolof that such an arrangement is possible – and is responsible for petrol, repairs and fines. These last are extremely heavy and are given for a variety of trivial reasons without appeal – having a companion on the seat beside the chauffeur, stopping on the wrong side of the road, hailing a prospective client instead of waiting till they are summoned, wearing native clothes, and other offences equally grave; if a chauffeur protests he knows he will have the police on his tracks for ever. The only possible way of living in peace is to acquiesce and to try to win the benevolence of the police by acting as unpaid chauffeur whenever they wish.

The job of taxi chauffeur, when obtained, is very insecure. It is an axiom which I have had several times repeated to me by Europeans that a native becomes useless as a servant and takes advantage of his position after a period which some people put at six months and others at eighteen, and at the end of the period one should dismiss the servant as a routine measure, to encourage the others. This is firmly believed and practised by the owners of taxis; moreover, they will often change chauffeurs to oblige a friend or to pay a debt. With the accentuation of the crisis the negro chauffeur has become doubly insecure, for there are now poor whites who will take the job under the same conditions. Fodé got and lost a great number of jobs, his personal character militating against him. For the greater part of his life he had been unwillingly solitary; he has great capacity for devotion which he is ready to lavish on his patron, with the result that he takes any reprimand terribly to heart and will either give up a job if reproaches are made to him, or sulk for days on end and in his misery do everything wrong. Except for this morbidly sensitive pride he did not look or behave like the average Wolof; he was fairly small with very sharp features, economical and not ostentatious. It would be difficult to find a better servant, for he was always willing to do whatever he could to be useful, and very quick to learn and foresee what was wanted. He always used to carry my accursed camera and plate-box, and knew its ritual better than I did myself. When I had to take him to task I would use the blackmailing method – you have hurt me so much, you have made me so ashamed – which was despicable but effective. Fodé considered me as a young child whom he had to look after and protect – I was to the chauffeurs an extraordinary phenomenon because I talked to them, looked after them when they were sick, and particularly because I ate the same food as they did, a thing which had never been imagined before; I was not a 'toubab', the semi-mocking name for a European, but Geoffrey (in conversation among themselves: to my face I was Monsieur) – and he made it his particular business throughout the journey to see that I was not cheated and did not spend too much money; he would walk for miles to save centimes at distant markets, would bargain endlessly on every occasion, and would hardly allow me to make the necessary repairs to the car. When the car had to be put on the train at Bamako he wanted to be allowed to go by the semi-direct train, which took over five days on the journey but cost fifty francs less. He was responsible for the car and looked after it very thoroughly, getting up before dawn to wash and polish it. He was a good driver in towns, but I did not feel so safe with him on bad roads.

When Fodé was introduced to me he was working for a government functionary, which was strictly illegal: no government functionary is allowed to engage in any sort of business, but they nearly all do, using some accommodation name to cover themselves. It was through Fodé that we hired the car. During our absence a friend of the functionary asked him whether he could find a job for his (the friend's) chauffeur while he was in Europe; the functionary said he could and dismissed Fodé on his return without even a reasonable excuse; he also attempted not to pay Fodé the wages that had been agreed on, on the ground that some repairs were necessary to the bodywork, and the threat of a lawsuit was necessary to make him pay the greater part. The last news that I had of Fodé was that he was again workless and alone.

Alioune Diouf is a colossus of a man, very tall and very broad, with a skin so black that it seemed as if it would leave a mark on whatever it touched. His skin was very smooth, close-knit and satiny in texture; it may be said indeed as a generalisation that the darker the skin, the farther evolved epidermically from the ape. The European with his coarse hairy skin and straight lanky hair is uncomfortably simian; the Oriental is a less hairy animal, but a woman's coat could as well be trimmed with Annamite's hair as with monkey's fur; it is only the negro with his almost complete absence of body-hair and his short curly head-hair whose surface does not recall the ape's. (We can console ourselves with our superiority in the matter of lips and noses; even if our sense of smell is practically atrophied, the organ with its thinness and prominence is most distinguished.) Alioune has a large and column-like neck, a completely spherical and rather small head which he keeps shaved; viewed from the back in the car his silhouette was extremely strange. He limps slightly, owing to a sore on his ankle contracted during childhood which was treated by magic, and as he is justifiably vain of his personal appearance he refuses to wear European clothes which would emphasise this deformity while the boubou hides it; he prefers to pay the resulting fines.

Alioune is a member of a large, proud and well-to-do peasant-farmer family in the province of Baol. Until he had to do his military service he had never been more than a walk from his native village. His family are extremely devout Mohammedans and he received a very thorough Koranic education. He follows all the ritual scrupulously and was constantly quarrelling with Fodé because the latter smoked. He obeyed scrupulously the prophet's injunction to divide all he had with the needy. At Bamako he met a comrade in tatters who appealed to him for help; he gave him two of the four boubous he had brought with him for the journey. He complained that he was never able to wear out his clothes; before he had had the full use of them he was always forced to give them away. All the time that he was in work he had a large army of dependants. One of the chief incidents he remembered of his childhood was that he had blasphemously picked some ears of grain before the first fruits were offered at the mosque; he came back from the fields with his head twisted to one side.

To his great distress he and his mother and all her family were psychic. His mother and sisters were m'Deup and would fall in catalepsy at the sound of the tomtom. He feared that he, too, had this gift of Eblis, and kept carefully away from the sound of dancing all the time he was with us. He had ghostly attendants which he had seen and heard from his earliest childhood; bluey-grey shapes would float past his eyes from right to left, similar to humans in flowing robes from the knees up, save that all but a little of the face was invisible; they would speak to him in boys' voices, foretelling the future and advising him on his conduct. If he was ever lost on foot they would set him on the right path. He was much perplexed by these ghostly mentors, for they were completely unorthodox; at the same time he was in no way frightened of them and they had always served him well. He always took their advice, even when it seemed meaningless or stupid; on different occasions they had told him to retrace his footsteps or perform apparently meaningless acts, and on each occasion he had profited strangely by their advice. He had never told anybody about these visions; when they appeared to him when he was in company he was forced to withdraw and lie down.

He told me about these visions at Abomey. As we got deeper into the fetishist country he was distressed with more and more horrible night-mares; several times he had woken us up with his screams, and the morning before he told me his story he had bitten through Fodé's arm in a nightmare struggle. The curious thing about these nightmares was that he was menaced by the different fetishes, and especially the smallpox fetish, in their esoteric shapes with all their proper attributes; but it was practically impossible that he should know this (in fact, he did not know that his mare was the fetish), for the fetish is never under any circum-stances pictured in even vaguely human shape; nor did I know it when he described his dream to me, though my suspicions were aroused and subsequent conversation with the fetish priests confirmed my diagnosis.

All the time we were in the country Alioune never went outside the rest-house and he could not communicate with the natives; his French was fragmentary and otherwise he spoke only Wolof and Arabic.

I was able to cure his nightmares. He had considerable belief in me as a magician – I had told his hand correctly – and he already knew the use of the pentagram. And for some unanalysable reason I massaged his shoulders and neck, pressing very heavily; I did not at the time know why I did this, but two nights later when I was being initiated in a fetishist convent the same massage was done to me. I also became strangely clairvoyant in that curious atmosphere, an ability which I have not possessed before or since.

After Alioune had completed his military service he returned home for several years. He got married, but his wife who came to live with his family quarrelled with everyone; she thought she was superior and they knew they were, and he was quickly divorced. He was very sober temperamentally and remained celibate for several years. He had married a young girl a short time before he left with us.

It was only when the crisis deepened and the price of groundnuts fell to nothing that he came to Dakar to earn a living. He had learned to drive a car at home and was a first-class chauffeur and mechanic and worked tirelessly; but he was terribly proud even for a Wolof and was constantly having rows.

As I have already explained, he came with us at very low wages (his own terms) to escape his hangers-on. He hated the journey with its discomfort and strange food – in the end he always cooked the rice for all of us as no one else could do it to his satisfaction – and despised all the other negro races as pagans and savages, who put up with intolerable treatment through poorness of spirit; he said that on his return he was going to offer a large thank-offering for being born Senegalese. He had a very retentive memory and got by heart the whole route and the distances between every village. He and Fodé did not get on very well together, though they had long been friends, for the latter saw that we much preferred Alioune as chauffeur and was bitterly wounded, and Alioune to keep the peace and to preserve his dignity withdrew himself more and more. He never offered his services as Fodé did, but whenever he was asked to do anything he did it willingly and well. The only aspect of the journey which interested him was the money-making possibilities of the different places; the plantations of the Ivory Coast excited him, for he thought that anyone as sober and industrious as he was could do well there. He had an amazing facility for falling asleep anywhere at any time and in any position (he had acquired this when looking after a taxi at night), and for continuing sleeping for an indefinite period. When I asked him if he was champion sleeper of his home town he replied truthfully that he was a triple champion: for sleeping, for eating and for working. He was always joking and had a very pretty wit; Benga said that he spoke remarkably pure, picturesque and subtle Wolof, but that of course I was quite unable to judge; for although I picked up a smattering of the language my vocabulary was strictly utilitarian.

7. Dakar Nigger

From certain points of view the population of Dakar can be divided into two classes – those connected with the administration (whether civil or military) and the rest. The functionaries number about three thousand and are in every sense the masters of the city; the seventy-odd thousand of Europeans, Syrians and negroes exist chiefly to pay taxes, which will keep their masters in the necessary comfort. These taxes are as high as they are numerous; besides death duties and income tax which are reckoned as in France, seven per cent is levied on all rent paid and on the assessed value of all furniture down to photographic enlargements – obviously necessary if the functionaries are to live rent free; water and electricity are excessively dear – both are measured by meters – but if the functionary is going to pay twelve francs quarterly as nominal rate for his water it is obviously necessary that an ordinary house with, say, three taps, should pay perhaps four hundred francs for the same period; there is the head-tax and the personal-service tax (prestation), but obviously the wages for the servants and the cars that a grateful republic supplies free to those who serve her must be paid by someone. The railway is extremely dear; but all government officials have free passes and an enormous allowance of personal baggage, and after all the railway cannot be run for nothing. The list could be continued indefinitely. It may be remarked that by English standards all except the highest functionaries receive ludicrously small salaries; their perquisites, however, are endless, and it would almost certainly be cheaper to pay them adequately and be done with it; if the weeding out of supernumeraries, started by Monsieur Laval as an emergency measure, were carried out thoroughly, the colony might even become self-supporting.

This weight of taxes is chiefly borne by the negro, though the traders and people in independent professions are kept near bankruptcy; but few Europeans have property in Dakar. The heavy import duties and market taxes fall naturally on the consumers.

At the beginning of this century negroes owned nearly all the town of Dakar; taxes and death duties have gradually forced them out, but this action was much hastened by the Crédit Foncier (Building Society) which in 1929 visited all negroes owning property in Dakar and offered to rebuild their houses, enlarging and modernising them; this philanthropic work would be paid for out of the increased rents which would be the result. There was a housing shortage at the time, and the negroes, humanly anxious to get something for nothing, nine times out of ten signed on the dotted line. The houses were built, the crisis came, the housing shortage vanished and building after building was foreclosed upon. The dispossessed negroes went to live in the Medina, a geometrical ghetto of one-room stone huts, built by a thoughtful government a little way out of the town.

The colour bar is extraordinarily strong in Dakar. Negroes are practically never seen in the cafés, restaurants and hotels; indeed, the *patronne* of the 'Atlantic', where we stopped, voiced the popular sentiment when she said I had lowered the tone of her hotel by bringing niggers (Benga) into it; niggers were only seen in her establishment as 'boys' or porters; everyone had complained. It is true that I had protested at the bill, which was far higher than the agreed price.

The racial discrimination is started by the missionaries. There is a club attached to the mission in the rue Malenfant; but although the congregation is predominantly negro you can seldom find one in the club, nor would he be welcome if he came. The little negroes at the mission school are used as unpaid church servants; it is perhaps one of the reasons for the strange fact that in recent years not a single negro has won any of the open State scholarships.

In theory all professions are open to negroes; but since to study medicine or law properly it is necessary to take a degree in France the number who can qualify is strictly limited; the highest position they can reach in Africa is that of auxiliary doctor (partially trained) and midwife. A certain number of medical scholarships to France have been given, but the students have only been allowed to become veterinary surgeons; I know of two cases personally in which the young men moved heaven and earth to be allowed to study human medicine, for which no one denied that both showed considerable aptitude: the official reply was that there was no need for negro doctors and they could either become vets, or forfeit the scholarship. One acquiesced, the other did not. There are now probably more horse-doctors than man-doctors in AOF.

The visitor who only spends a few hours at Dakar might reasonably wonder whether he was in Africa at all; except for the dockers and taxi drivers there are not so many negroes to be seen as at Marseilles. A European will sell you stamps and cigarettes, a European will try on your shoes, a European may even drive your taxi and carry your bag. In the government buildings the greater number of typists and clerks are white. The brothels are naturally stocked with and controlled by Frenchwomen, and the casual whores in the dance-halls are white. A great number of the governmental and commercial employees are (quite illegally) the wives or relations of minor officials and soldiers.

In the barracks the Europeans and negroes, though serving under the same conditions, are scrupulously segregated. For some reason the coal-black Martiniquais are counted as Europeans.

A certain number of negroes get positions in the administration; but the government employees are divided into two classes or cadres, the

European and the native; it is only the former which carries perquisites with it and it is very difficult for a negro to get into it; and I know of a number of cases in which a negro and a European do identical work side by side and the European receives double salary.

With so many careers closed to them and so many poor whites ready to take their job, it is small wonder that unemployment among the negroes is chronic and that they accept it as normal that one in five should work and should support the four idle; but despite their ever-growing pauperisation and exclusion these French citizens are far happier and better off than the other French negro subjects; if they are too badly cheated or abused they have some redress in the law courts; and they cannot be really badly manhandled without their assailant being reprimanded.

The mortality among young negroes is unaccountably high. Tuberculosis, generally fatal to negroes, is now, of course, common in Dakar, plague is practically endemic, and there are periodical outbreaks of yellow fever; but it is not from any of these recognisable causes that the young people die. I do not know how many times Benga asked after a schoolfellow and was told that he had died some time ago; and on every occasion when the cause of his or her death was asked, we were told 'He just died; in the morning he seemed quite all right and he was dead by nightfall.' During the first week of our stay in Dakar two young men whom we had met and talked to, and who had seemed in robust health, died in this mysterious fashion. They were both educated and unemployed; and it seems as though in West Africa, as has happened already in Melanesia, the natives are so overwhelmed with the hopelessness of their position that they have lost the will to live. It is noteworthy that such unaccountable deaths are far more common among the educated classes than among the proletariat.

ITINERARY TWO

The Horrible Journey

FODÉ BROUGHT THE CAR ROUND to the hotel at five. After nearly a fortnight of very mixed emotions in Dakar we were leaving for the interior. The peripeteias by which we had finally got a suitable car on possible conditions would fill a volume. Twice when we thought we were settled negro information made the car or the chauffeur undesirable. We had interviewed everybody of any consequence in practically the whole of the administrative service; they had been kind but vague; and the only piece of information that we had got was that the rains were due to commence, that if we did not arrive at Bamako that week we should never get there at all (the road was open for another month), and that once there it was extremely improbable that we would get farther. Acting on this advice we left extremely precipitately, missing by two hours the Governor-General's letter of introduction; if we had waited for it our journey would undoubtedly have been simpler, but we should have seen quite a different Africa. If you are recommended to the administrators, the administrators look after you; your time and your movements are planned.

There was one man who did know the conditions in the interior, who had motored throughout the colony; he gave us a great deal of the most helpful advice. It was thanks to his advice that we bought water-bottles – we had thought that two small thermoses would be sufficient – and took pieces of corrugated iron to put under the wheels of the car when it got stuck in the mud. He advised us to take a spade and hatchet, but we had no room for them, and only once felt the lack. He also told us that only fairly high-horsepowered American cars could cope with the roads we should meet; French cars had not enough pulling power, and were all too low for the very uneven roads. Thanks to his advice, we avoided some of the most painful errors, but it was quite a little while before we learned enough to take proper provisions of food, water and petrol with us. To start with I adopted the negro belief that 'something was bound to turn up'. We were both completely inexperienced in solitary travelling and at first often went hungry in consequence.

The car was a 15-horsepower four-seater Pontiac with a touring body; it had just been run in when we hired it. The first morning we spent three hours packing the luggage and loading it; subsequently we got this down to three-quarters of an hour. On the luggage carrier were three small tin trunks – we had been told to get them to guard against termites – which contained our clothes, the medicine chest, books and playing cards – most useful in the very long evenings and during rain – cooking utensils, tinned food, photographic plates and – until it made a lordly present for Prince Aho at Abomey – the chemical ice-making machine with its salts. I never found out if it was able to make ice, for it took half an hour to produce sufficient to cool a long drink, and I could never wait that long. The folding table and the pieces of corrugated iron lay on top of the trunks and the lot was covered with a waterproof sheet. On the front mudguards were tied the two green waterproof sacks which contained the camp beds, with their mattresses, pillows, rugs, and mosquito nets. We did not take any linen. The bags also contained the folding chairs, old clothes which we had taken to give as presents and which the chauffeurs greatly appreciated on our return, the chauffeurs' belongings tied up in bundles and anything else which was too knobby to fit in elsewhere. In the body of the car where we sat were the camera and slide-case, a one-pint and a three-pint thermos, when possible filled with ice, my typewriter, a loose coat, mackintoshes, a Woolworth (or rather Prix Unic) hatbox which we had bought at the last minute in Paris and which stood the journey valiantly, which contained a few tins of sardines, emergency medicines (bandages, permanganate of potash and at one moment chlorodyne), towels, tin-openers, toilet paper – in fact everything which might be needed in a hurry – the petrol-burning lamp which was shaped like a hurricane lantern but which burned a fragile mantle and consequently had to be wrapped in coverings and treated with the greatest care, a basket to hold fruit and cooked food and occasionally a four-gallon tin of petrol. There was not too much room inside the car and the tinted glasses were always getting mislaid. Beside the chauffeurs were usually eight gallons of petrol – the reservoir only held ten – a large tin container, which served as cauldron at nights and as pail by day, with the cooking stove inside it, a petrol tin with one side taken off which held the metal drinking bottles, and various other bottles containing methylated spirit, petrol for the lamp and stove, a spare bottle for melted butter, a bottle of vegetable cooking oil, and fruit, and usually a little spare motor oil. At first we thought we would only have room for Fodé, but when everything was placed we saw that two men would not be more uncomfortable than we were, and Alioune came with us at literally five minutes' notice, as auxiliary chauffeur and help. We had already had experience of his excellent driving.

As the luggage was being put on to the car a strange man came and held Benga in conversation, saying that his wife had just had a child which he would name after him. Benga was at a complete loss, for the man was a stranger, and was hesitating when his sister pulled him away and dissolved into tears. The man was a notorious sorcerer, the son of the most dangerous sorceress of Dakar. Marie fetched her bottle of holy water and drenched us and the car with it, which effectively prevented any evil result.

When we were finally ready to start it was discovered that Fodé had not got the necessary certificates of vaccination and immunisation against plague, without which we could not leave the neighbourhood. We went to the native Service d'Hygiène, which was already full of negroes who had arrived that morning, but I used my pigment prestige and got Fodé treated before any of the others. I never got over the shame of taking advantage of my colour, but it was so useful and saved so much time that I constantly traded on it. For anyone who has not a naturally Imperialist constitution this is one of the most disagreeable facets of African travel.

At last we got started, and for twenty miles drove over asphalted roads – the longest finished stretch of asphalted road that we found in

French West Africa – to the town of Rufisque. A few years ago Rufisque had been an important and prosperous port, for it had handled the groundnut trade, Senegal's unique export; but the price of groundnuts had fallen from 200 to 50 francs a hundredweight, and the dwindling export trade had been taken by the improved port of Dakar; the small trolleys stood rusting in the empty streets.

After Rufisque the road changed to a narrow, shifting, sandy track, scored by deep gullies of which a few had been bridged, and except for small stretches kept the same character till Bamako, a distance of about eight hundred miles. The road is purposely kept in an almost impassable condition to divert as much traffic as possible to the State-owned railway, whose track runs parallel with the road; but its charges are so high that nearly all goods are conveyed by road.

The landscape was monotonous and dismal. No rain had as yet fallen and all the undergrowth was burned brown; most of the country was covered with a thin scrub of acacia and other thorny shrubs, too mean to make a forest, but dense enough to prevent any distant view. Many of the shrubs had their dead leaves still hanging to them, though a few were putting forth their new green. Some parts where the scrub was less thick had big trees dotted about; in Senegal these are mostly the baobab, which looks quite nice when in leaf and seen from afar, rather like an old oak in form, with curious flowers like inverted magnolias hanging down with stringlike stalks; but when it is bare, that is, from October to June, it is probably the ugliest vegetable in creation, with an enormous squat trunk, many yards round and generally rotten, with a tangle of short branches on top from which point out measly little fingers. Despite its unpleasant appearance this tree (*Adansonia digitata*) is of the greatest use to the natives; the couscous is flavoured with its young leaves, cord and rope are made from its bark, and the fruit can be used for glue or as a substitute for curdled milk! The noblest tree in the West African landscape is the cotton tree (*Eriodendron anfractuosum*), which is practically evergreen with leaves like a chestnut; its silver-grey trunk sometimes goes as high as two hundred feet before the branches commence. The trunk is covered with large thorns which make it impossible to climb and it has usually near the base curious thin outgrowths like buttresses. The cheesy wood is quite useless except for pirogues, but the fibre which surrounds the seeds makes a very good substitute for cotton wool and is generally used in the colonies for stuffing pillows and mattresses. This fibre is a strong irritant, and in the places where kapok is cultivated nearly all the natives suffer from ophthalmia during the harvesting season.

Of the other common trees the flamboyant (*Poinciana regia*) is the most spectacular with its numberless panicles of bright scarlet flowers; and the mango tree (*Mangifera indica*) the most grateful to the senses, with its solid crown of glossy pinnate leaves and its hanging loads of green and yellow fruit. The mahogany tree is surprisingly drab, and the teak with its large pale leaves commonplace.

After the first rains a number of bulbous plants come into flower, the most common being a pinky-white amaryllis, incarvillea, a low-growing purple flower like a cross between a colchicum and a catleya which I could not identify, nerines and unnecessarily phallic black and green arums; but they are not common and hold their bloom for a very short time. In the forest the vegetation was more varied.

Just after the rains have fallen, before the grass grows too high, the savannah has a pleasantly domestic park-like appearance; but although it is no longer painful to the eye it is terribly monotonous. Except in sandy regions the earth is as red as Somerset clay.

The most vivid note in the landscape is provided by the birds; they are numerous and with the most varied and lovely feathers, scarlet and green, royal blue and amethyst, yellow and flame colour. They have the added attraction of being songless. Unfortunately I am no ornithologist and could not identify a single one of them. We saw some big birds; a variety of scavengers, vultures and hawks and carrion-crows, the big black marabout stork, a few crested cranes and great numbers of guinea-fowl. The butterflies are varied and lovely, with the most eccentric colour patterns and silhouettes, some with windows in their wings. We occasionally saw a few monkeys and antelope, once a horse antelope (coba), but otherwise no large mammals.

The monotony is broken by infrequent villages. The character of the villages varies with the races inhabiting them; in some the huts are isolated, in others joined together into large family groups by a united exterior wall. Among the Bobo the huts have tall conical roofs and are mingled with narrow storehouses; they are joined together with earth walls and look like squat Gothic castles. The materials of which the huts are made also vary considerably; the greater number are made of vegetable matter – straw, brush, palm leaves, withies – but in some localities they are made of earth or clay. The villages are, however, all made on the same plan, centring round an open space shaded by a large tree under which markets are held and where the village worthies can sit together and chat; often the village well is in the marketplace, and when the radiator boiled – a common occurrence – we would stop and bargain for tins of their inspissated mud while we were surrounded and stared at for the freaks we were. The villages mostly swarmed with pot-bellied naked babies, many with navel hernia, and with numberless chickens. These miserable fowl, dwarfed and wiry from the endless search for food (they are seldom given anything to eat), for three months became my most constant article of diet. They are horribly tough and flavourless and have to be eaten fresh-killed; their tiny eggs accuse them of exaggerated fertility. In many regions they are the only available meat, and many unhappy colonials see them on their table fourteen times a week; no wonder they are soured. The birds cost very little to buy, and outside the administrative centres we were usually presented with a brace by the local chief on our arrival. In the North there were some biologically very curious strains; one race nearly twice as big as the normal, another with frizzled feathers, a third with naked quills.

I did not foresee the serried ranks of chickens whose death I was to cause, the morning that we left Dakar, and I stared excitedly at everything we passed, pleased because it was so exactly like what the films had led me to expect: I felt as if I was having the satisfaction of saying 'I told you so' to the African continent. The road ran parallel with the railway line, through Alioune's home country, and he was soon telling stories. He was driving, for nobody unused to the soft sand could have gone a mile without getting bogged.

About twenty years ago the piece of rail that we were passing would not stay laid. Every morning it was put down afresh and every night it was torn up. People became afraid to pass there at night, and even the useless guards that were left were nervous, for such acts were obviously due to an evil spirit. And such indeed proved to be the case. A man who understood the ways of these gnomes advised surrounding the site with mirrors. This was done, and the next morning the manikin was caught peering at the reflection and walking round, trying to make out the mystery. He was immediately surrounded by planks and was slowly starved to death in this improvised cage. While he was dying he sang:

> *'Koo dan rere talalé;*
> *Té 'nga rere n'eti biskit,'*

which being translated means 'He who used to dine richly and well now has only three biscuits to eat.' This song was learned by all the children. The manikin looked like a small human being, but with a distorted face.

Fodé capped this story with another about a goblin which had been captured in Dakar last winter. A man went into his room with a lighted match, which the goblin swallowed. Every light which was brought into the room the goblin ate, so that the room became uninhabitable, and the services of a magician were called for. The magician captured the goblin by the simple expedient of popping a packing case over its head. While he was engaged in this a telegram came from his father in Guinea, who was also a magician, saying, 'Let it go at once.' He refused to do so and has since been sickly. The goblin was exhibited to the curious at Dakar, and Fodé was taken by his patron to see it. His hair stood on end with fright. The goblin was shaped like a man but smaller, covered with hair, and with his eyes continually downcast. His body was palpable, but it was impossible to touch his head. The goblin was eventually sent away, it was said, to the Institut Pasteur at Paris.

The morning passed in agreeable conversation and it was past midday before we arrived at Diourbel, where we hoped to lunch with the king, Ely Manel Fall, who was Benga's uncle. He had the official position of *chef de canton* of M'Bayar. After a little delay he received us most kindly. He is the most regal man I have ever seen, very tall and very broad, with a huge face like a kindly Roman emperor, his greying hair descending to a very pronounced widow's peak. His house was practically European in style and furniture, with comfortable chairs; Japanese reed pictures and Turkish prints decorated the walls. We sat in a through draught, for it was really hot; the clouds and breezes of Dakar were left behind. He was attended with considerable ceremonial; everyone who approached him took off their shoes and bowed or squatted so that they were always on a lower level than he. When he heard Alioune was with us he sent for him and enquired after his family, to the remotest cousins. He was a cultivated man and spoke French perfectly. He introduced us to his chief wife and some daughters, resplendent with jewellery, and to his little only son; he had been unlucky with male children. The little boy had just returned from Mauretania, where he had been in a Koranic school; he did not know any French. The king gave us a sumptuous meal, more delicious dishes and vegetables, locally grown, than I could eat; he regretted that we had not warned him so that he could have prepared a meal. He served wine but did not drink it. More useful still, he gave us a circular letter of recommendation to the most important princes and kings in West Africa, which proved absolutely invaluable. After lunch he took us to see a sacred tree, accompanied by his chief griot, who was also his mouth-piece; all orders were given to the griot, who passed them on to the people. The griot did not appear to approve of me, and refused to let the king be photographed. It was almost impossible to photograph Mohammedans except surreptitiously.

The sacred tree was a gigantic cotton tree. It had always been sacred but had not always been there. About a century ago it had been in a village some way away, where a blasphemous woodcutter had tried to cut it down. At the first stroke of the axe the tree had disappeared and had planted itself in Diourbel in the middle of the night. To bless its adopted town it had surrounded itself with wells of sweet water which would never run dry while the tree was there; the wells were present for all to see, but it needed an instructed eye to make out the axe buried high in the trunk. He told us the story of another sacred tree a few villages away. The administrator ordered the Public Works man to have the tree cut down; no one from the neighbourhood would do such a thing, and even the prisoners refused when commanded to do so; eventually a soldier from another province, who was afraid of nothing, cut it down. Within a week of its felling the soldier, the Public Works official and the administrator were dead.

Diourbel is the chief Mohammedan centre of Senegal and is noted for its marabouts and magicians. We did not have time to see anything of them, however, for it was getting late and was overpoweringly hot. The magnificent modern mosque built by Serine Bamba looked very ugly.

We had thought in our folly that we could reach Tamba Counda that night; but we barely covered half the distance. This was unfortunate, for there was no accommodation for passing travellers in Senegal – it might encourage them to use the road. When night began to fall we decided to stop at Kaffrine, where a colleague of Ely's lived. But he was away travelling, and we were at a complete loss when an unsuspected assistant administrator arrived on the scene, put a newly completed hut at our disposal – so new that it smelt of paint – and asked us both to dinner. This was almost the only time that Benga received an unsolicited invitation. He did not accept, however, as there was the unpacking to be seen to and the mysteries of the folding beds, lamps and stoves to be solved. He and the chauffeurs were starting to prepare a meal when an excellent couscous was sent round from the chief's house. I, however, was pleased to accept – indeed, it was impossible to do otherwise – and we went over to the administrator's house. He had living with him another European connected with the administration, a soured and embittered man who hated the colonies; this latter was separated from his wife and any other white man by nearly a hundred miles. I was inevitably given whisky to drink – it is technically illegal in the northern portions of French West Africa, and consequently no self-respecting man will drink anything else – and later a fairly indifferent dinner at which I made my first acquaintance with African chicken. The servants were prisoners, as they are in most West African outposts, and the soured man teased them continually – he probably thought he was being genial. He hated the negroes – they were lazy, dirty ('So would you be if you didn't have more and better water than they have,' interrupted the other) and untrustworthy. The assistant administrator on the other hand liked and was interested in the negroes – I had no experience to know how very exceptional he was both in his enthusiasm for his work and his frankness – knew their language, and when he made his frequent tours on horseback would sit beside the story-tellers in the evening and listen to their conversation. His chief complaint about the negroes in the district was that they were unambitious and incurious. About forty days' agricultural work a year supplied all their needs and no incentive would make them do more work. The only thing to do was to create more needs for them; a start had been made with clothes. A couple of villages away was a perfect and inexplicable mono-lithic stone circle; the negroes had made no legends about it; they were just stones. He had only been in the colonies about eighteen months and was full of enthusiasm; he had had rest-houses built and sanitary work done by the prisoners; if he could have got money grants he had numerous plans for the development of the neighbourhood. Unfortunately he was being transferred, probably to a place with quite different conditions, inhabit-ants and language, and all his plans would remain uncompleted or would be altered by his successors. He spoke with bitter envy of the district commissioners in the English colonies – the minute colony of Gambia was quite near – who often did all their service in the same district. Then you could get to know the people you had to deal with and could carry projects through; in French Africa you were seldom left even in the same colony two years. An enthusiastic and potentially most useful servant of the State was being made quite needlessly embittered, cynical and discouraged.

After dinner I went back to our hut to write. It was nearly full moon and a dance was going on, but we were both too tired to go out and look at it.

We got up at four the next morning and for the first and only time I washed in boiled water. I had been much frightened by the tales of bilharzia and other intestinal worms which could be caught through water, and I had been advised to have no contact of any sort with unfiltered water. But all colonials used the ordinary water without bad results, and boiling water took so much time that after the first day I washed in what water I could get and was thankful for it. It was only when the livestock in the water was excessively visible that I abstained.

We set off with the dawn and drove over dull and dreadful roads for eight hours; the only incident was a puncture. We arrived at midday at Tamba Counda, a fairly large town, and were given lunch by the local midwife, who was a friend of Benga's sister. Her house was in disorder, for a week ago she had received notice to report immediately to Dakar, as she was being transferred. She had sold her larger furniture and had taken the smaller objects with her. On arrival at Dakar she had been told that the official mind had been changed and she was to return to Tamba by the next train. A great deal of her crockery and instruments had been broken with the double journey. The game of General Post is a mania with the Dakar bureaucracy; as soon as anyone is settled anywhere he must be shifted to somewhere else. This works particularly hard on the midwives and auxiliary doctors who frequently marry one another; when the marriage takes place it is an incentive to the directing powers to put a couple of colonies between husband and wife. The girl was just succeeding in gaining the confidence of her patients, a difficult job, for she was a Catholic among Mohammedans and spoke a different language. A few weeks after our passage she contracted a civil marriage with a Mohammedan pharmacist; it is very difficult for a Catholic girl to marry another Catholic, for the few who can afford to marry are chary of engaging themselves irrevocably. Her mother was heartbroken at her marriage; she did not dare to appear to countenance her, for fear the priest should excommunicate her, as he had already done with another mother in a parallel case.

After lunch we did a little shopping and saw the native weavers making long narrow strips of material in different patterns of blue, black and white; the warp, always white, is several yards long and fastened some distance away from the weaver; the near ends are fixed to a primitive wooden contraption which is worked by the feet, or rather the big toes; the woof is of different-coloured cotton in shuttles and is worked by hand. The weather was very hot.

For several more hours we continued our dreary drive, the roads getting continuously worse; the heat and the jolting, combined with lack of sleep, made me feel very ill; I had a splitting headache and nausea and rheumatic pains all over my body; when I tried to stand I nearly fainted and, as always happens with me when I am very tired, I broke into tears. The others were much alarmed at this exhibition, which relieved me; Fodé advised me to eat sugar, and with a little brandy this greatly relieved me and I had some sleep. After night had fallen we had to cross a ferry, a wooden raft propelled by poles; this was the first of many, and on nearly every occasion the ferry was on the wrong side of the river. All the French ferries are primitive and slow; there is no charge made for them, however, and the modern steam-driven ones in the Gold Coast are very dear. A little while later we ran over a small antelope in the dark and the chauffeurs roused me from my torpor to borrow my penknife; the animal's throat had to be slit before it died or the meat would not be kosher. It was some time after nine when we arrived at the hotel of Monsieur Ferari at Kayes. As soon as we had driven into the courtyard Alioune lay down on the ground and went to sleep.

I went to the dimly lighted bar to get some beer and on my way there tripped over what I had thought to be a stuffed lion. I was somewhat taken aback when the lion rolled over on its back. As I stood in amazement the proprietor cried 'Grattez-le' and I rather gingerly tickled the lion's chest. It purred like a mowing machine.

Monsieur Ferari is the most extraordinary animal tamer I have ever come across. Besides the lion, who was called Toto, there was in complete liberty a most engaging young warthog who answered to the name of Hippolyte; besides knowing his name he would obey orders like a dog; moreover, you could set the clock by him. Every morning early he would go round the marketplace and shops to collect titbits; he would return at nine punctually and would sleep under the dining-table till three, when he would make another round for an hour; after his return at four o'clock he was willing to be sociable till sundown. The ostrich Josephine Baker was becoming a bit of a nuisance and Monsieur Ferari feared that he would have to get rid of her; she had fallen violently in love with one of the chauffeurs and spent her time stealing cola nuts which she would bring to him in her beak; followed by the irate vendors. Chewing cola nuts replaces cigarette smoking for most negroes; the nuts have a pinky skin and are very crisp with a rather bitter astringent flavour which I personally disliked; the pith is not swallowed but is spat out when thoroughly chewed, by which time it is a rust-red colour. The nuts, which grow in large pods (the tree is *Cola acuminata*), divide into four quarters when peeled and are much used for divination. A considerable tax is collected on them in the Ivory Coast, where they are cultivated; the very profitable trade in them is almost entirely in the hands of the Syrians. They have a stimulating and hunger-quelling effect.

A serval which Monsieur Ferari had recently acquired was still bad-tempered and was kept chained; he would not yet join the other beasts and the dogs and cats at the communal trough. Earlier Monsieur Ferari had had many other animals, including for some time a young giraffe, a female panther to whom he was devoted and who had once saved his life by clawing him out of a burning bed; a sheep and a marabout stork who had been inseparable; and several hyenas and lions. All the animals had been house-trained. He had a large collection of photos of his different pets; his chief interest was in making incompatible animals get on together and in changing their character; he had absolutely no fear of them and never hit them. He was unmarried. Kayes is in the midst of the game country and we were promised that we should certainly hear, if we did not see, hyenas and lions. We did neither.

Kayes is proud of being one of the three hottest places on earth. The heat is so fantastic that I have been frightened to talk of it for fear of being set down a liar. It reached 53 degrees Centigrade (about 127 Fahrenheit) in the shade at midday, and seldom falls to below 40 (102 Fahrenheit) at midnight. The well and tap water is so hot you can barely put your hand into it. When I went to do my packing in the hermetically shuttered and verandahed room, I scorched my hand picking up a thin silk dressing-gown.

We were given a room for form's sake and to put our luggage in, but nobody could, or was expected to, sleep in rooms. Beds were laid out in rows on the terrace roof, and everyone, men and women alike, lay on them and sweated silently in the moonlight, hoping for a breeze and sleep. Toto slept at the head of the staircase. At dawn we trooped down to our rooms which had got slightly cooler in the night, and tried for more sleep in a through draught with an electric fan a few inches away.

The only way to resist this heat is to keep active; if you lie down under it you sicken. Iced beer is not permanently refreshing, but it is very pleasant and we drank gallons of it; we even breakfasted off it. To get a drink reasonably cool the glass must be stuffed with ice (there is, fortunately, an electric ice-making machine at Kayes); liquid can be brought down to drinkable temperature by wrapping a bottle in wet cloths, or by putting it into a gargouillette – a very porous earthenware vessel – and standing it in a draught.

It was impossible to contemplate motoring in such a heat, so we decided to travel by night, which should be less tiring and would possibly stop the radiator boiling over so often and the inner tubes of the tyres bursting so frequently. We saw little of Kayes beyond the orphanage directed by nuns and consisting exclusively of mulattoes.

We set off about five and travelled without incident till sundown, when we lost our way among sisal fields. A couple of hours later we had a ferry to cross; Fodé routed out the ferryman by explaining that I was a commandant on important business. I tried to look as official as possible on such short notice. Running the car off the ferry Fodé cut his foot badly and I bandaged it; we took the opportunity to dine off bread and sardines; this was accomplished with considerable difficulty as no tin-openers could be found. After this I dozed fitfully as we drove on; a little after midnight the road ran along a river flanked on the other side by high cliffs; above the noise of the engine a number of voices could be heard calling, as it seemed to us, speaking urgently but incomprehensibly. Nobody said anything at the time, but about an hour later Alioune asked if we had heard the spirits. We had. I have no explanation to offer; whatever the noises were they were certainly not echoes. About four we had another ferry to cross, and by an extraordinary stroke of good luck the ferryman had just been roused by some Syrians who were returning to Dakar and the ferry beached almost the moment that we arrived. It was the only piece of good luck that we had; four tyres burst during the night and early morning and the hand-pump broke. At the worst and longest puncture I sat by the side of the road and wrote my diary.

About ten o'clock we limped into a pretty little town called Kita, picturesquely situated amongst hillocks with the huts built on stilts. We bought curdled milk and luscious but very messy mangoes for our breakfast, and then called on the administrator to borrow a tyre-pump and to beg drinking water, for we had finished all ours. The administrator was an angel and lent us a pump and chauffeur, and gave us water 'with something in it' to drink. He remembered Benga well from having seen him dance in Paris. There were a remarkable number of albinos in the village; and it is difficult to imagine anything more repulsive than a white negro, with a very coarse, pinkish, maculated skin, pale yellow curly hair and crimson eyes. The red albinos come near them in hideousness; their hair is carroty and their skin a particularly loathsome orange brown. I do not know the genetical explanation of this phenomenon; it seems possible that it is the same variant which causes our freckled eyelashless redheads. Negroes also suffer from a skin disease which turns them white in patches; the negro in the post office at Bamako had white hands and a negro priest at Joal had one half of his face white, like a restored 'old master'. It is not the same as leprosy, of which we saw a good number of cases. We left Kita a little before midday in stifling heat and travelled for eight hours more, with two punctures amidst continual flights of locusts. I survived the journey fairly well, feeling slightly light-headed, probably on account of an empty stomach; but I made a resolution, which I nearly kept, of never doing more than two hundred miles in a day; and I was so tired and bored that any favourable combination of circumstances would have brought me straight back to Europe.

We reached Bamako at sundown, having motored for sixty-six of the eighty-four hours since we had left Dakar; we had covered about eight hundred miles, and had had no food solider than sardines for the last three hundred. Lorry drivers habitually do the journey in two days, by heaven knows what superhuman efforts. It is the most unpleasant journey I have ever made.

Bamako is the capital of the French Sudan, and is a large and important town. It is divided into three sections: the administrative town pleasantly and coolly situated on a hill, some miles removed from the lower town, which consists of a fairly well planned European quarter surrounded by a number of native villages. It is on the left bank of the Niger.

It is always a mistake to see things with romantic names. The Niger calls up such glorious visions, such happy memories of Mrs Jellyby's philanthropic efforts; and at Bamako it is a shallow stream flowing in a number of channels with a broken-down wharf and a semi-smart Lido for dinner, dancing and bathing. Of course no negroes are admitted and full bathing dress is compulsory. Both the scene and the people recall some drab river restaurant just outside Paris. The French have an unrivalled facility for carrying their dowdier suburbs wherever they go.

We had asked a pleasant-seeming mulatto the way into the town, and when he directed us he advised us to go to the 'Hotel du Commerce'; we consequently went there and I booked rooms. I had hardly settled down and was attempting to scrape a little dirt off me when the proprietor broke into my room. He hadn't understood that the other room was to be for a nigger; that was absolutely impossible in his establishment. Very well, I replied, I was willing to have my luggage taken down; we would go elsewhere. Oh, no; that wasn't what he meant; he didn't want to turn me out; the nigger could find somewhere to sleep in the native village. I said that we had travelled together from London and Paris, and I didn't see any reason to change now; if Benga wasn't good enough for the hotel, the hotel wasn't good enough for me. Then he changed his tone; of course in that case circumstances were different; he had thought he was my servant; sometimes people wanted their servants to stop with them, and that was impossible, for then if anything was stolen his servants would be blamed. With the same argument he refused to let the chauffeurs carry the baggage upstairs, with the result that the hood of the car was torn, my fly-fans lost and one of our precious 'Termide' thermoses, which keep ice three times as long as any other make, was smashed. The hotel was uncomfortable and outrageously dear – hotels in Africa represented by far the biggest single item on the trip; and it was only fatigue and the necessity for having the car oiled and overhauled and of getting new tyres which made us stay there two days. After the first skirmish the proprietor was very obsequious; his wife was a slightly cockney very genteel blonde from Greenwich.

When we returned to Bamako a couple of months later the chauffeurs insisted that we should go to the unpretentious 'Niger', whose proprietor had housed and fed them when the 'Commerce' would have nothing to do with them. The proprietor was an incredible creature, a female impersonator who was taking a year's rest before continuing his world tour. He had had considerable success in the big Paris music-halls, and had created a furore in the colonies. He was short and very fat, with a blue chin; his hands and feet were tiny. He made us extremely comfortable, looking after all our wants, and doing the more elaborate cooking himself. When we left he made us up a picnic basket to save the expense of restaurant cars, and gave us special artistes' terms. When he was not busy with the housework he spent all his time gossiping; he told us practically the whole of his life history. His parents were Spanish born but naturalised French; they had a hotel in Fez, but were so strait-laced that he could not stop with them. His speciality was Spanish dances; he knew the whole classical repertoire, and had dozens of costumes in his room, besides a valuable collection of shawls which he used to exhibit in the lobby of the theatre where he worked. For ten years he had had a partner to whom he had been devoted; he had been gassed in the war, and was so strict, my dear, you can't think; I like to have a laugh, but no, he was always against anything which wasn't properly correct. When we were at the Scala in Berlin the management of the Eldorado wanted me to dance there; but my partner wouldn't hear of it. Is the *petite chaumière* still open in Paris? And who's So-and-so living with now? Have I played you my Albeniz record? This is how I dance it – and he would fetch his castanets and dance some peasant dance with all the appropriate expressions, far funnier than he could ever be on the stage with his sweaty short-sleeved shirt, his apron and his bright blue beard. Bamako is a horribly tedious town, and without his entertaining company the three days we were forced to spend there waiting for the train on our return would have been dull indeed.

Most of the actors in French West Africa are of the sort which the newspapers call 'described herself as an artiste', though they can usually sing and dance a little as well, which pays for their hotel room. We met one company on the road, which consisted of an extremely sissy young man who had been one of the boys at the Casino de Paris, and who staggered on hearing Benga's name, a thin brunette and a burly blonde fishwife. They were accompanied by the local administrator, a fat middle-aged man who was obviously having the time of his life, and who gave us completely misleading information so that he should not be parted from them. White prostitutes are forbidden in the interior; however, they frequently come by train into Bamako and are able to make sufficient money in the six days which elapse before they can be sent back to make the trip a very profitable one. There is a large garrison at Bamako.

The mulatto who had shown us the way to the hotel turned out to be a pest of the worst order, a limpet with a grievance. He pursued us wherever we went and poured out his sad story into our unwilling ears. His mother was Madagascan, his father Corsican – 'our name has been known in Corsican history for a thousand years' – and he had some post in the administration. His pretentiousness and his flashy appearance made him intolerable to the Europeans, and of course he could have nothing to do with negroes. He claimed he was slighted out of jealousy, and made up for it by telling long and completely unfounded stories of sexual successes, and in planning vague vendettas.

Two mulatto acquaintances of Benga saw us at Bamako, and we spent some time in their company. They both came from Saint Louis, the town of mulattoes par excellence; the mulattoes there form a race apart, marrying exclusively among themselves; after the second generation they become aristocratic – 'old mulatto families'. The genetics of mulatto crosses – West African by European in both first generations – have not, I think, been worked out, and such casual observations as I was able to make seem contradictory. Girls seem to be lighter in colour than boys, and later children than earlier children in the same family. A full range of pigment and hair variations can be seen in the same family, but white would appear to be dominant. The first generation of mulatto by

European did not present any superficial negro traits; with mulatto by negro the white stigmata had not disappeared in the third generation.

Of Benga's two acquaintances the elder was completely negroid in appearance; he had been for a great number of years in the administration at Saint Louis, but he had opposed Diagne and had consequently been shifted to the Ivory Coast. He identified himself with the negroes and was constantly protesting; he was proud of his reputation as a *rouspéteur*. He had some terrible tales to tell; among others the story of a negro who had been to Diagne to protest against the scandalous conduct of one of the latter's protégés. Diagne had soothed him with promises and sent him back to the Ivory Coast; meanwhile he telegraphed that if anyone gave the man food or shelter he would break him. The only person who dared oppose this veto was a European planter. When it was seen that the man was still alive a dinner was given in his honour, apparently by the anti-Diagnists, during which he was poisoned.

The younger mulatto, R, seemed physically like a South American with sharp features, wavy hair and café-au-lait skin. He was far too elegant, with a wasp-like waist, and was always dressed in riding clothes with a crop in his hand, as if he had just returned from an (imaginary) polo field. He spoke French with a preciosity of accent which is usually only heard in parodies of the Comédie Française, and took great care to insinuate into the conversation the names of the great and good whose houses he had managed to enter. He had spent several years in Paris in the unavailing attempt to make a good marriage, and had but recently returned to Africa; he had first taken a position in a lawyer's office, for he wanted to go into politics, but had then transferred to the administration as more stable; he was working in the customs. Before we left he presented us with copies of a pamphlet he had edited about colonial policy; even from the viewpoint of the *Action Française* it was reactionary, with its repetition of ragged clichés about security, 'la mission civilisatrice française', the AOF as a 'réservoir d'hommes', and panicky about the menace of Bolshevism and Islamism. I had meant to write him an ironical note about it, but forgot to, which may have been the reason why he cut the two appointments he made with us on our return to Bamako.

Or perhaps we were merely too shabby. The mulatto who denies his negro blood fills me with the same kind of disgust as the loyal Jews who protest to Hitler their solidarity with the Nazis.

In every town of any size in French West Africa there is a large orphanage kept by nuns and exclusively filled with mulattoes. Any unmarried Frenchman who comes to the colonies takes as a matter of course a 'mousso', a young virgin negress whose dowry he pays. If the girl produces a baby the European has to keep the mother and child for three years, after which the nuns take the bastard. Comparing the number of mulatto children with the number of adults I saw, I should imagine the mortality among them must be very high; they are susceptible to the diseases of both stocks, and do not usually enjoy the hygienic precautions which surround European children. It is probably better for them to die, for those that survive have a miserable life, rejected by both races; occasionally the father creates some sort of position for them, usually in the administration, but unless they become rich they are not accepted anywhere. The negro attitude to this cohabitation and the results has greatly changed recently; until the present generation it was held to reflect a certain honour; now it is a complete disgrace and many races refuse to countenance it at any price. The greater number of mousso are Peulh women – a curious pastoral race in Guinea with practically European pigmentation, features and hair; nearly every anthropologist has a different theory about them.

Bamako, and the greater part of French Sudan, is inhabited by the Bambara, a handsome race (particularly those from the banks of the Niger), fanatically Mohammedan and reared in a warlike tradition. They are many of them pedlars or 'dioula' and are to be found all over French West Africa; their language, called Dioula outside their country, forms a lingua franca for the whole colony. Their character is unpleasant, servile unless they are in authority, when they become brutal bullies. They are the great stand-by of the French administration. According to Fodé, the women are all whores, and dishonest at that; we were very glad to leave them for the Ivory Coast.

BOOK TWO

The Desert

Solitudinem faciunt, pacem appellant

1. The Administration

THERE IS A STORY which is often told about a famous French author who went to his native village to announce to his mother that he was leaving for the United States to give a series of lectures there. 'Go then, my son,' said the old lady, 'since you will gain money by it; but don't let any of the neighbours know.' Very few provincial French people think this story funny; the old lady was so obviously and instinctively right.

The French are by nature parochial. If a Frenchman leaves his family, his home town, and how much more his country, there must be some very peculiar, and probably disgraceful, reason for such an act. (When I was living in French families to learn the language I was never able to persuade people that it was normal for me to have been to boarding schools.) Consequently there is no tradition of colonial administration, and the posts are usually filled with influential hotheads who for some reason cannot be fitted into the home administration, or by poor people who have passed the necessary examinations and hope to make their fortune by work in the colonies. The chief exception to these groups consists of the relations of people who have important colonial positions. Of the administrators who have passed through the schools the few who are not Corsicans come from the neighbourhood of Marseilles or Bordeaux.

There is little which can attract men of ability in the French colonial administration. The few plums – such as governorships – are usually given outside the administration, and except for the men who have great

93

influence in Paris colonial administrators are grossly overworked and ludicrously underpaid. From the point of view of salary administrators are divided into several classes; there are slight family allowances. In 1927 an unmarried first-class administrator received 24,600 francs a year – the equivalent of £200 – and this has since been cut. This was the most that could be earned in local work. A monthly allowance for travelling expenses is added, on which an unconscientious man could save; servants, house and furniture and so on are provided, and also six months' leave every three years on full pay with all expenses paid to and from their home, and a retiring pension proportioned to the length of service. Even with such perquisites it is financially an unattractive prospect. With a few honourable exceptions Frenchmen who come to the West African colonies, whether officials or traders, do so with the intention of accumulating as quickly as possible sufficient capital to retire in a little house of their own in their native town; consequently the natural French parsimony receives a further impetus, which manifests itself in a number of ways; besides such illegal actions as saving on government grants and so on, a special price-list for goods to be sold to Europeans has been imposed on the natives, sometimes as much as three times less than the current market price; and occasionally an administrator might do a little private trading.

To guard against this eventuality Monsieur Carde, the then Governor-General, invented in 1924 the principle of the 'wheel' by which no administrator should serve in the same colony two terms running. This device may have discouraged trading: it was certainly effective in discouraging any more altruistic motive. Who would bother to get to know the language or customs of the people they were set over for so short a time? (Native languages are not represented in the admission examinations.) Who would try to develop or improve a district which he would probably never see again? Who would waste thought on schemes that his successor might or might not carry out? Original initiative, at all times subject to the whim of Dakar and Paris, was completely quenched. All that was left to do was to get through the daily grind sufficiently well to avoid criticism.

The work of a district administrator is manifold and endless. He is entirely responsible for the administration of his 'circle', which in some cases may have an area of ten thousand square miles. His chief pre-occupations, the collection of taxes and recruits, will be dealt with more fully later. He is responsible for law and order, roads and communications, and should deal with famines and epidemics. If the post is an important one, he will have to help him an assistant administrator, a special officer responsible for the policing of the district, and a doctor. Very occasionally there is an agricultural expert and a man from the Public Works department, but usually their functions fall on the administrator. In the most populous areas there are a few sub-administrators in the larger conglomerations.

Besides having to be judge and jury, road builder, real-estate agent (the administrator grants land to European and occasionally native planters), labour recruiter, tax collector, sanitary officer and agricultural expert, the administrator has to fill in an endless number of forms. The system under which French colonies are governed was laid down by Napoleon, and has since been modified but not recast; this fact, added to the excessive centralisation of the government, gives the administrator a great deal of often completely useless clerical work.

The task is made somewhat easier by the fact that provided his returns of money and men are satisfactory an administrator is practically omnipotent in his district. Except for an occasional and heralded visit of an inspector or governor he is in no way controlled. The negroes, with the exception of citizens, are ruled by the administrator's interpretation of the interpreter's version of tribal custom. The administrator's word is law, from which, as far as I know, there is no appeal. He is a little god. There is little responsibility combined with so much power; an administrator's tenure of office is so short – it is seldom that one stays a whole term in the same district – that any faults he may commit can seldom be visited on him; if he is not already removed he can blame errors on his predecessor. At Dakar they are judged by their returns.

Such a combination of circumstances – too much work with inadequate pay, too much power with too little responsibility – would be trying for any man, whatever his abilities. And French West Africa does not on the whole get able men: there is nothing to take them there. The climate, though extremely varied, is almost universally unpleasant for Europeans – the chief exception is French Guinea, which is mountainous and has an almost European climate: it is a very isolated colony and is notoriously a haven for people with influence – and people who enter the colonial service naturally prefer if possible to work in the pleasanter colonies. French tropical Africa gets the candidates at the bottom of the list.

There is a great deal to be said against a ruling caste founded on money and birth, such as we possess; it is obviously unfair and excludes a great number of competent people; but it has many advantages over the French system founded on examinations and influence. Men who are trained in the belief that they are born to command may lack many qualifications, but they are unlikely to lose their head when they do get authority in the same way that people who have lived their lives in subordinate and mediocre positions do. They are so certain that they are the salt of the earth that they take it for granted and presume that everyone they deal with will also do so; consequently they can treat subordinates with the same consideration and impersonal politeness with which they treat servants; they do not have to insist on their superiority and prestige. Most of the French administrators I met were not bourgeois turned 'gentilhomme': they were petits bourgeois turned Caesars. The results were equally deplorable for rulers and ruled. An evilly disposed or cowardly man can create almost intolerable misery; I was in two areas in which the negroes would run and hide if possible at the approach of a white man; in one the present and in the other the last administrator would have anyone, man or woman, who did not leave what they were doing and salute him as he passed manhandled by his guards and imprisoned; sometimes the ill treatment was ordered because he thought the man was looking impertinent. There have been some notorious criminals – such as Blocquard who was finally arrested – who spent their time devising tortures for their own amusement. I have also heard a number of extremely circumstantial and detailed stories of rape. But more aggravating than these Neronian proclivities are the endless petty annoyances. In towns where officials live dancing is generally not allowed after eight at night; and at least in one district any noise after that hour is punished with a fine and prison. Fines are freely and arbitrarily imposed; it is a very general practice, both with officials and planters, to impose fines for various misdemeanours and deduct them from contracted wages, so that it very frequently happens that a negro will find he has worked for a month for nothing, the money he should have earned being taken for fines. A young agricultural expert told me that the negroes resent this more than anything. It seems to me probable.

A constant and regular supply of prisoners is absolutely essential for French administrators. Their own comfort depends on them. In some cases they are domestic servants – in all, gardeners, fetchers of wood and water, latrine emptiers and usually town cleaners; they build the houses for the Europeans, and rest-houses, and generally make themselves useful. An empty gaol is unthinkable. The attitude of the negro to prison is difficult to define. Little stigma is attached to it; if the man is unmarried, the sentence not too long, and the food adequate (which is scandalously not always the case), I do not think they mind much; though to assert as Paul Morand does that they seek prison for the security, food, comfort and distinction to be gained there is obviously incorrect; nor is the underlying imputation much to the credit of the administration he seeks to defend.

What continually surprised me in the administrators I came in contact with was their ignorance. Communications with Europe are difficult, so it is not surprising that they should know little of home affairs; but they usually knew nothing whatsoever concerning any part of the colony outside their own circle, and very little about that. I was practically never able to get any information about the habits or customs of the negroes they were ruling; they were almost all convinced that there was nothing of interest to be found. The great majority disliked and despised the negroes they were set over; their attitude varied capriciously between familiarity – 'a loving father with his children' as the propaganda speeches say – and a sergeant-major-like brutality, too often accompanied by physical violence. I never met one who was independent of an interpreter.

On the whole they regarded me as a nuisance. They feared that they would be forced to entertain me and arrange dances and so on for me – as, had I waited for the Governor-General's letter, they would have to have done – and grudged the time. When they found that I was unrecommended and only required the use of the guesthouse and permission to make my own arrangements to organise dances with the local chiefs they mostly left me alone; a few were most kind and hospitable; a certain number set themselves the mission of thwarting me and getting me out of their area. These last were not numerous, but I came across a number at the beginning of my journey and consequently acquired the habit of avoiding them and stopping in villages off the main road where I could see what interested me. It was entirely owing to the action of these obstructive administrators that I was driven to take notice of the local conditions, in which I had originally had no interest; and since it was generally the most disagreeable administrators or those that had most to hide who acted in this manner they forced me to see much of the worst side of the administration. On my return journey I travelled with a number of administrators who gave me a good deal of information.

A sort of indirect rule is maintained. Under – a long way under – the administrators are the native kings and princes who are made 'chefs de canton', district chiefs, and a long way under them are chiefs of each village. In theory these local chiefs rule under the guidance of the administrator: in practice they are the scapegoats who are made responsible for the collection of money and men. While they enjoy the administration's favour they have certain privileges, usually good houses and land and in a few cases subsidies; but unless they are completely subservient they risk dismissal, prison and exile. In principle the eldest son succeeds his father, and there is a special college for the sons of chiefs on the island of Gorée. But at the least protest they are displaced. A typical case can be quoted from the Ivory Coast, in the forest region. There is there a compulsory subscription of two francs per head per annum for a Société de Prévoyance, a sort of Farmer's Aid Society; the district had within two years subscribed 40,000 francs and had with difficulty received two thousand francs' worth of seed. The acting chief protested at this, and demanded that the Société's lorry should be at the service of negro as well as European planters; it was the only way of getting their products to the coast. For this impertinence he was exiled and another chief, a stranger and a Catholic, appointed. This chief was accepted by the natives as a figurehead and a scapegoat; but secretly another chief was elected from the proper family who had all the real prerogatives and homage; except for religious reasons he does not leave his hut, and his existence is unsuspected. Such 'double' chiefs are not uncommon, especially in the many cases where an old soldier with fifteen years' service to his credit has been installed. The position of 'chef de canton' has certain advantages; that of village chief practically none, for it is on him finally that the onus of tax collecting falls.

2. Taxes

'The idea of colonisation becomes increasingly more repugnant to me. To collect taxes, that is the chief preoccupation. Pacification, medical aid, have only one aim: to tame the people so that they will be docile and pay their taxes. What is the object of tours, sometimes accompanied by bloodshed? To bring in the taxes. What is the object of ethnographical studies? To learn how to govern more subtly so that the taxes shall come in better. I think of the negroes of the AOF who paid with their lungs and their blood in the 1914–18 war to give to the least 'nigger' among them the right to vote for M. Diagne; of the negroes of the AEF who are the prey of the big concessionary companies and the railway builders . . . ' So writes Michel Leiris in the diary which he kept while working for the Griaule ethnographical expedition.* It is, at least as far as concerns French West Africa, a judgement which it is difficult to quarrel with. (Except that the negroes did not even get the right to vote for M. Diagne by the sacrifice of their lungs and blood; they had had that for several years before. The victims of the 1914–18 war were simply blood sacrifices on the altars of the

---

* *L'Afrique Fantôme*, p. 169.

white fetishes Gloire and Patrie; they didn't get any more out of the transaction than sacrificial animals usually do.)

All negroes, with the exception of a few town-dwellers, are subject to taxation in two forms – 'capitation' or head-tax, and 'prestation', which is defined by Larousse as 'a local tax used for the upkeep of roads in the neighbourhood, payable either in money or work'. As far as I know this latter is assessed everywhere except in the towns at twenty francs a head; but except as a favour negroes are not allowed to pay in money; they have to work off the tax under conditions which I shall describe in the next section.

The amount and incidence of the head-tax vary with each district. In the most favoured it is only levied on all males over the age of fifteen; in the majority on all people over that age; in the most unfortunate on all people. The amount varies between six and fifty francs a year. It is usually the smallest sums which are the hardest to pay, for the taxes are assessed more or less according to the richness of the country; if they are under fifteen francs a head it is a pretty safe bet that there is no work to be found in the district and no produce which can be sold.

The district administrator is instructed from Dakar of the amount of taxes he has to collect – a sum usually calculated on the last census figures; the administrator is made responsible for seeing that the stipulated amount is brought in. He in turn assigns to the *chefs de canton* the sum for which each is responsible in his district, and they in their turn tell each village chief how much his village must contribute. The village chief is personally responsible for the taxes of the entire village; if he is unable to get enough out of the villagers he has to make up the sum himself; if the village does not pay to the full, the administration takes a hand, and the village chief is the first to suffer. The village chiefs will consequently go to almost any lengths to collect the required sum, and it is on them that the chief onus is thrown.

If money can be earned, either by selling produce or labour, the tax is not unduly hard. Moreover, the census figures – which were, I think, last taken in 1931 – then probably bear a reasonable relation to the population. But the districts which fulfil these conditions are almost exclusively situated within a hundred miles or so of the coast – that is to say, the forest region of the Ivory Coast, with its numerous and flourishing coffee plantations, the banana area of New Guinea, and at any rate until the slump Senegal and lower Dahomey, with groundnuts and palms respectively. But between this prolific band and the Sahara to the north there is a large area of savannah, save on the banks of the Niger indifferently watered, which can produce little beyond the food needed to support a scanty population. It is this very extensive region on which the taxation falls hardest. There is no money to be earned locally; except for rice or cotton in a few small areas there is no exportable product; however moderate the tax it is almost impossible for the natives to acquire any money unless they go south to seek work. A considerable number do this, and all do not return, which is one of the numerous reasons why the census figure is in most districts far higher than the present population – in Bodi in North Dahomey, for instance, the 1926 census figures on which the tax is collected give the population as three thousand: according to a native estimate it is now six hundred, a statement which the number of abandoned huts confirmed – and consequently the tax which is demanded of the village works out at far more per head than the official figure. To pay the sum required is almost an impossibility; and there are numerous cases of unscrupulous administrators and/or chefs de canton demanding the tax two or three times in the year. There is no redress against this, except a personal appeal to the governor; and that is made very difficult.

When a village fails to pay its taxes the administration steps in brutally and ruthlessly. When punitive measures are taken, as they frequently are, the administrator himself is never present, and therefore has a complete alibi; he sends his negro soldiers – naturally always of a different race to the people they are sent out against, most usually Bambara – with instructions to collect the money. It is axiomatic that no one treats servants so badly as a servant set in authority: no one could be more heartlessly brutal to the negroes than the uniformed negroes who act for the administrators. This employment of negroes for the dirty work serves a double aim; it keeps lively the interracial hatred

which is so essential for colonies where the subject races are so much more numerous than the colonisers, and it enables the administration to deny forthright the more inhuman practices in which they tacitly acquiesce, or should the facts be irrefutable, to lay the blame on the excessive zeal of their subordinates.

I heard on my journey a very great number of stories nauseatingly horrible, but obviously unproved. I shall only tell of those incidents which I know to be true, either from personal experience or from abundant evidence. I am not indicating the district exactly for fear of getting my informants into trouble. None of the cases is exceptional.

A village in the Southern Sudan was unable to pay the taxes; the native guards were sent, took all the women and children of the village, put them into a compound in the centre, burned the huts, and told the men they could have their families back when the taxes were paid.

In North Dahomey two men who had not paid their taxes fully (they were twenty-five francs short of the hundred at the proper date) were flogged with the *chacoute* – a heavy leather whip – in front of the assembled village until they fainted, were taken to prison without medical attention, where they had to work for fifty days, and were then sent back with the remainder of the tax still owing. I spoke to one of the men in question and saw his back covered with suppurating sores.

In a village in the Northern Ivory Coast the chief's son had been taken as hostage until the tax was paid. The chief had not seen his son for nearly two years. Incidentally this practice of hostage-taking is very common; and I cannot remember how many times I have been offered young girls and boys to enjoy or keep as servants for the price of the head-tax.

The following letter was received by the servant of a doctor from his father: 'Envoie vite 30 francs pour impôt. Ils nous avons pris tout le bétail et tout le mil et nous crevons de faim.' (Send thirty francs for taxes at once. They have taken all our animals and millet and we are starving.) In a village in the Upper Volta people were collecting winged ants; they explained that they had nothing to eat, for the whole of their livestock and grain had been taken for taxes.

In the whole of the Western Ivory Coast flogging with the chacoute –

legally non-existent – and imprisonment follow unpunctuality in tax-paying.

On the way to Abengourou in the Ivory Coast, though not in that 'cercle', I was stopped by a native guard who mistook my car for the administrator's. The guard was slightly wounded in the head and had with him the most miserable man I have ever seen. He was naked with his genitals much swollen, his belly puffed and bruised, his eyes closed and bloody, and blood pouring from his nearly toothless mouth. His hands were tied, but he could barely stand, much less run away. The guard explained that the man was behindhand with his taxes; he had therefore gone to fetch him to work on the road, and the man had refused on the ground that if he left his plantation at such a critical moment he would never be able to pay taxes. He had tried to resist, slightly wounding the guard, who thereupon 'lui avait foutu dans la gueule'. He was obviously very pleased with himself and waited anxiously for my commendation. I told him that he deserved the legion of honour.

3. Labour Service

'Forced labour' and 'prison labour' were a few years ago the two most popular anti-Bolshevik war-cries; with Russia's increasing respectability they have now become rather old-fashioned; but they are very adequate descriptions of how nine-tenths of the public work in the French West African colonies are performed. Fifty centimes – one penny at the normal rate of exchange – is considered the proper rate of remuneration for a ten-hour working day; and the 'prestation' or work tax, fines and arrears of taxes are worked off at that rate. Consequently every adult male negro – in some districts also women and children – does at least forty days' work for the State, chiefly road-making, and if it happens that he has to make roads when he should be cultivating his fields, that is just too bad. The more conscientious administrators try to avoid this contingency, but the fields have to be worked during the rainy season, which is also the time when the roads need the most attention.

Except in the districts where there are railways the roads in French

West Africa are reasonably plentiful and good. They have been built and kept in repair by unpaid labourers working without any tools except the short-handled hatchet which is the negro's sole agricultural instrument. The roads are made of earth, and in the southern part of the colony the soil is laterite, which makes a particularly good and hard surface. The best roads are slightly raised above the surrounding country, on account of the rains; the earth to make them up is scooped out of the neighbouring land with these hatchets into wicker baskets which are then carried on to the road and dumped. The surface is smoothed by having mud poured on to it which is beaten by women standing in serried lines holding pieces of wood and beating the earth to the time given out by the forewoman. They keep up this work for ten hours, continually stooping, many of them pregnant or with babies strapped to their backs. Unfortunately a photograph I took of these 'tapeuses', as they are jovially called, at work was not successful.

Except in the case of a couple of bridges being built by private contractors I did not see any instruments of any sort being used in public works in French West Africa. Albert Londres has already described the building of the Congo-Océan railway, where each sleeper literally represents a negro life, and where the only instruments he found were one hammer and one pickaxe, for making tunnels,* and I have no reason to believe that conditions are better in French West Africa. Negroes cost far less than shovels, not to mention cranes. I did not see any railway building, but the Thiess–Niger line is so bad that part of it will have to be relaid shortly; still, after the strike of 1925 the government may take a few more precautions.

In the forest regions of the Ivory Coast there is a great deal of work to be done with woodcutting and plantations and a very sparse population; consequently workers have to be recruited elsewhere, and particularly among the Mossi of the Upper Volta (now part of the Ivory Coast) who were by far the most populous tribe of the savannah; this is done both by public and private enterprise. On several occasions the administration

---

* *Terre d'Ebène*, p. 234.

have settled large groups of the Mossi in the Ivory Coast – sixty thousand have been moved to the neighbourhood of Yammossoukro, in the middle of the forest, this year; but the negroes support the changed climatic and dietary conditions so badly – not to mention hard work on inadequate pay – that something like half die in the first year. Private woodcutters and planters can also get permission to go and recruit the men they need; the local administrator merely tells the chiefs that so many men are required and are to be delivered at such a place and date. The men cannot refuse to go.

When men are working away from their village they are meant to be fed and housed. What is more, they sometimes are, though in more than one case that I have seen the Society for the Prevention of Cruelty to Animals would have prosecuted me if I had given a dog the same quantity and quality of food and shelter.

4. Military Service

For more than a century France has made use of negro soldiers. At first they were merely used for subjugating other negroes, but from 1870, if not earlier, they have been employed in every quarter of the globe in which France has been at war. Up to the beginning of this century volunteers were relied upon, but various decrees between 1904 and 1919 instituted conscription, under terms which have since been only slightly modified. During the 1914–18 war all negroes between the ages of eighteen and thirty-five were conscripted, and in 1917 there were thirty-one negro battalions on the Somme; large numbers were later garrisoned in Germany. Since 1919 the quota for West Africa has been fixed at 23,000 men annually, but the physical standard is so low that it is doubtful whether more than half that number are actually taken.* Except for the negro 'citizens' who do their military service for the same period, though not under the same conditions as Frenchmen, the conscription period is for three years. A negro is allowed to re-engage himself voluntarily after

---

* In 1934 there were 13,500 negro soldiers from the AOF.

his conscripted service: if he completes fifteen years' service he gains a number of privileges, such as a pension, immunity from certain taxes, the right to certain positions in the administration, and I think citizenship. Old soldiers are often made village chiefs.

The quota for each district is fixed annually after a visit by a recruiting officer. The negroes are on the whole extremely unwilling to become soldiers, and very frequently I found that on my arrival in a village all the young men had hidden themselves, fearing that I might be a recruiting officer. Even after they have been designated for service they frequently try to run away and have to be caught by press gangs. The usual method of capturing runaways is to lasso them from horseback, after which they are tied to the horse and brought back to the depôt.

The usual training for non-citizens consists of three months' instruction in Africa, after which they are shipped to the South of France for another three months; they then complete their service in France, West Africa, or more often in Morocco, Algeria, Syria, or Indo-China. When they are stationed in Africa they are housed in separate huts and are allowed to have a wife with them to prepare their food. When they go abroad the wives are occasionally allowed to accompany them, but this is fairly uncommon, and French prostitutes are usually put at their service. These wretched women are numbered, so that if a negro catches a venereal disease he can tell the doctor from which number he caught the contagion, and sanitary measures can be taken. The prostitutes have to be renewed fairly frequently, for there is such demand on their services that the negroes have not time to undress and the women develop sores on their thighs owing to the continual friction of fly-buttons.

When a negro is conscripted he is mourned by his village as a dead man; justifiably, for the chances that they will ever see him again are slight. The mortality among conscripted soldiers is extraordinarily high; I believe the official figure is somewhere near fifty per cent. During the two days I was at Ouagadougou over twenty men of the new draft stationed there died. The sergeant whom I overheard mentioning this did not regard it as anything exceptional. Negroes in the more primitive communities adapt themselves very badly to a changed environment;

they seem unable to resist comparatively slight changes in the humidity of the atmosphere. Once they leave Africa their case is far worse; the negro is peculiarly susceptible to pulmonary and bronchial affections of all kinds, and although all do not succumb there are comparatively few who do not come back contaminated, with the result that a particularly virulent form of tuberculosis is now endemic in the greater part of French West Africa. The danger of tuberculosis is enhanced by the abuse of alcohol, to which they are quickly accustomed. If a negro survives his three years' service he will usually re-enlist, preferring the comparatively carefree life of the soldier, with its attendant pleasures of women and wine, to a return to village life with its continual anxieties about crops and taxes; moreover, old soldiers have got so accustomed to an alien way of living that it is extremely difficult for them to re-adapt themselves to tribal life. They usually finish up in the service of the administration in a different part of the country.

It is arguable that a conscripted negro has a higher standard of living than the average, at any rate while he is in Africa. The negro soldiers are housed in relatively well-built and sanitary huts, which they make themselves under orders; they have regular and sufficient food, which, although it is considered inadequate by people from near the coast, is probably a considerable improvement on the diet of the inhabitants of the savannah; and they are provided with clothes of a sort. These clothes generally consist of a flannel vest, which they have to wear as a health measure, khaki cloth trousers reaching to the calf and a khaki coat. These generally fit very badly and are often extremely shabby. Even when stationed in towns they are not provided with any sort of footwear. They are taught a sort of French in parrot fashion by negro sergeants. I had noticed most of these details myself, but they were confirmed by conversation with a young Dahomeyan doctor. He was as over-cultured and educated as a negro can be, speaking French far too well with many quotations from the classics; and he had been made unhappy and ill by having to go barefoot after having been shod all his life and having to speak the sergeant's completely inaccurate French to avoid corporal punishment. Immediately after his service was finished he was given a far too important medical post. The Dahomeyans, who are by far the most Europeanised of the negroes of French West Africa, are extremely jealous of the Senegalese citizenship. The Senegalese have at present only twelve months' service and are not meant to be sent abroad.

Service in West Africa is the paradise of the professional white soldier, and particularly the non-commissioned officer. They are better paid than in Europe and have far greater privileges; they are nearly independent and have very little beyond office work to do. The non-commissioned officers have very comfortable huts, and inevitably a 'mousso' or native woman to look after them. These sous-offs, or gobi as the negroes call them, are the great terror of civilians. They have almost unlimited power, for it is very difficult for a charge to lie against them, and they abuse it mercilessly. They are usually drunkards – indeed, most Europeans in West Africa could be so qualified – and by tradition and education extremely brutal. They are not on the whole malicious, and the scrounging, rape and arson in which they so frequently indulge is regarded, by them, as practical joking. The blame for the great harm that they do should be laid less at their doors than at those of the authorities who place uneducated men in positions where they are under no restraint and have no distractions save drink from the pervading boredom. I spoke to several and found them individually pleasant and unconsciously informative.

The greater number of French officers are stationed on the frontiers and particularly on the edges of the Sahara, where the Moors are still very imperfectly civilised. They seem to lead a very pleasant *Boy's Own Paper* existence. The medical officers whom I met seemed to know their job far better than their civilian counterparts.

A large number of Europeans do their military service in West Africa, and it is from their ranks that the greater number of planters are drawn. A Frenchman can take a special engagement by which, after nine months' service in the colony, he can leave as soon as he can find a job. Plantations are usually given for the asking.

Of the conditions of negro soldiers outside Africa I only know what regular soldiers on leave have told me. In Europe they are shod, and housed in barracks; they complain that they are very cold, and the floors terribly hard to sleep on. They are chiefly fed on rice. Outside Africa they receive three sous, instead of one, a day.

Perhaps the thing which surprised me most in French West Africa was the excessive militarisation of the country. In any conglomeration of any size was a barracks; and it was comparatively seldom that an hour passed without hearing a military bugle. Indeed, the bugle has completely ousted the tomtom as a background to local colour.

One of the most intelligent administrators I met was a Monsieur V, who travelled back on the same boat as I did. He said to me: 'We French have really very little use for our colonies. We do not need them for a surplus population, we are not to any extent dependent on their products for our food, we make practically no use of them as a market. [This is certainly true; practically the only French goods you see in West African stores are drinks and cosmetics; most machinery and metal goods are American or German, most textiles English, Japanese or Russian, in that order.] A few private companies have had concessions to exploit the rubber and minerals, but they have on the whole harmed the colonies without enriching themselves. Consequently the only group of people who have a permanent interest and influence on colonial policy are the militarists. Roads and communications are developed on the basis of military strategy, naturally about fifty years out of date; military interests are always paramount. The colony is run like an armed camp. We are destroying our colonies by stupidity and you English are losing yours by sentimentality;* the Dutch are the only people who know how to run colonies.' Although I am not certain of Monsieur V's exact words, I am sure I have not distorted the gist of his remarks, which I noted immediately; it is as far as it concerns the French colonies on the whole a judgement which concurs with mine, and which is founded on far greater experience. It is curious to note that every administrator of whatever nationality I spoke to always thought other nations managed their colonies better.

* This 'sentimentality', of course, only applies to our West African colonies, and possibly India.

5. How to Empty a Human Reservoir

No French politician can make a speech, and few French journalists can write an article, about their West African colonies without dubbing them 'un réservoir d'hommes'. This metaphor, a human reservoir, is indeed so frequently used that it has become a synonym. When a Frenchman hears a speaker refer to 'ce grand réservoir d'hommes prêts à défendre leur patrie' he smiles knowingly at such an elegant method of describing French West Africa.

French West Africa is extremely sparsely populated. With an area about eight times that of France it has a population of less than a third of the mother country. According to the last census it has a total negro population of fourteen million. Despite the efforts that I have made either directly or indirectly I have not been able to find the statistics which could show the movement of population;* but the figures given by Marcel Sauvage in his articles on French Equatorial Africa (an adjacent colony with a similar system of government) which he published in the *Intransigeant*, 28 July–17 August 1934, under the title *Les Secrets de l'Afrique Noire* are sufficiently revealing: in 1911 French Equatorial Africa had twenty million negro inhabitants, in 1921 seven and a half million, and in 1931 two and a half million! These figures were given in a responsible French conservative paper and have not been denied; moreover, scattered observations elsewhere, and the prevarications of the information bureau for the colony, make it seem certain that the almost incredible state of affairs that these figures show – the population reduced by ninety per cent in twenty years – is a sober statement of fact.

The depopulation of French West Africa is not proceeding at so vertiginous a rate, but the trend is undoubtedly the same. The drop in population does not represent only deaths, though mortality is extremely

---

* As far as I can interpret the figures at my disposal, the population of recent years has remained more or less stable; but the figures are too inadequate for me to be able to gather more than the fact that the influence of civilisation, contrary to usual practice, has not brought about an increase in population.

high; very great numbers of negroes emigrate to the English colonies, fleeing from the conscription for military service, and forced labour, whether for the State or for individuals. Within the years 1926–29 it is calculated that over two million negroes passed from French territory into British Nigeria (which has about a quarter of the area of AOF and about one and a half times the population) and the better part of a million into the Gold Coast. Since 1929 the rate of emigration has slowed down somewhat, owing to the slump and the consequent fall in the demand for labour, particularly porterage; but it is still going on regularly, and villages on the routes to the English colonies do a continuous business, hiding the fugitives by day, and feeding them. The French authorities do what they can to stop this efflux, but it is practically impossible; the negroes are uniformly in sympathy with the fugitives, the frontiers are wide, and as soon as a negro has crossed them and destroyed his papers it is impossible to reclaim him. The tiny colony of Gambia, which is sandwiched into Senegal, has had to guard its frontiers very thoroughly to prevent unbearable overcrowding. This evasion is most constant in the colony of the Upper Volta (now part of the Ivory Coast) and the neighbouring territory; we passed whole districts inhabited entirely by old people and children. On more than one occasion we heard of whole families which had just set out for 'England'.

The Upper Volta, the land of the Mossi, was at one time comparatively thickly populated, and was the chief recruiting ground for soldiers and labourers for railways and plantations. It is now fairly empty.

Mortality among the negroes in French West Africa is extremely high, even disregarding the death-rate among recruits. The chief causes of this are, firstly, diseases imported, like tuberculosis and syphilis, or caused from urban conditions, like the various epidemics; and, secondly, malnutrition. As far as I can see, the French have not improved the standard of living, as far as food goes, of the negroes in any way. I never saw a modern agricultural instrument or mill, or a well protected from infection. Famines caused by drought and locusts are still common, and are not always relieved; a locust famine in villages near Tenkodogo in 1933 sent the whole population into the Gold Coast. Far from improving the standard of living, the French may be said to have lowered it, for the grain which the negroes cultivate, and which practically constitutes their diet, formerly sufficient for their needs, has now to be sold to pay taxes, and, if there are any public works in the neighbourhood, at an extremely low official rate. Moreover, their diet, while sufficient for the relatively easy life of a cultivator, is grossly inadequate to support life under the strenuous efforts exacted from the working negro. The twenty thousand deaths (up till 1931) of the workers on the Congo–Océan railway were undoubtedly chiefly due to privation. The successful efforts of missionaries have largely added to the infant mortality. It was the custom of negro mothers to suckle their children for three years, for animal's milk is scarce and the ordinary diet is not sufficiently nutritive for young children. During that period the husband would not have intercourse with her, for otherwise she would become pregnant again and stop lactating. Under monogamy this practice obviously falls into desuetude. The heavy work which pregnant and nursing mothers are in some parts made to do is a contributory cause.

The medical service, on the whole overworked and badly equipped, has been able to do something to alleviate certain diseases, particularly yaws – a non-fatal venereal skin disease – and sleeping sickness, which now yields very well to a treatment of injections on a base of arsenic; it is no longer a fatal disease, though the tsetse is spreading rapidly. Other less common tropical diseases such as elephantiasis and ainhum can also be cured, and vaccination has done a great deal to lessen the terrors of smallpox, formerly the greatest scourge. But the best-equipped doctors in the world are powerless against a policy which has malnutrition and tuberculosis as its inevitable fruits. An unhappy negro at Bodi said to me that that part of the country (North Dahomey) would be completely uninhabited in fifty years' time. If the present methods continue, this man seems to me to have set an over-generous time-limit for France's 'mission civilisatrice'. To paraphrase Tacitus, they are making a desert and they call it a colony.

6. Voiceless Protest

When I started on my journey in West Africa I hoped that I should be able to ignore completely the political and administrative conditions of the negro. I was completely ignorant on the subject, and had no background of comparison by which I could judge what I saw. I wanted to concentrate exclusively on the more picturesque aspects of the district, particularly dancing and magic religions and their place in ordinary negro life. It was the churlishness of certain administrators, particularly in the savannah, which first forced my attention on the economical and political aspects of the situation, by their refusing the negroes permission to dance for me; when dances were organised I was far too busy photographing and noting to have time for snooping and questioning; when these distractions were refused I had to occupy myself somehow. But an alert observer would have to be conducted very carefully through French West Africa for most of the facts given in the foregoing pages not to be brought to his notice; they assume such an overwhelming importance in the negroes' outlook on life that any account of them in which such subjects were ignored would be intolerably falsified.* As far as possible I have used official figures, but I admit that I have on the whole presented the case from the negro's standpoint, and that there is probably something to be said from the other side of the question, the imperialist side. I am not writing, at least I am not intending to write, a book about politics; what I want to do is to write about the negro as an individual and as I saw him. To avoid being endlessly anecdotal it was necessary to collect the scattered observations and conversations of three months into some sort of order. I want to make a few generalisations on the attitude of the negro to the various manifestations of civilisation described above; after which the subject can be dismissed and the stranger and more picturesque aspects dealt with.

* This is indeed the case with Paul Morand's *Paris–Timbuctoo*; the picture there given of the carefree, laughing, dancing, childlike, handsome negro bears no relation to anything I saw; but then he was an official guest.

West African negroes are divided into a very great number of different races, with distinguishing physical characteristics and languages, but they can be conveniently divided into three groups, according to their religions and geographical situations. The negroes near the coast are mostly Christian and have been in contact with Europeans for a considerable time; to a varying extent they have adapted themselves to European modes of thought and life and are consequently fairly much at home with present conditions. The Mohammedans to the north have with the religion acquired much of the mental background of the Arab; they are not on the whole agriculturists, but either hunters, shepherds or traders, and consequently seldom much attached to any special area of land; they have been reared in a warlike tradition, and for the greater part take kindly to soldiering. As members of a worldwide religion their outlook is not wholly parochial; they have perhaps exaggerated the inherent fatalism of Mohammed, and console themselves for their present sufferings with the certainty of paradise. Between these two groups of people who have both been subject to alien influence is the savannah and the forest inhabited by a number of races which are predominantly agricultural, and which have each their own magic 'animistic' religion. It is only within the last fifty years that these people have had any continuous contact with outside influences, and in large areas it is practically only within the present century that they have been colonised. Until the advent of Europeans their ways of life were stylised and practically static; the tribe and the family group were the two economical units; the individual had very little importance. The incidents of every man's life followed a set pattern; every possible eventuality could be dealt with by precedent; all non-human occurrences were given a satisfactory explanation by the magic religion, and established ritual taught them how to deal with every emergency. It was a life without surprises, and on the whole without misery or want. War, waged with the most primitive instruments, played a certain part in their lives; but except in the case of large conglomerations like the Mossi and the Dahomeyans, who were able to dispossess their neighbours and take them as slaves, these wars had chiefly a sporting interest; they probably did not produce many more casualties than, say, an American football match, though some sides might devour their fallen adversaries. It is easy to sentimentalise this primitive society: it is now in the process of being destroyed and can never be reconstituted; but whatever its ethical and cultural drawbacks it suited admirably the negroes who had composed it and had followed its routine for an incalculable number of centuries; and it is obviously going to take a considerable time before another and better civilisation can be evolved in which the negro can feel at home and which will free him from anxiety, misery and distress as adequately as the earlier one. It is with the relics of these primitive societies that my interests lie, and it is the reactions of the members of these to the process of colonisation that they are now undergoing which I shall try to describe.

In principle the negro does not object to the head-tax. Tribute from the conquered to the conqueror is not a foreign notion to them. It is noteworthy in this connection that in Dahomey and the Ivory Coast events are always dated 'from the French conquest'. This does not mean that it does not lie very heavy on them and cause them great anxiety; one man said to me: 'I can't sleep for thinking of the taxes; if I am put in prison what will happen to my children? If they let us alone we could get the money; but they force us to make roads and don't pay us; they don't give us any time to make up; what can I do?' But the idea of the head-tax doesn't shock them, though individual methods of assessment and collection may do so.

The speech quoted above also gives the general reaction to forced labour. The idea of slavery or peonage, under which a man and his family belong to another and work for him, receiving in return food and shelter, is quite in accordance with their outlook, but they cannot understand and do resent intermittent unpaid work, which often interferes with their agriculture and consequently their ability to pay their taxes. It would probably suit the negro mentality better if a man could do his whole labour service in one stretch, provided he was not taken outside his tribal district. It is this forcible breaking up and destruction of the family and tribe which rouses the negro's keenest resentment and misery; in a manner of speaking they do not live as individuals, and to separate a man from the environment in which he was born is to cause distress to the whole group. This is the reason why the recruiting officer, whether he is looking for soldiers or for labourers for another part of the country, is more feared and hated than the greatest bully and extortioner. Most negroes would prefer death to military service.

I have not found anybody who has been able to put up a reasonable defence for the existence of a negro army outside Africa from any point of view. Negroes who have imbibed the French ideology consider that it is right that there should be a negro army which is capable of defending its own country; but all Europeans and negroes with whom I have discussed the subject are unanimous in considering the employment of negroes abroad a stupid barbarism. I should also have thought it a very short-sighted policy, from the imperialist point of view, to teach a profoundly discontented people a common language (hitherto the greatest bar to negro solidarity), a discipline and the use of arms. It is to escape conscription that thousands of *families* cross the English frontiers every year.

There is no doubt that the negroes of French West Africa are a dispirited, miserable and resentful people, who can now only be ruled by fear. It is not merely the colonial policy which has brought them to this state, but the brutal and abusive manner in which the French treat them on nearly every occasion, and the systematic way in which they are cheated in every transaction, which the cheaters quite erroneously believe their simplicity prevents them from realising. Actually it is their fear and their experience with the results of complaints which keep them apparently quiet. The following quotation from André Gide's *Voyage au Congo* (p. 113) is unfortunately too typical. He is describing a conversation with a trader.

He told me he had spent a long time in the Gold Coast and when we asked him which country he preferred he replied: 'In the Gold Coast you can't do anything. Imagine, down there nearly every nigger can read and write' . . . He couldn't hide his anger against the English traders who are stupid enough to pay directly to the negro the market price of his goods, which 'spoils the business'. He admitted cynically that when there was not sufficient profit on the goods he made up for it by 'faking the weights' . . . He complained loudly against the administration 'which is destroying business', but only the upper branches of the administration; he was full of praise for the sub-administrator of the district where he was working: 'A nigger can go and complain if he likes: he'll soon put him in his place for you.'

Similarly Albert Londres* mentions the weighing machine of a cotton buyer on which a man weighed seventy kilos before the market opened, and fifty kilos after. Any number of similar examples could be given. My reason for preferring to quote French books rather than give my own observations is, I should think, obvious; it is not for lack of material. Mention has already been made of the ludicrously low prices at which negroes are forced to sell their provisions to Europeans and those working for them; in some regions, indeed, they are not allowed to name a price, but should receive thankfully whatever is offered for their goods. The negro cannot even always buy where he likes; in some districts seed must be bought from the government store. A further piece of chicane is the fines that public and private employers can inflict arbitrarily on their work-people and deduct from their wages. The truck system is also extremely common. Paradoxically enough, it is the negroes who are given the reputation of being dishonest.

I was universally informed that the only treatment that negroes can understand is physical violence. It is certainly the only treatment they ever get. When I told Frenchmen that a negro in the English colonies who was maltreated by a white man could bring an action for assault they were incredulous and horrified. (This was the chief reason for Monsieur V's accusation of sentimentality.) To watch the average overseer or planter at work you would imagine that all that was needed to produce good results was a sufficiency of kicks, blows and lashes. An administrator from the Gold Coast visited some American missionaries recently; after he had left

* *Terre d'Ebène*, p. 150.

117

they told their 'boy' who he was. 'What, him a governor!' the 'boy' said; 'I don't believe it. He didn't hit or kick a single person while he was here.' When I was in Assinie I had to spend a considerable time with the local administrator, who was extremely kind to me, while the chauffeurs had to wait in the car; when I passed them I apologised for keeping them waiting so long. 'You apologise to them!' said the horrified administrator; 'you want to give them a kick up the arse!'

The language of uneducated negroes who have been in contact with the French is extremely coarse and brutal; it is the only language they ever hear. The way French men and women taunt, nag and bully their servants is extremely embarrassing to witness. One really gets the impression that they do not consider them as human beings. I was considered criminally eccentric because I bothered to see that the chauffeurs got food; I was frequently told, as was André Gide,* that if I started bothering about what my 'boys' were going to eat I should be done for; they'd manage all right and wouldn't let themselves starve. One of the first ladies of Dakar advised me always to throw away any food which was left over from a meal, since I couldn't give it to the dog like she did; otherwise the cook would prepare much too much, so as to have the remains. I know of only one person who feeds his servants and workers properly.

If a negro is constantly knocked about and abused as a thief, a liar, a shirker, a dirty nigger, he takes on those qualities. The uprooted negro's character is extraordinarily plastic; within certain limits you can make him what you like. If you treat him as a villain he will quickly become a villain; if, as I did, you assume he is honest and conscientious, he will, after he has got over the first shock, be honest and conscientious; the only exceptions I met were Catholic converts, who were uniformly rogues, a fact due to their unfortunate but wholehearted belief in the efficacy of confession and absolution. If you can watch a man dealing with negroes you have no need to ask his opinion about them; and if you can watch a man's negroes you will know the chief points of his character. They mirror their masters faithfully and terribly.

* *Voyage au Congo*, p. 184.

As soon as negroes have got over their fear of being trapped into making compromising statements for which they will be punished later – a not uncommon practice – they will pour out their woes in a flood. But except for sporadic rioting, such as has occurred at Lomé, they don't do anything about it, partly because they are too miserable and browbeaten, but chiefly owing to their character. Interracial dislike and the lack of a common language prevent them acquiring any sort of unity; although kind and generous they are rarely capable of any altruistic action, or indeed of one that has not their direct personal advantage in view; their religious fatalism prompts acquiescence. Worst of all the negro's indolent reliance on something being bound to turn up saps all initiative; and many times educated negroes have whispered to me that the 'something' they hope will turn up will be another war, in which France will lose her colonies to some other nation. *Omne ignotum pro magnifico.*

Mandate

W E HAD NOT ORIGINALLY INTENDED going to Ouagadougou (Wagadugu on English maps). We had been told, as it happened quite truthfully, that there was nothing there of interest beyond the many-times-described court of Moro Naba, and that the country surrounding it was exceptionally ugly. But we were practically forced there by the yellow-fever quarantine in the lower Ivory Coast, which had been our original objective. I thought that the quarantine was strictly applied, and that once in the suspected area we should have great difficulty in getting out. Later I discovered that all the quarantine meant was the possession of a sanitary passport which was automatically signed by the overworked doctors. Moreover, King Ely had given us an introduction to Baloum Naba, the Moro Naba's first minister, and we hoped by that means that we should see more than others had done. So when we arrived we went straight to the house of Baloum.

The poor man was terrified, so frightened he could hardly keep seated. We had committed the unpardonable mistake of visiting a negro potentate without first getting permission from the local administrator; we might be disliked by the government, and in that case if the wretched negro gave us something to eat his tenure of office would be short. Stammering, Baloum gave us a drink and then hurried round with us to see the administrator, who told us we must stop at the hotel. We weren't pleased at this; we were hoping to be given a spare room at the palace.

The hotel was mud-built and mouse-infested; it consisted of a hall and three stifling bedrooms. It was slightly more expensive than the Ritz – five hundred francs for three nights and five meals. After we had received that bill we decided to avoid hotels for the future; and, indeed, we only spent three more nights in them while we were in Africa. The hotel was run by a man who was working his way round the world. He was a curious little man, afflicted with a painful stammer, which did not prevent him composing poems and monologues which he recited at every opportunity. He romantically identified himself with the wandering troubadours of the Middle Ages. His poems were sad idyllic dialogues in mechanical alexandrines; the personages had the most resounding names imaginable. The monologues, on the other hand, were learnedly humoristic; they mostly dealt with literary history, and contained more puns per sentence (each one explained in brackets) than any other writing I have ever seen. He had a passion for puns and had a huge manuscript collection of them. He presented me with some of his works, which he had had printed; on the covers he described himself as 'le troubadour moderne', 'le jeune et vaillant globetrotter' (which he pronounced globby trotair), 'l'illustre Humoriste', or 'l'homme jazz unique'. It was by this last function that he earned his living; he had a complicated contraption of percussion and wind instruments, so arranged that some played automatically, while he could work others with his hands, feet and mouth; the result was surprisingly loud and efficient, rather like a mechanical piano with effects.

Ouagadougou is the most depressing town I have ever seen. It is in the middle of a burned, treeless and desolate plain; from any vantage-point the eye is carried straight to infinity; you feel that you are at the end of the world. The big town is entirely built of grey mud; it was designed to hold a far larger population than has ever inhabited it, and whole quarters are falling into ruin without ever having been lived in. Such inhabitants as there were, were the ugliest, most degenerate and most diseased group of people I have ever seen.

Ouagadougou has had an unhappy history. Up till 1920 it was merely the town in which resided the Moro Naba, king of three million Mossi; the region in which the Mossi lived formed part of the French colony of the Niger, with which it has climatically much in common. In 1920 the colony of the Niger was cut in two, and the lower portion made into the colony of the Upper Volta; Ouagadougou was designated for its capital and the town was laid out on an extremely generous scale, and all the government residences and offices were built, except the governor's palace. The building of governors' palaces is the most spectacular and the most costly colonial enterprise of French West Africa; it is done extremely thoroughly. When the crisis came in 1931 economies were imperative; the great sacrifice was made; no governor's palace would be built in Ouagadougou. But if there was no palace there could obviously be no governor, and the colony of the Upper Volta must again be attached to some other colony; the obvious solution was to re-attach it to the colony of the Niger where conditions are very similar; but Niamey, which is its capital, is so badly served with communications that the practical difficulties would be great, and it was impossible to shift the capital, for at Niamey there were the beginnings of a perfectly stupendous governor's palace, which had already cost several million francs, and which was likely to cost several million more before it was completed; and so the Upper Volta was attached to the Ivory Coast, and all the offices at Ouagadougou dismantled. In some ways this was an unfortunate decision, for the conditions in the Ivory Coast and the Upper Volta are very different; moreover, the Upper Volta has its own customs barrier which is still maintained, for it is not bound by the convention of the Gulf of Guinea. But one day the railway from Abidjan may reach it, and then things will be better. Shortly after this momentous decision was reached it was discovered that there was one more governor than there were palaces; this problem was neatly solved by making Dakar and its dependencies a separate unit, and a most beautiful palace, which looks like the largest Swiss sanatorium ever built, is nearly completed in Dakar.

On the Sunday afternoon when we first visited it Ouagadougou was particularly dismal. The native quarter was full of negro soldiers getting drunk, rowdy and quarrelsome on millet beer; the market had an extremely mean selection of articles for sale and little trade was being done. Cowries were the principal coin; the people are far too poor to work in sums larger than a fifth of a centime. The one remaining European store had practically no stock, and the proprietor announced his intention of leaving the dying town. The Mossi were friendly, but extremely repugnant to look at; they seemed more simian than human, with their prognathous skulls, short bodies and, it seemed, disproportionately long arms. They were riddled with Guinea worm, leprosy, yaws and other diseases; many were malformed and crippled. (They probably represented the dregs of the nearly emptied human reservoir.) And everywhere was the pervading sound of the bugle, impossible to escape from by day or night; the only populous parts of the town were the military camps. The whole effect was unpleasantly macabre.

Within the limits set by his nervousness Baloum was very kind to us and sent round to the hotel twice a day two big pots, one filled with several boiled chickens and one with a mess of rice. This was intended for the chauffeurs' food, but it was much too much for them, and we occasionally helped them out. These pots were brought over by Baloum's *sororés*, or boy servants; they are the chief peculiarity of the courts of Mossi notabilities. These boys enter the service of the Nabas at the age of eight, and stop with them till they are given in marriage; until that time they have to remain virgin under pain of death. They have the exclusive privilege of being allowed to wear broad copper bracelets on the upper arm; the number they wear represents their rank; when they are married they have to give them back. Baloum's sororés were fairly normal in dress and behaviour, though they used to present the pots to me with a deep curtsey, holding the pot in both hands above their bowed heads; but those of Moro Naba were clothed and coiffed like women, and were exaggeratedly graceful; Moro Naba has also an incalculable number of wives, and it is uncertain if these ingles are for use or just for ornament. They are traditional.

Baloum arranged for us to have an audience with Moro Naba, but after the arrangements were made we were rather embarrassed, for Woolworth gifts were obviously unsuitable to a monarch who received a subsidy of ten thousand francs monthly from the administration, and we did not feel inclined to give up our ice-making machine for a mere interview. As a solution to the difficulty I wrote the Moro Naba a sonnet in English, which I copied out on a nice piece of paper and gave to him with a French translation; it was a very bad sonnet, but I introduced his name in capitals three times and I am sorry I didn't keep the rough copy; it surprised him considerably.

The Moro Naba is pure musical comedy, despite the fact that he is the most powerful West African king, and that no order of his is ever disobeyed (which is perhaps another reason for the disestablishment of Ouagadougou). His whole life is spent in pantomime; every morning he prepares to ride forth to war against his hereditary enemy; and every morning he is persuaded not to, with exactly the same words and gestures. Every quarter of an hour throughout the day he has to drink a pot of beer; and he never moves without the crowd of sororés who crouch in a tangle at his feet and whisper to one another; whenever their master happens to belch or sneeze or hiccough or cough or spit or in any other way ease his over-stuffed body, they click their fingers together for about a minute, making a considerable noise. I thought this little courtesy pretty and trained my chauffeurs to do it. The Moro Naba is very well in with the government, and every Friday pays a visit in full state to the military club. He is an imposing-looking person, much taller than the ordinary, very stout from his ritual diet of beer (he and a couple of other chiefs were the only fat people I saw in French West Africa) with a little straggly pointed beard and extremely cunning and cynical little eyes. He was magnificently dressed in a hand-embroidered dark-blue robe and a little gold-trimmed toque. He came on to the steps to greet us and seated us in a couple of European chairs, facing his low throne which was surmounted by a palanquin. The audience room was a long chamber open to the air on one side, and decorated with photographs of the Moro Naba, cheap prints and tinsel flowers. Besides the bevy of sororés who lay in a graceful tangle at the Moro Naba's feet, there were present a number of magicians in full regalia, most of the cabinet, including Baloum, who acted as our interpreter – the Moro Naba understands but refuses to speak French – some mangy dogs and a couple of extremely distinguished and silky goats. I have an idea that if we had given a proper present we should have been presented with these goats. They wouldn't have been easy to deal with, but we felt slightly cheated when we went away without them. Conversation was heavy going, for the Moro Naba just stared at us and waited for us to speak; it was rather embarrassing. The only remark of mine which had much success was the statement that prayers were being offered up in English churches for rain to break the drought; this tickled him very much, for he was in his Own Person Lord of the Water, and he obviously considered that the prayers were being sent in the wrong direction. Otherwise the interview was impressive rather than amusing.

The only prosperous concern in Ouagadougou is the Catholic mission. As the Catholic father who showed us round rather naïvely observed, the fetishists were very easy to convert as the two religions were very similar; the catechumens already believed in a Creator and the spirits of their ancestors; only a little dogma was wanted. Besides building the largest church in the interior of Africa, with the help of its converts, the mission also ran a cotton and carpet-making factory. The carpets were excruciatingly ugly imitations of Moroccan patterns, and were made in a most primitive way by a host of women and children under the super-vision of nuns as forewomen. The spinning and carding machines, on the contrary, were the latest Manchester models; they were not fitted with any safety devices, and there had been a number of distressing accidents. The converts had their breasts as immodestly exposed as the heathen, and indeed showed no superficial differences. I have not been able to under-stand exactly how making negroes work ten hours a day for fifty centimes is considered to be pleasing to the Lord, unless it was a mortification of the flesh; the converts looked distinctly undernourished.

Except for conversations with the non-commissioned officers Ouagadougou offered no distractions and we were glad to leave it in the direction of Togo and Dahomey. The water of Ouagadougou is so disinfected as to be almost undrinkable, and I think it was probably the cause of the slight attack of dysentery from which I suffered in the next few days. Our first stop was inevitably Tenkodogo. The landscape on the way was horribly parched, for no rain had yet fallen; the rare villages were very small, practically family groups, standing among what would be green fields. The negroes were very ugly and poverty-stricken – and terrified. I was accustomed to men standing at attention and saluting as soon as the car came into sight, but in this district all who could ran to hide: those who could not stood at the salute as long as the car was in sight, men, women and children, old and young. All dropped whatever they were doing; if they were on horseback they dismounted; palsied old crones, their heads shaved and their dugs shrunk till they looked like Shaw's she-ancients, tottered out from the shade in which they were sitting and held their hands quavering to their foreheads. At a crossroad we had to ask the way; the only man in sight had tried to run away, and when Fodé got out of the car to question him, he stopped dead with his arm over his face, shivering. It was a horrible and humiliating experience; I have never in my life been so bitterly ashamed of being a member of a group – in this case the white-skinned group. It wouldn't have been so unpleasant if they hadn't been so grotesquely ugly, almost subhuman; they were like bullied cripples.

I went to see the administrator with my usual request for permission to use the rest-house and organise dances; but I could get nothing definite out of him. He spent about half an hour reading my passport, looking for I don't know what – 'I'm not blind yet, young man,' he said when I offered to find him any relevant stamps – and finally wrote on it and stamped it. Rather discouraged, we went and saw the local chief, who played at being a Naba with a court of three in a hut decorated with apéritif advertisements. He promised to organise a dance for the morrow, and we presented him with a watch and cigarette case.

The village was surrounded by trees which the Wolof call oulh, and Mungo Park – as far as my knowledge goes the writer of easily the most accurate description of West Africa – the Nitta tree. It may be *Parkia africana*. It bears long bean-like fruits, full of little black seeds surrounded by a yellow pith. This pith, of a sweetish rather soapy taste, is eaten and the seeds spat out; these seeds are collected and put into water and buried for several days to ferment; they are then kneaded into balls which serve as a butter subsitute and stink more abominably than any foodstuff I have ever come across. There were also frangipani bushes, with waxy sweet-scented yellow flowers on the ends of leafless stems.

There were some American missionaries in this village, a whole family living in a house filled with texts; I do not know what creed they preached, or with what success; they looked more like American missionaries than I had thought anyone could have done off the films. They were very kind to me and gave me fresh drinking water; they spoke with a dispassionate 'none of our business' disapproval of the ill-treatment of the negroes, who they said were ruled entirely by fear. They also told me about the ravages wrought by lions in the rainy season when the grass was high; according to the official figures twenty-five negroes lost their lives; the survivors say eighty.

The rest-house was next to the school, and we talked with some bright little boys who spoke French quite well. One was particularly informative; he talked about all his friends who had left for the Gold Coast, which is quite near; in his mother's village there had been a famine in the winter, owing to locusts, and since no help was given the whole village crossed the frontier. The inhabitants of the village Bakou, which is on the frontier, have no taxes to pay. One of the child's remarks was 'Il n'y a plus de jeunes gens ici; tous les garçons et les filles s'en vont en Angleterre; les tirailleurs ne reviennent pas.' He also told us that the real chief was in prison at Ouagadougou, for having protested at the treatment his subjects were receiving; the present chief was an old soldier who had been appointed by the administrator, and none of the people would salute or acknowledge him. This may have been the reason why he sent a message the next morning saying that no dances could be arranged as the dancers' father-in-law had died, though more probably it was due to the obstruction of the administrator whom he had been to visit on horseback, or his own laziness. Anyhow, I was furious at so rude a message – the least he could have done was to have come himself, after the gifts – and sent back all the insults I could think of. I wanted to leave at once, but Alioune wouldn't hear of going away without getting the gifts back and shaming the chief; he put on his best boubou and sat in the back of the car, while Fodé drove and acted as interpreter; in a little while he came back with the gifts, and said that he had reduced the man to tears. Feeling slightly revenged, we shook the dust of Tenkodogo off our car.

We could not go far as we had left after lunch; we stopped about thirty miles farther on at a pretty little village called Lalaguine. We had got into the habit, which had produced extraordinarily good results, of asking any negro we found on the wayside which villages had the best dances. In this case we had fallen on a sly little cripple, the village scribe, who told us quite inaccurately that there were wonderful dances there, provided we would give a present to the chief's brother; the real chief had gone to try to bail out his only son, who was held as a hostage. I replied that it was our habit to do so, and asked if he would prefer gifts or money. 'Money, of course,' said the scribe; 'then he will be able to get something to eat.' He showed us a wall-less barn where we could sleep the night; it would have been all right if there hadn't been a heavy thunderstorm. The dances were quite curious but tedious; they were danced by torchlight to the sound of drums and a one-stringed fiddle played by a blind man; the dancers were little girls, naked except for strings of red beads round their necks and waists, and a couple of young men. A doleful, almost Gregorian chant preceded, accompanied and followed the dances, which consisted of jumps and a curious undulating movement of the spine, accompanied by a quick, uneven and syncopated foot-movement; the men at the same time did a mock military salute. The dance was extremely difficult but not very interesting. The barn roof leaked and I was slightly unwell and much more alarmed, for I was excreting blood and terrified of bilharzia; but forty-eight hours' starvation diet removed the symptoms.

In the morning we crossed the frontier into Togoland. The landscape had changed considerably, for the land was undulating and slightly wooded and the small millet was already fairly high; the change from winter to high summer in twenty miles is very surprising. Although there were a number of deserted villages the country seemed comparatively populous, and it was a change to see young men about in the fields. Conscription had been in force till 1925; then the government, faced with the alternative of no population or no soldiers – for the former German colony was split between the English and French and the frontier follows the entire length – chose the latter solution.

We arrived at Dapango in time for lunch. It is a very pretty little village, situated on a group of small hills overlooking the park-like countryside; it is difficult to describe the almost physical relief that a slight break in the appalling flatness and monotony of the West African landscape gave. The local chief received us in the most lordly fashion, and presented us with all the provisions we could possibly require; there were also there a couple of young and highly educated Dahomeyans, the auxiliary doctor and the teacher, who acted as our interpreters and spent a good deal of time with us. Their chief distraction was reading the catalogues of smart men's clothes shops, and they insisted that I should give them the address of every good shirtmaker I knew. I hope Hawes and Curtis sent a catalogue.

Dapango was really a group of small villages, each village inhabited by a different race, which preserved its own dress and customs. Consequently the crowd was quite exceptionally variegated. The Haoussa from the North were dressed in boubous which swept the ground; on their heads men wore curious raffia hats, adorned with coloured patterns, which looked like the baskets in which Miss Jekyll would gather her flowers. The Bobo were naked except for two packets of leaves held in place by a girdle. The original inhabitants of the country wore a piece of cloth round their waist; their torsos were decorated with elaborate patterns in raised weals. The Peulh women were remarkable for their lighter skin and sharper features, and their hair dressed in a high crest running from the centre of the forehead to the nape of the neck, with the sides of the skull shaved clean. There were a couple of other groups which I was unable to identify.

The whole afternoon was occupied with various dances. First of all there were a series of ritual dances performed by boys and old men dressed in white shifts and carrying wands, dancing round a big drum. They were all dances for special occasions – circumcision, burial and so on – and several of them were very impressive. There was a very curious 'hate' dance, which was danced widdershins with the back turned to the drum, a regular witch dance. Most of our photos of these dances were spoiled by an old Bobo lady who insisted on stopping permanently in front of the cameras; she was old and wrinkled and her head was shaved, but her years did not prevent her dancing and singing with the utmost energy, holding a calabash in her right hand and waggling her greenery under our noses in a frenzied black-bottom. She probably did not think the dance of the Bobo women gave her enough scope. This was a country dance, a sort of Sir Roger de Coverley, in which the women stood in a circle singing and clapping their hands; pairs of dancers advanced into the centre of the circle in turns and performed a number of steps at one another, the pas de deux finishing when the two executants had bumped bottoms as hard as they could, after which they resumed their places in the circle and another pair started. After this interlude – as it were a Balanchine ballet after one of Massine's drearier symphonies-made-easy – there was the war dance of the Konkumba (?), one of the two most beautiful spectacles I saw in West Africa; the other was the dance of the Nesshoué (river fetish) at Djebbé, near Abomey. These dancers had extremely lovely bodies, slim and elegant, well set off by their costumes, which consisted of a wide belt of cowries to which a piece of antelope skin was attached like a tail; they had thick necklaces of cowries and white beads; their eyes were rimmed with black; round their forehead they had a fillet of cowries and above that a bright scarlet conical cap. They had cowries and pieces of jangling iron as garters below their knees and straps of cowries hanging from the elbows, and carried short axes. Their dance was a miracle of frenzied rhythmic precision, most complicated and controlled, an ordered savagery which it is impossible to describe. There was nothing of the accidental or extemporary which so often mars negro dancing; it was impossible to be patronising towards the dance; it could only be judged by the highest standards of choreography; and by those standards it seemed to me more moving than the Polovtsian dances of *Prince Igor*, to which it bore a considerable resemblance. It affected me physiologically as the other ballet does; my heart beat faster with the mounting rhythm; I forgot my watching body and seemed to dance with the dancers.

It would have been pleasant to have stopped some time in that neighbourhood, but I was anxious about my health and wished to consult a white doctor, so we went on to Sansanné Mango, the most important town in Northern Togoland. There was a charming and extremely competent old doctor there – a naturalised German, I was told – who examined me thoroughly and prescribed for me; but his advice to eat as much fruit and vegetables as possible was difficult to follow in a fruitless region. He and his wife were loved and respected by the negroes, who were much distressed at his imminent departure; he said he was leaving because it was too 'hot' for him; he had a pretty sense of humour. After I had consulted him I paid my regulation visit to the administrator; he was away, and we were charmingly received by his assistant, a very Parisian young man who spent a happy afternoon recalling Parisian scandal with Benga. This conversation took place on the verandah of the special agent's bungalow, in which we had been given a room; the other officials were also present and were much shocked at the depravity of fashionable life which the talk brought into prominence. Before he left us the assistant administrator had said that he would arrange for a tribe in the South-West to do their dances for us in a couple of days' time; we would all go together, for his newly married wife had never seen them. We had dinner with the special agent, who was, almost inevitably, Corsican; he was also a freemason, and suffered from an unquenchable thirst, an inferiority complex, and the feeling that he was hardly used. He had only been transferred from Lomé, the capital, where he worked in the treasury, three months before, and now he was ordered to return; this would put him about three thousand francs out of pocket.

The administrator returned early the next morning and sent for me. He was fairly young, and extremely courteous and diplomatic; he made us a very welcome present of bread and fruit and vegetables, and deplored the unforeseen difficulties which prevented the dances being organised, as arranged. Anyhow, they were of little interest, and he didn't approve of organised dances, which lacked the verve of spontaneity. If we could return on the fourteenth of July all the dancers would be in Mango. What was our intended route? All the way through Togoland down to Atakpamé and then to Abomey? Unfortunately floods had made that road impassable; now, if we left by Lama Kara, we could get to Djougou in Dahomey the same day and then there was a first-class road. A bit dazed by all this finesse – in the Nellie Wallace sense of the word – I said I was unwell and didn't like long journeys, and anyhow I couldn't leave that day as I had to see the doctor again. In that case, the administrator said, we could stop at Lama Kara and see the sleeping-sickness installations; he would telephone to the sub-administrator there at once, so that the rest-house should be ready for us. After a little cordial chat we went back to the bungalow, to discover that our Corsican host had suddenly remembered a long-standing engagement which would take him away for the whole day; he placed his house, his servants and his cellar at our complete disposition. The rest of the people with whom we had chatted the day before were also engaged.

I was rather taken aback by this quarantine. As I noted at the time, 'They want to get me out of the colony before I see – what? and to prevent people talking to me for fear they should say – what? It strikes me as an idiotic policy, for naturally one starts snooping... The panic of the people here is amusing though aggravating; aggravating, for unless you go off the road, the people don't dare do anything without the administrator's permission; amusing because they are forcing my attention on to things I had little curiosity about.' The kind doctor was able to explain the reason for our ostracism; the administrator had, for some unguessable reason, decided that we were spies sent by the League of Nations, and had consequently sent round chits to all the Europeans asking them to treat us with the greatest courtesy but not to say anything. The French are extremely sensitive about their mandated territories and frightened they will be taken away from them; and they are very indignant with the English because instead of making their slices of Togoland and the Cameroons into separate units, as the French have, they have, apparently illegally, incorporated them into the Gold Coast and Nigeria respectively. I still don't know what the administrator was afraid of my seeing; the negroes were certainly poor and frightened, but noticeably less poor and frightened than in the French colonies proper; there were more doctors and they were far better equipped and installed; the German plantations of teak and mahogany had been added to; the countryside looked relatively prosperous. The only possibility which crossed my mind was that the district we had planned going to was off the main road and on the frontier, and there might have been some military preparations; but it seems to me improbable. It was more likely just a bad case of ingrowing suspicion.

In the afternoon we drove across the frontier into English Togoland. The country was slightly less wooded but otherwise very similar; the road was considerably worse; the negroes seemed just as poor, and their huts and agricultural implements just as primitive. There was only one difference. On the English side when the negroes saw us coming they waved to us and went on with their work; on the French side they dropped everything and stood at attention. On the one side they smiled at you; on the other they saluted and flinched. I had been very depressed by the pervading atmosphere and thought I might be exaggerating the contrast, but the chauffeurs spontaneously commented on it.

In the evening our Corsican host had imbibed enough Dutch courage to break the quarantine; he was leaving in a few days anyhow. He told me about his work in the treasury at Lomé. Togoland is economically independent and consequently keeps all the money it raises, whereas the other colonies have to send all but the most meagre grant to Dakar. The territory is therefore relatively rich with considerable reserves; it was apparently our host's duty to scrutinise demands for grants and give them out.

The next morning, after an affectionate round of farewells, during which the administrator presented us with further vegetables, we left in the direction of Lama Kara. The doctor advised us to follow the administrator's plan, for the whole colony would be warned of our presence; he and his wife had been very nice to me. They were very humane people, distressed at the misery they saw and harried when they tried to remedy it; it was charming to watch them together with their little courtesies and private jokes. They were polite to the negroes, who worshipped them; they were ignored by the Europeans.

The countryside became continuously more edenic and idyllic, very green and pastoral, with many hills. The formless appearance of tropical landscape was broken by sudden outcrops of rock. The principal tree was the palmyra (*Borassus flabelliformis*) – a tall, very formal palm with fan-shaped leaves and clusters of fruit like big oranges – undoubtedly the most decorative of all palms. There are two types of vegetation which give a landscape an exotic air: plants with a stiff symmetry, like these palms, or euphorbia and traveller's trees; or plants so tangled as to appear completely formless. Trees which make an irregular pattern immediately seem homely.

About midday we were stopped by a torrential downpour; luckily we were near a village with a sort of rest-house, where we took shelter. The village chief organised a little dance in our honour; the dancers wore little toques trimmed with horns and feathers and a number of white feather bands round their legs as well as jingle-jingles made from folded pieces of lead with a pebble inside; between showers they shuffled in circles, dancing from the knee down. When the rain stopped we went on and shortly saw our first Cabrai. All the men and most of the women go completely naked, without even a string when they are in the country; both Benga and the chauffeurs were so surprised and shocked that they were never able to pass one without laughing. What embarrassed the chauffeurs even more was the rather disconcerting habit that both sexes had of pissing while engaged in conversation; but I think it was less the act than the position in which it was performed that upset them, for as pious Mohammedans they knew that a piddle was only pleasing to Allah if performed in a squatting position. They were a happy and handsome people, shining with palm oil; they greeted us merrily with an open hand to show they were unarmed. I determined to spend a little time to try and find out about these people who seemed so different from any I had seen; and luckily the sub-administrator, who had just arrived, was too busy putting his house in order to bother with us. He put at our disposal a most sumptuous furnished guesthouse. Lama Kara is a pretty garden town, laid out by the Germans on a spacious scale with plantations between the houses, the only planned small town we saw in West Africa; it is on the banks of the Kara.

The Cabrai are a relatively small race, inhabiting a region about fifty miles long by thirty wide; as far as my experience goes they are completely different from any other race of negroes which has not been exposed to alien influence. To start with, they are the only group of uncivilised

Africa Dances

negroes I met who are not mad: that is to say, that their minds work on lines which Europeans can follow – a statement which I will amplify in the next section. Magic religion which fills the larger part of the life of most negroes has very little place with the Cabrai. They carry no amulets; their dead stay dead; they have no initiation ceremonies; they are not circumcised. They indulge in a very vague sort of nature worship; certain trees and pieces of ground are holy – but only trees which are of no economic value and land where nothing else will grow; and the chief function of these sacred places is to serve as abattoirs; when an animal is going to be eaten it is slaughtered on a holy spot; the divinity gets the spilt blood.

Their mode of living is as practical as their religion. They go naked because they consider clothes a useless expense; on the whole they refuse to accept them as gifts, though missionaries and outside influence are now getting some of them to wear loincloths in the villages. They are scrupulously clean, for their country is well watered and they bathe several times daily; after each bath they anoint themselves with palm oil, which leaves the palms of their hands and the soles of their feet a brick-red colour. They are the best cultivators I have seen, not merely in Africa, but, considering the primitive instruments they use, in Europe. The fields are planted regularly and thickly – a great change from the haphazard planting of most negroes; the ground is hilly and stony, but they have utilised every corner of available earth and built up small terraces and pockets of earth flanked with stones. Some hills which seemed entirely covered with millet we found to be quite arid; the millet plants were in groups of three in little walled pockets of earth which had been brought up in baskets from the plain below. Agriculture is chiefly the men's business; the women, who are in a very inferior position, are chiefly occupied with preparing the food and other household business. Their domestic architecture is the most elaborate, the cleanest and the most practical I saw. They live together in big family groups, and each group of huts is like a small village; each individual except the smallest children has his own hut with a raised sleeping-place, covered with animal skins; there are huts specially adapted for hens, horses and goats; there are special

138

granaries, and places devoted exclusively to various domestic tasks such as breaking or kneading grain and washing. All the buildings and the paths between them are made of mud worked to the consistency of cement; each path has a hollowed drain in the middle which is periodically sluiced; there are also drains in the floors of the huts. All huts have their floors raised a few inches above the ground to guard against floods; the step which leads into the hut is usually decorated with an inlaid abstract design in cowries. The exterior walls of the hut are coloured and worked till they look like carved wood. I visited three of these groups of buildings and found each one spotlessly clean, quite unlike any other African huts; in each case they were the homesteads of chiefs, and their greatest pride was their own rooms with a cheap European bed, photographs and gewgaws. The chiefs were dressed after the Haoussa fashion, very fully; their numerous wives were adorned in the most eccentric manner; many had clothes painted on their naked bodies with white chalk; and several had smothered their face and neck in white powder. Polygamy is very general, but women enjoy great sexual licence; when a woman feels excited, I was told, she will place a certain leaf some way in front of her and behind her in the field path, and will remain between them with another leaf in her teeth until a man comes along who is willing to gratify her. They are also much addicted to pederasty, if the very pointed and public advances of a young man made to me and an elder one to Benga were not exceptional.

Their laws are very just. All crimes are punished by fines roughly double the value of the damage caused; half goes to the injured person and half to the chief. Hereditable property, which devolves exclusively on males, is divided in the following way: the chief arranges the property in portions which are several times the number of heirs; the heirs then choose portions in turn, starting with the eldest, minors and absentees being represented by uncles; at the second round the youngest chooses first and the order is reversed; at the third round the second heir has first choice; and so on till the lots are exhausted.

They have to rely on hunting for most of their meat, for the tsetse have killed all the cattle; they chiefly hunt the antelope with bow and arrow, though there are occasional lions and leopards which they spear. They make elaborate dishes with the many varieties of fruit and vegetables they grow. They brew millet beer, on which they get gloriously drunk.

Their chief diversion is dancing which, as far as I could discover, had no ritualistic significance; nor, as far as I know, do they believe in sorcerers. We saw a number of their dances in the villages – for, as usual, the presence of a European in a town stops dancing there. The dances are of two sorts – warlike and orgiastic. At Loudina the war dance was almost frightening. All the young men danced in a ring round the drums; they were armed with bows and slings, cutlasses, and hatchets; they most of them wore some sort of head-dress, but otherwise their costumes were arbitrary and fantastic; one man was completely naked except for a small-sized straw roof on his head; several had animal pelts covering their backsides; a few wore drawers. They pranced round in a circle, shouting and grimacing; they challenged one another to mimic, but extremely realistic combats; as the dance continued they got more and more ecstatic and uncontrolled, until I was quite relieved that another appointment forced us to leave; I am not happy with a murderous-looking knife being twirled a few inches from my face, even with the best intentions.

Our other appointment was at Lasa, a village a few miles away; the entertainment which we found there is quite impossible to describe, even if it were permissible to do so. The dance was a mixture of Brueghel and Bedlam, semi-erotic, semi-ecstatic and quite cuckoo. The dancers, who were old men and youths, were nearly all stark naked except for head-dresses ornamented with horns and cowries and necklaces of black and red seeds; as for the dances – one old and bearded man danced chiefly with his left foot which he waved in the air; another did the most surprising things with his more private parts, throwing them about rhythmically and peculiarly; they were of extraordinary size and plasticity. At one moment everyone sat on the ground and did the most eccentric things, advancing with a sort of woggle of the haunches. One young man with an extremely elaborate helmet had danced himself into a mediumistic frenzy in which he stuck feathers and thorns into his arms; the other dancers threw him about like a ball. Another young man ate earth and smothered himself in it; he was continually being sick and swallowing his own vomit; he had reached a stage at which only the whites of his eyes showed. He continually fell exhausted to the ground, but the music of the drum and the whistly flutes would bring him to and he would start off again. The native guard who was meant to be keeping order was seized by the contagion and did things with his rifle which weren't quite nice. It was the oddest evening I have ever spent.

There are three blots on the Cabrai's otherwise idyllic life: taxes, locusts and disease. The labour tax they don't mind so much, for they can work it off locally; but although they have everything they need themselves they handle very little money, and it is almost impossible for them to collect the eighteen francs which is demanded for every male over fifteen; some go out to work, but many just say they have no money and can't pay; since Togo is still mandated territory, and the negroes there, as in Dahomey, know the address of the ILB at Geneva, the administration has to leave it at that. Locusts were causing great damage while we were there; women and children tried to prevent them settling by making as much noise as possible; it is the only remedy they have. But disease is their greatest trouble. The mountain water gives them goitre, and their heavy work hernia; we also saw several cases of elephantiasis and leprosy. But these maladies are relatively unimportant compared with the havoc worked by sleeping sickness, which is now endemic among these people. The banks of the Kara are haunted by tsetse; the only way by which it might be exterminated is if a space were kept permanently razed and out of bounds on either side of the river, a difficult work to accomplish. All that can be done is to try to establish a sort of quarantine and to cure those of the sick who come up for treatment. Until recently a fatal disease, sleeping sickness can now be cured in the greater number of cases with Fourneau's arsenic injections, especially if the illness is caught in its first stages. But in the first stage, when the trypanosome is in the blood stream, there is little beyond the swollen glands at the base of the neck to mark the infected person, who is also at that time a source of further contagion; they merely look slightly plumper than usual. It is only when the trypanosomes have got into the central nervous system and the invalid is no longer a danger to his fellows that the horrible symptoms occur – the wasting till a man is reduced to a skeleton, the painful and often dangerous madness, the paralysed lethargy – which last over a considerable period and make sleeping sickness one of the most fearful of lingering deaths which consumes a man piecemeal physically and mentally. Even in the last stages it will often yield to treatment, if there are doctors and the necessary drugs. In Togoland there are both, in French Equatorial Africa, which is being depopulated by this plague, on the whole neither; in the lower Ivory Coast sleeping sickness has been spreading for a number of years; but until it had got a thorough hold on the country the administration refused to admit that it existed, on account of its bad propaganda value; any mention of it in a doctor's report was erased by superior functionaries. It was only after an administrator's wife fell a victim that occasional cases were grudgingly admitted; and the overworked and unbelievably badly equipped doctors can do no more than treat such cases as come to them when they receive supplies of the drugs. There are few sights more revolting and more pitiable than a man in the later stages of sleeping sickness.

On the way to visit the new installation which was being erected to deal with this disease we passed some villages on the edge of the Cabrai country where the negroes' bodies were so tattooed that they resembled mosaics. On our return to the guesthouse we found that in our absence someone had deposited a magazine in French dealing with a mystic cult called Mazdaznan. I fell on it with avidity and learned that the secret core of the doctrine was that breathing was absolutely essential to life. As long as you breathed you were sure to be fairly all right, and if you breathed deeply two or three times a day there was absolutely nothing you couldn't do. An even surer method of gaining health and success was to 'vibrate the glands'; but which glands, and how they were to be vibrated, the brochure didn't tell. People were also told to take air baths and mothers were advised to give their children 'genital massage'. People had to be vegetarian, and a long list of suitable foods was given – as far as I could gather the suitability of, say, rice as a food depended on the position of the sun in the zodiac. Chocolate creams, I was happy to see, were always wholesome. There was something unbelievably incongruous in finding this advertisement of a synthetic religion, presumably designed for neurotic middle-class town-dwelling women, in the midst of the one race of happy naked negroes who were not swamped in religious systems of their own.

It was with great regret that we left this country. On our way out of the town we stopped at the only store for petrol and nasty cigarettes. The old negro storekeeper came out and addressed me in excellent German and was almost moved to tears when I answered him in that language. He insisted that we should come into the store and drink a glass of beer with him; and over the beer he poured out his heart to us. He had been educated by the Germans and remembered their rule as heaven. They had been very hard – they did not make prisoners, but used to flog offenders – but there had been money to earn and work to do under them, whereas the French try to get everything for nothing. In those days, so peaceful and contented was the country that a small child could carry money from the coast to the frontier without anything happening to him; now he couldn't cross a village. The Germans were starting to exploit the colony; the French were only interested in getting taxes out of it. Although he probably saw the past in a very rosy light a great deal of what this negro told me was later confirmed by an Englishman who had been in Togoland with the British occupation during and after the war. He was full of respect for the thoroughness with which the Germans had planned the exploitation of the colony. They had started by sending engineers and agricultural experts to make a thorough survey of the whole country so that they could know what each district might one day be expected to yield, and had then planned their roads and railways to be of the maximum future utility – a foresight which, as far as my informant knew, was unique in colonial exploitation. Once the roads were planned the Germans built new villages about every ten miles along them in those parts which weren't already inhabited, and forced the negroes to move to them, so that the road could be kept up without the negroes having to leave their homes. Little now remains of their planning save a few plantations of timber trees and the spacious lines to which Lomé and the smaller towns have been laid out. The Germans, my informant added, had been very harsh with the negroes, but just and generous, and were generally liked; of course they had no race theory then. He also told me that when war was declared the Germans packed up their supplies of gold and divided it into cases; each was taken up into the hills by a trusted man, accompanied by five negro porters; when they got to the secret place where the chest was to be buried the white men shot the negroes and buried them with the chest, a precaution which the negroes thought extremely sensible, not only because it would prevent the secret being divulged, but also because the spirits of the dead porters would guard the treasure from unauthorised hands.

After we had left the valley of the Kara the country turned very dry and barren; the north of Dahomey is a very poor land. A few miles before we reached Djougou we came upon a band of musicians playing under a tree. The musicians were dressed after the Dahomeyan fashion, a *pagne* or large piece of cloth wrapped round their waist like a skirt. Their instruments were a huge double drum which gave out a most doleful sound, a couple of smaller drums, and several hollowed horns which may have been small elephant's tusks, covered with leopard or antelope skins and with small worked-ivory mouthpieces. Although I was unable to distinguish any tune in what they were playing the effect was not displeasing, and even rather impressive in its mournful rhythm. It was a funeral concert to mark the end of the mourning period for the death of an elderly or noteworthy man; when the man had died his eldest son had had to go into the wilderness for a certain time, and it was to mark his return to the community that the concert had been organised; the musicians would play with short intervals from sunset to sunset; on the second evening a bull would be sacrificed and the musicians would receive the head and the chief the chest. From time to time during the twenty-four hours handfuls of cowries were thrown into the air by the female relations of the deceased, to the accompaniment of wails, and the children would scramble for them. This rite is not performed after the death of women or of young and unimportant men.

Djougou is an ugly and uninteresting town, full of corrugated iron and Catholics, and we left it as soon as we could to go south. The farther south we went the more 'tropical' the landscape became, particularly by the numerous watercourses; big trees were masked with a tangle of undergrowth, especially wild bananas and varied creepers; rope-like lianas hung down from the branches as though arranged by a film producer for a rather nervous Tarzan. We stopped at a few villages to see the dances, but we soon found out that there was only one type of profane dance in the whole of Dahomey. A number of young men sit in a row behind one another on a log of wood; the drummer stands in front of them. One of the men is song-leader, and he chants a phrase to which the other men and the crowd reply in chorus, beating time with bits of wood. As the spirit moves them the young men get up and do a few steps with a rhythmic movement of the shoulders and arms which are held forward and away from the body, finishing with an abrupt half turn. The singing is often quite pretty, but when you cannot understand the language it quickly palls. Until we reached Pira the only incident of any interest was a m'Deup who fell into a trance and started dancing at Bodi; but she was forcibly removed by her companions.

The Dahomeyans are mostly tall and too thin, which gives them a rather weedy appearance; they are not very dark in colouring. Men and women dress practically exactly alike in long pieces of printed cloth which are arranged over the shoulder, under the arms or round the waist as occasion demands; they always fall in a skirt to the ground. Except for the elaborate methods of dressing the hair – they train it into whorls and loops and every manner of curl – which the women cultivate on the rare occasions when their heads aren't shaved for mourning, and the short pipes which the older women smoke, it is extremely difficult to tell one sex from the other; in some cases we were never able to decide. The Dahomeyans are extremely tasteful and coquettish in their dress; any article which accompanies their pagne is always well matched to it. They make an extremely picturesque crowd, for their costumes are very bright and varied, usually in a bright blue cloth with designs and patterns stamped in black and different colours. These materials nearly all come from England and as a whole strike me as the most beautiful group of stuffs I have ever come across. The successful audacity of the decorative motifs – letters, figures and conventional signs are used with astounding effect – should, were they known, stop all the amateur arty craftsmen from ever spoiling good linen again. But these cloths and their designers are completely unknown to England; they are secretly designed and printed in Manchester and shipped abroad, without Englishmen ever getting a chance of admiring what is perhaps their pleasantest craft. It is a pity, for they would make a pleasant alternative to the flowered patterns and gracelessly rectangular modernistic designs which are at present our only choice in upholstery cloths.

We were much struck by the relative paucity of schools in Dahomey. In the Sudan every fourth hut seemed to be a schoolhouse, and in the rest of the French colonies they were fairly frequent, though the instruction gained in them was not always what was intended – witness the school in the Ivory Coast where the (inevitably) native teacher had a coffee plantation in which his young pupils were given 'practical work' and were severely whipped if they didn't gather the proper quantity of berries. The reason for Dahomey's comparative lack of schools is, I think, that the Dahomeyans take to education far too well. They seem to show a capacity for acquiring European knowledge far in excess of any other negro race; they win most of the open scholarships and examinations with great regularity, and consequently if they once start learning they continue until they have got a probably useless diploma. There is in Dahomey already a large population of intellectuals who are unemployable under the present policy; they are the administration's greatest danger, for they are extremely vocal; the tiny Dahomeyan seaboard, about a hundred and sixty miles in length, has in its towns about a dozen small and scurrilous newspapers, owned and written by negroes; which is perhaps one of the reasons why in the last few years no governor has stayed in Dahomey more than six months. These educated Dahomeyans are not pleasant people; they ape European manners to an idiotic extent; they are most of them dishonest intellectually when they are not actually; they are all Catholics; and they have the most bitter scorn of their illiterate fellows and their beliefs. 'On fait ça chez les indigènes' – that's what the natives do, is their constant and scornful reply to any question about negro practices; the despised natives usually being the greater part of their family. Dahomey was conquered only in the nineties, and without the retarding influence of Islam the negroes have evolved too quickly.

Pira is the most important centre for fetishism in the northern part of the colony of Dahomey (as opposed to the kingdom of Dahomey). By this I mean that negroes in need of magical aid in the surrounding district will come from considerable distances to Pira; but as far as I could find out this was not due to any special sanctity of the place or to any highly organised religion, but to the great occult powers of one man, Banoué Ajouba. I was not able to find out very much about the beliefs of the country, for the barn where we put up was quite uninhabitable. We arrived in the middle of a terrible thunderstorm to find that the roof leaked in nearly every part; moreover, all the insects of the neighbourhood seemed to have settled on the rest-house as a sanctuary; the floor was alive with enough varieties of ants and beetles to delight a coleopterist, as well as scorpions and rather alarming millipedes; the walls were covered with lizards, mason flies and big furry spiders, of which I have an uncontrollable horror; large bats hung from the roof which was luminous with thousands of glow-worms; moths and other winged creatures actually obscured the light, so dense a cloud did they form; and for a final touch there were a couple of sloughed snake skins on the verandah. Moreover, we had run very short of food and there was very little to be purchased at Pira; for the thirty-six hours we were there we ate practically nothing except yams dipped in coconut oil.

Owing to the ascendancy of Banoué everything in Pira is doubled. Banoué ranks quite as high as the real chief, and is attended by a greater retinue and ceremony. The fetishist dancers are more important than the lay dancers. This duplication is carried down to the smallest details.

We were awakened at dawn the day after we arrived by a tremendous noise; we were being serenaded. We dressed quickly, for the water was so full of livestock that washing seemed out of the question, and found the chief outside with a large group of men and women singing to the sound of drums and flutes. As soon as we had settled in the shade of a gigantic cotton tree they started dancing, and continued for several hours. After a couple of hours Banoué Ajouba arrived, escorted by a couple of old men and a crowd of women. He had one of the most impressive appearances of any man that I have ever seen. Although not much past middle age, he walked with a long stick with a slightly syncopated movement for the sake of dignity. He was dressed in an immense flowing robe of dark blue; a snow-white turban surrounding a scarlet skullcap covered his head; he held a very large round white fan, which had magic properties, in front of him. His dress successfully set off his truly remarkable face. His features were very refined and his face was far longer than is common with negroes; his large eyes had an extraordinary fixity and strength. He is the only person I have ever met who has given me the impression of possessing a sort of power which was indefinable but quite definite. While he was present it was impossible to forget him, and he made all other people seem rather shadowy. His head made the same sort of impression on me that certain pictures of Indian and Chinese sages do – I was particularly reminded of the porcelain statue of a Lohan in the British Museum.

When he arrived he took a seat opposite us slightly in front of the chief, and he and I engaged in a staring match – none of the negroes would meet his eyes. I felt that for some reason it was necessary for me to meet his gaze, and I continued staring at him across a space of about thirty yards till all the surrounding people and the landscape became an indistinct blur and his face seemed preternaturally distinct and as it were detached from his body and nearer to me physically than it was in reality. I wondered whether I was being hypnotised, when Banoué dropped his eyes and sent a messenger over to me to tell me I had great magical power. Somewhat flattered, I replied that I knew that his power was far greater. After this exchange of courtesies his women started dancing.

Their dance was the usual trance dance, accompanied by the curious pantomime of awakening and the cataleptic falls. We had seen it in many other districts and were not much interested. After a time Banoué came over to greet us, advancing with a curious shambling trot, while the whole of his retinue fell flat on their faces. He took my right hand in both of his and held it to his forehead for a little time and then returned to his seat. After a little more time he sent to ask if we would like to visit his shrine; and on our saying we would he told us to follow him in a few minutes. We went through the village, where I saw for the first time the little roofed shrines covering wooden figures (*boitchyo*) and wooden phalluses in a mound of earth (*legba*) which are so common a feature of lower Dahomey and whose significance I learned later, and eventually arrived at an open space in the middle of the village; in the centre of this space was a low, spreading tree with pieces of wood laid in its branches; under the tree was a low bench of logs on which Banoué and his two male assistants were sitting; behind were two or three straw-covered altars. On Banoué's left there was a row of young women holding purple-dyed besom brooms in front of their faces. At a sign from Banoué they started singing a sort of canticle, the most impressive and 'musical' tune, in the European sense of the word, that I heard in Africa, and in time with their song performed a rhythmic and ritualist brushing of the ground round the tree with a curious slouching step. The effect was far more solemn than any other negro daylight ceremony I saw. Benga was so impressed with Banoué that he wanted to make use of his professional services, and as I was very curious to see him in action we arranged to visit him privately later in the day.

When we returned, accompanied by an interpreter, we were led to Banoué's hut. It was fairly large and the outer walls were covered with inexplicable stylised drawings. Banoué was resting inside in deep contemplation, and we were told not to disturb him. We therefore sat down and looked at the surprising collection of grigris on the walls, strange heterogeneous objects made of animal and human bones and skulls, crabs' claws, fur, bits of cloth and other objects not easily identifiable. Our interpreter, noticing which way our eyes were wandering, told us on no account to look at the one in the niche above Banoué's head. It was so dark there that nothing could be distinctly seen. After a little time Banoué took notice of us, and told us to follow him. Accompanied by his acolytes, one of whom spoke French sufficiently to dispense with our interpreter, we went out into the shade of the tree. Once there Banoué held a long discourse, much of which wasn't translated; among other things he said that I was the third European to 'sit beside him': the two others who had done so had achieved their desire and had written to tell him so. One was an administrator who had become, as he had prayed, a governor while unusually young. He showed us the letters, which seemed genuine; we knew the name of the governor. After this preliminary he asked us our names and the boons that we desired from the fetish; Benga's request was of a definite and private nature, but I had nothing I particularly needed, so asked that my next book should be successful. If it is I shall certainly write and tell Banoué so. We then gave him the price of a bullock, for an animal was not immediately procurable, and the prayer was made. The acolytes hid their faces, and Banoué took off his head-dress and shoes and made us do the same. We all crouched on the sacred spot in front of the tree; Banoué held a calabash of millet beer in his hands, and spoke to the ground in a low and urgent voice, spilling the beer as he did so. As soon as he had finished speaking he poured the lees of the beer on our hands and his own and we rubbed them together, while Banoué listened carefully to a low rumble which seemed to come from under the ground we were standing on. He then took another calabash of beer from which we all drank a little and the remainder was poured on to the ground. Banoué studied intently the puddle it made and the patterns formed by the innumerable flies which settled on it, and then told us our requests had been granted, but that neither would be fulfilled for several moons.

We went on our way somewhat bewildered. For the next few weeks we were more engaged with the invisible than the visible world.

BOOK THREE

Fetish

Foreword

Before a description of negro magical religions it is essential to give some
sort of definition to the words used. To avoid obscurity I have used native
words as little as possible; for the same reason I have avoided technical
anthropological terms such as 'mana'; also these terms do not always
correspond properly with my observations. Consequently I have been
forced to use words which are already in current English use; but since
most of them hold a variety of meanings I am giving the senses in which
I have employed them herewith. When I use the word NEGRO I refer
exclusively to the people inhabiting the parts of tropical West Africa that
I visited.

At the head of every negro theological system I came across is a god
who created all things visible and invisible. Each tribe knows him under a
different name, but they are all agreed that this creator is too far removed
from human beings to influence them or be influenced by them. This
God created a number of forces which I have called fetishes; these forces
are part of God and are as it were the canalisation of a section of his power.
God can be worshipped only through these forces, which bear in negro
eschatology much the same relation to the godhead that saints and the
BVM do for Catholics. Each fetish has some object, usually an animal, in
the physical world which has the same characteristics as the force or fetish;
these objects, whether animal, vegetable or inanimate, are therefore signs
of the fetish and have the same name as it. This is the only sense in which
I use the word fetish; originally introduced by the Portuguese, who
applied the word 'feitico' from its contemporary meaning – relics of

Africa Dances

saints, rosaries, images, pieces of the true cross with miracle-working properties – to similar manifestations in Africa, it has come to be loosely applied to all African religious manifestations and as such is too indefinite. For the same reason I have not used at all the English coast word 'ju-ju'. The power of the fetish can be reached through the medium of a priest, a person who claims and is granted special influence with one of these fetish forces, part of which has descended into him; he is helped in his rites by fetishers, people who have been consecrated to the fetish and have learned the proper ritual. The laity are fetish worshippers. The most general way of gaining the fetish's favour is by a sacrifice, usually an animal killed in some place impregnated with the fetish's strength, and offered in thanks or in hope of benefit to come. If on the other hand it is desired to avert present or threatened illness or misfortune, it is necessary to make a *vô* (Dahomeyan) or special sacrifice into which the ill-luck can pass. For everyday personal use it is necessary to have private charms or grigris, either as amulets to be worn about the person or as private magical objects to be used with a special ritual. They are made either by or under the direction of a fetish priest. This side of religion is known in Dahomey as *Tovôdoun*, which the negroes exported from the slave coast to the New World called voodoo. An equally important side of religion is *Akovôdoun*, or worship of the dead. The dead may be divided into two groups, the ancestors, all the anonymous dead of the tribe, and the recently dead, who are still known by name, and whose individuality in the land of the dead is still distinct. These latter are very important and dangerous; for they represent the soul of the dead man, without the hampering of his body. The soul can be roughly defined as the animating principle of all life; in normal circumstances it is coexistent with the body; but in certain states parts of it, for it is indefinitely divisible, can be active elsewhere. The most important of these states are sleep, trance and death. A sorcerer is able to exercise his terrible and antisocial power by sending his soul abroad into other objects. Besides sorcerers evil can be worked by discarnate devils or imps; they are malicious sprites which can usually be controlled.

The first five chapters of this section deal exclusively with the religion of the ancient kingdom of Dahomey – that is to say, with an area which roughly corresponds with a circle of fifty miles' radius of which Abomey is the centre. Nearly all my information is derived from Prince Justin Aho, chef de canton d'Oumbégamé, who with the greatest kindness gave me every facility I demanded, made it possible for me to go everywhere and see everything I wished, and put at my disposition both his own considerable knowledge and his notes, and when he was unable to accompany me himself gave me as guide and interpreter some other member of the ex-royal family. I have verified some of the statements in the first chapter by the aid of M. Le Hérissé's *Ancien Royaume du Dahomey* and Richard Burton's *Mission to Gélélé*. The sixth chapter is more general in character and also takes into consideration my subsequent investigations in the forest region of the Ivory Coast. For the information in the last chapter, which concerns the tiny kingdom of Dassa Zoumé, I am indebted to the Reverend Mr Buckley, who had collected the statements of his catechists.

1. The Kingdom of Dahomey

In 1625 Dako, one of the sons of the king of Allada, moved north because his brothers would grant him no position in his father's town. He settled at a place called Uhwawe, near Abomey, first as a guest and later as the usurper of a chief named Awesu. He started encroaching on a neighbouring kingdom called Danh, and the king of that country one day remarked in anger, 'You will soon be building in my belly.' Dako accepted this as a challenge, conquered the kingdom of Danh and built a palace which he called Danh-ho-men, which in the Ffon language means in-Danh's-belly. It was and always has been customary for Dahomeyans to take symbolical names representing special events in their lives; on this occasion the king, his people and his country took the symbolical name of Dahomey. Danh is also the name of the snake fetish, and an alternative derivation is therefore given; but since ophiolatry has never been popular in Dahomey it seems improbable. In Ouidah on the coast the snake fetish was the principal object of worship.

At this period the kingdom of Dahomey was no more important than any other of the myriad African kingdoms: it was merely a town with a little surrounding country of which one man was the chief. But Dako had strangely ambitious blood in his veins; and when he handed over the most sacred amulet, the Dahomey, to his son he made him swear to leave a larger Dahomey than he found. This oath was sworn and kept by the nine successive kings who make up the Dahomeyan dynasty; from the beginning of the eighteenth century Dahomey had access to the sea; the area under the sway of its kings continually expanded; with the kingdom of Ashanti, to which it for a time paid tribute, it was by far the most powerful and organised group in West Africa, and in the nineteenth century it was continually threatening what is now Western Nigeria. At the beginning of the nineties of the last century the French, with the agreement of the other imperialist powers, invaded and conquered the country, with the aid of the Wolof; they sent into exile the tenth king Béhanzin, the man who sold Dahomey, whose name none of his subjects will mention; they tried to install a puppet king but failed, for Béhanzin had taken the Dahomey with him; after this abortive attempt the same sort of administration as in the other colonies, with chefs de canton, was set up.

The chief cause of the kings of Dahomey's power and wealth was the slave trade. Their numerous wars were really slave raids and the Dahomey coast was known as the slave coast. These slaves were sold to Europeans who were allowed to settle on the coast, the chief buyers being Portuguese, Brazilians and Englishmen. With the profits of this trade the Dahomeyans were able to buy European rifles and cannons by which means their army became practically irresistible to the less organised surrounding tribes. Their most consistent customer and merchant was a Portuguese named da Souza, and for him and his family a special rank was created at the Dahomeyan court.* When England decided that slavery was uneconomic and righteously interfered with those who still found it profitable a great deal of Dahomey's revenue disappeared;

---

* It is probable that the Marquis de Sade drew on accounts of Dahomey for his symbolical description of the kingdom of Butua in *Aline et Valcour*.

thereupon Glélé, the last and greatest king, turned his attention to the profit to be produced from palm oil and copra and had palm plantations made; these are still the greatest sources of the colony's wealth.

In the nineteenth century the name of Dahomey was sufficient to curdle the blood of Europeans; the most fantastic and horrible legends were told about it, and the not infrequent travellers made up the most astounding fictions concerning it. The two details which most struck the European imagination were the women soldiers, or, as they were called, Amazons, and the human sacrifices, especially the Customs. The religion was merely devil worship and idolatry and never excited much interest; to the best of my knowledge Richard Burton is the only nineteenth-century writer who dealt with the subject, and he is hopelessly inaccurate, possibly owing to incorrect information, but chiefly on account of the open hatred and scorn with which he viewed the Dahomeyans and negroes generally. To explain the Amazons and the Customs it is necessary to consider the position of women in Dahomey and some of the religious beliefs.

In all probability the Dahomeyans were originally matriarchal; for although women were considered as chattels a child usually belonged to his mother's family. To this day the position is extraordinarily complicated; there are half a dozen different types of marriage, ranging from complete marriage by purchase (*akumosi*) when a husband buys the woman and all her children, to *bossudi nobossi* (give the she-goat to the he-goat) in which the husband enjoys the wife but has no claim on her or her children, nor is he responsible for her taxes or other expenses. There is nearly every variant between these two extremes, and in the greater number the children go to the mother; the chief exception is the princely marriage – *avonosi*, married with cloth – in which the prince has all the enjoyment and none of the cost. All the king's children belonged to him, but none of his daughters could keep children, for dynastic reasons; they were consequently notoriously licentious.

Under the kings women and children were the only hereditable property, and that only by favour; the whole of Dahomey, and everything and everyone that therein was, belonged absolutely and only to the king.

People were granted as a favour the use of land or women, but it could always be withdrawn from them.

For a long time the queen mothers had, as in Ashanti, considerable powers, and had control of the treasury; but one of them abused her position and this power was taken away from them.

Unless there was some reason against it, succession went to the eldest son, except in the case of kings; these latter were never legitimate, but were chosen from the children that the heir apparent got on the slave-women which his father presented him with when he set up house for himself; the heir was not designated till he had got a child by a similar mother. The only exception to this rule was the third king Akaba, who was the brother of the second king Aho; the reason for this was that Aho had a twin sister; twins in Dahomey are considered with special reverence and are always treated exactly alike; Aho's sister had reigned with him, and normally her heirs should have stood equally with his; to avoid this dangerous situation Aho chose his brother to succeed him.

Like nearly all negroes, the Dahomeyans were polygamous, for wives are the greatest wealth; and logically the king had far more wives than anyone else. This collection was constantly being added to, for at the death of any of his subjects all the dead man's property was brought to the king to be regiven, and he habitually kept a few of the wives as death duty. The fourth king, Agaja, used part of his superfluous wives, firstly as a bodyguard, and later as soldiers; this practice was continued till the destruction of the kingdom, and this force of Amazons was feared far more than men soldiers. It is reckoned that besides about a thousand Amazons Glélé had about eight hundred wives in his palace, and about a thousand female slaves to attend to them; chastity was enforced on all these women under terrific penalties; since the whole population of Dahomey was probably not more than 500,000 a system of sexual starvation, which cannot be paralleled elsewhere in Africa, was forced on to a large part of the population, with the result that sexual perversion and neurotic curiosity were developed to an almost European extent. To this day the Dahomeyans make groups of little bronze figures of an obscenity which resembles feelthy postcards; and I am told, though I did not witness one, that they hold consciously shameless orgies. Most negroes take their sex calmly and simply – the accounts of nameless orgies are chiefly due to the perverted daydreams of sex-obsessed missionaries – and as far as I know the Dahomeyans are unique in their almost Asiatic approach to the subject.

As a result of this permanent women's army all the positions in the king's court were doubled, every male officer having his opposite number among the women. Today women fetishers are as numerous and as important as men; Dahomey is again unique in having no religious rites from which women are excluded.

The Customs were an occasion for uniting filial piety with criminal justice. It is a tenet with all negroes that when a man's body dies his soul (*yé* in Ffon) goes to the kingdom of the dead, where he will occupy exactly the same position as on earth. Consequently, when a king or great man dies it is necessary to furnish him with wives and slaves and so on, so that he can take up his position fittingly. This was known as the Grand Customs and was performed only once after the death of the king. But every year there were the Small Customs, during which devotion was paid by the reigning king to his father's spirit; among other ceremonies he sent as servants to his father some prisoners of war and the criminals of the country (who were not executed at any other time). Also whenever any event of importance occurred the king would send news of it to his father by telling it to some bystander and immediately killing him. The negroes' view of the after life has a great resemblance to that of such spiritualists as Vale Owen; but although they are really sincere in this belief they are very frightened of death, a subject which could only be mentioned in the king's hearing by circumlocutions.

Although the kingdom is now destroyed great reverence is still shown to the tomb of Glélé. (It may be mentioned that all the kings on their accession took a symbolical sentence for their name, of which the first syllables passed into common use; Glélé is short for Glélé na myonzi which means 'no man can lift a furrow', i.e. the king is so much part of his country that you can no more separate him from it than you can lift a furrow out of a ploughed field; that is a very good example of the symbolical and shorthand way in which the Dahomeyan language and mind work. Dahomeyans constantly change their name throughout their lives, after any important event, and it is extremely rude to address them by any except their present name; at their birth they are given conventional names depending on their position in the family or on some peculiarity attending their delivery; their next name is given to them at puberty by the Fa or oracle.) By a courtesy which has hardly ever been shown to any other foreigner we were allowed to see Glélé's tomb and some of the rites attending it; great men are always buried in some part of their house which is kept secret from everyone else lest a sorcerer might learn of it.

Glélé is buried in a hut in his extensive palace. Except for a curtained recess in which are his most personal possessions the hut is empty; in the middle is a broad bed under which his body lies; the bed is covered with a large piece of red and green striped silk (the royal colours); at the head and the foot are silk cushions embroidered with a panther and a cross with equal-length arms. The people who were slain at his Customs are buried elsewhere. The simplicity was very moving; before we could approach the tomb a couple of his surviving wives sacrificed a chicken and stayed crouching and praying for some time before and after our visit. Seated against a wall a little way from the tomb was an incredibly old and withered hag spinning cotton; her name was Yahi, and she was the last of the Amazons who had fought with Glélé against the Yoruba and with Béhanzin against the French. There was something very pathetic and romantic about this battered old relic of a completely dead age; she who had once proudly boasted that she was no woman, but a man, was now reduced to the degradation of spinning; she who had once captured her own booty with her musket and cutlass was happy for a few sous to hobble into the sun and be photographed. She must have been well over eighty. Several other blood relations of Glélé, including his second son, live in the palace, now apparently unimportant people, mere guardians of a tradition.

Glélé's palace was enormous – it had housed in its time more than two thousand people – but the great part is falling into ruins and the red swish walls which surrounded it have only small portions unbroken. The chief courtyards, however, have been turned into a sort of museum, and the big huts have been re-roofed with corrugated iron. This palace is by far the biggest and most elaborate piece of negro architecture I have seen; with Great Benin I imagine the most important in West Africa. The entrance lodge and the buildings surrounding the two chief courtyards – perhaps fifty yards square – are made of plaster covered with painted bas-reliefs. These bas-reliefs are inset into the wall, each being about a yard square. There are a number of heraldic devices, but the greater number are records, sometimes of a highly stylised nature, of the most notable deeds of Glélé and his father Ghézo (short for *ghézo emasigbe* – 'the flame-coloured bird can't set the bush on fire' – i.e. the king's enemies may look fierce but they can't do anything), and many of these are of an extremely bloodthirsty nature; one shows Glélé pounding a vanquished king's head in a mortar with the unfortunate man's leg – the treatment that the vanquished man had threatened to apply to Glélé. The general effect of these courtyards is curious and oddly Byzantine, especially in the treatment of the animals; negroes are coloured a brick red, the other colours used being green, blue, yellow and black on a white ground. In the rooms adjoining these courtyards a number of relics of the kings are kept, including their thrones, or stools as they are called in Ashanti; they are of elaborately carved wood and a few are decorated with silver and copper. Ghézo's is extraordinarily high and is mounted on four skulls of vanquished enemies; that of Glélé's mother is also mounted on skulls, but except for these rather grisly legs resembles a country-house pouf. Besides these stools there are a number of cumbersome arms; some very handsome *assan* (ancestor altars) in silver and copper; some horse-tail fans mounted on skulls and set with silver; an elaborate silver pagoda covering a leopard which was on holy days placed over the fetish hut, and some curious pieces of bent wood surmounted by a bird which were used on the same occasions. The Dahomeyans have been and still are extremely expert carvers and designers in wood and metal. In a hidden room are the only representations of fetishes I saw in Dahomey – fabulous birds with smaller birds in their beaks (belonging to Ghézo), panthers with antelopes in their mouths, and a unique human figure, sacrilegious but from its antiquity extremely sacred. The panther, Agassou, is the fetish animal of the royal family, which is stated to have sprung from the union of a woman and a speaking beast; to recall this miracle all the members of the royal family have small parallel scars cut on either side of their face above the cheekbone, representations of the panther's claws. Never more than three people at a time have had all five marks cut; these were the king, his heir when he was definitely designated, and the chief jester. Only the last was ever allowed to expose all the marks to the common gaze. The rest of the royal descendants have four, three or two cuts according to their relationship with the king. These marks are made at a very early age. On all the bare plaster surfaces of the royal palace panthers are painted.

During the days of the kingdom the relationship between the king and the priests was somewhat peculiar. As is usual in absolute monarchies, the throne and the church were closely united by a host of common interests; but the Dahomeyan kings believed in the power of the priests and were very frightened of them; they feared both their magical powers – particularly the wonder-working adepts – and their possible influence and wealth. Over the wonder-workers they were able to exercise a sort of supervision; and to prevent the Church accumulating too much wealth or influence they decreed that there were to be no permanent priests; while people were performing the sacred rites they had a holy power, but between these occasions they were merely private individuals, with no special privileges, except in the case of women fetishers who had always a certain control over their husbands; in this way their influence was kept within reasonable bounds. After the conquest the conditions remained the same, except that it is now the descendants of Glélé (particularly Prince Aho and the other chefs de canton) who control the wonder-workers.

Present-day Dahomey offers many curious anomalies. The conquest is so recent that all the older people can remember clearly the epoch which preceded it; and although they have been quick to adapt to their own use all the advantages which modern civilisation and science can offer them, as well as a developed language with the difference of mentality that implies, the great majority have not abandoned in any jot or tittle the customs or beliefs which they had held before, with the questionable exception of those which are now considered criminal. The old traditions have had no time to lapse; in the kingdom of Dahomey missionaries have made very little headway; with the result that you have educated men following minutely and piously a primitive religion. For although the fetishism of Dahomey is far more elaborate and varied than that of more primitive races – the size of the population makes this possible – it is not, as a religion, fundamentally different from those of the most primitive negroes. Where it does differ considerably is in the relatively restrained importance it holds in the worshippers' lives: that is to say, that for most people it is very little more important than Christianity was for zealots in the Middle Ages; there are portions of their everyday life which are not permeated by religion, and their treatment of 'practical' matters is fairly material; on non-religious subjects Europeans can follow the way their minds work.

2. The Fetishist Religion

The name the Dahomeyan fetishers give to the Creator of all things visible and invisible is Maou; His symbol is the sun. It is necessary to remember Him in your prayers, but He is far too remote from human beings for it to be possible to influence Him and He is far too powerful to be called down by any priest, however adept. Consequently He has no altars and no servants, no formal worship. But Maou is a Trinity; the two other forces which go to His composition are His Mother, Lissa, whose symbol is a chameleon, and His Son, Gou, whose symbol is the crescent moon, and who is lord of all the sand. Although these two are His relations and are part of Him, they are creations of Maou, and differ only in sanctity from the other fetishes; they are equally susceptible to worship and influence. The antique and sacrilegious human figure in Glélé's palace is a representation of the Trinity; it represents Lissa, dressed as one of her women fetishers, holding Maou, the sun, in one hand, and Gou, the moon, in the other. At least that is how she originally was, but when the statue was exposed to the vulgar gaze the symbol of Maou was removed, partly perhaps because the sun was of solid gold, but chiefly to avoid idolatry. After Maou had created the world and the fetishes the Trinity walked about the new earth; where they stopped to converse the rock was marked with an equal-armed cross, and some of these marks can be seen to this day; the equal-armed cross is a holy sign which is incorporated in the decoration of most sacred vestments and paraphernalia.

This combination of the Trinity with the sacred cross seems at first glance to show obvious Christian influence; as a matter of fact I believe it is purely coincidental. Firstly, Christianity has been preached in the interior of Dahomey only very recently, and the use of the cross is commented on by early travellers; the statue of the Trinity is certainly a century old. Also the idea of three persons or forces in one is far less alien to the negro mentality than it is to ours; the whole basis of fetish worship is the calling down of the fetish's force into the body of the fetisher, who is then, at least temporarily, two-in-one; that the same situation should be ascribed permanently to the Creator of all things is only logical. It is obvious also that the other forces incorporated in Maou must be weaker than Himself, for there is nothing stronger. The use of the cross as a sacred emblem is, of course, extremely general; it was found on the excavated altars of Cretan Knossos.

Maou, and to a much smaller extent the other members of the Trinity, are objects of universal but private worship. But when Maou created man He also canalised the different aspects of His force into certain powers or fetishes, as an intermediary between Himself and men. These fetishes are purely 'spiritual' in nature, and are conceived as abstract forces which it is impossible to represent; but each of these forces has on earth some object which stands as a symbol of its power, and which is consequently identified with it and given the same name. Thus the symbol of the royal fetish Agassou is the panther; the panther is the king of the beasts, the strongest, bravest and most cunning of animals; Agassou may be said to represent the principle of predominance, of which in the animal world the panther is the symbol; for the sake of convenience Agassou is called the panther fetish, but it must always be remembered that the panther, as a panther, is not an object of worship or reverence; it is only because it symbolises in the highest degree the power of Agassou that it is subject to any special treatment.

In the kingdom of Dahomey there are a great number of fetishes, perhaps as many as fifty, one for each tribe or family-group. A man has no choice as to which fetish he will worship; each clan has its own special fetish which everybody belonging to that clan will revere as a fetish worshipper; and the fetishers (wives or servants of the fetish) will all be chosen from the one clan. It follows that each fetish has its own more or less defined geographical sphere of influence; in the region round Abomey where we were staying the chief fetishes, besides Agassou the panther and Lissa the chameleon, were Nesshoué the river, Héviosso the thunder, Danh the snake and Sagbata the smallpox. Sagbata has had a curious history; it was the fetish most feared by the kings and its worship was frequently forbidden. There was reason for this; the priests of Sagbata undoubtedly knew how to spread the infection by means of dried scabs; it is probable also that they had discovered some form of immunisation, either through the blood of an infected animal – an idea which would certainly not be disagreeable to the negro mind – or by some homeopathic treatment. With such very material powers – for until the advent of Europeans smallpox was the greatest scourge of that part of Africa – the priests of Sagbata were evidently a very great danger.

For the whole race the great God; for each tribe the Fetish; for each individual his Legba, or devil, and his Fa, or destiny. The Legba is a completely personal devil; each person has his private altar to it, and if a man does not keep his legba permanently appeased with offerings of food and so on things will go badly for him. Legba has his shrine before the door of each house; this shrine consists of a low mound of clay, sometimes vaguely formed into human shape, from which protrudes a very realistic phallus; the whole is covered with a small straw roof. This phallic devil is for the master of the house alone; ranged beside it, or occasionally against the wall of the house, are a number of small clay pots, one for each member of the household. In some places there is a big 'crowned' legba, much more human in design, which serves for the whole village. The pots are regularly filled and the legba anointed with palm- oil and millet flour; on certain occasions a chicken is sacrificed to it and some of the feathers are plastered on to the tip of the phallus and the wall above the pots. In the legba shrines can often be seen little wooden figures called boitchyo; these ugly little figures are dedicated after certain rites to Legba, and may very possibly be a symbolisation of human sacrifice. It seems almost certain that this phallic worship was the religion of the original inhabitants of the country, and the general rule has been followed by which a deposed god becomes a devil. If W. Seabrook's account of the Habbé is accurate, it would seem as if this devil was still their god. Legba is associated with the rites of Héviosso, the thunder fetish. I did not find a corresponding 'devil' in any other primitive religious system.

The Fa, or destiny, is in many ways the most fundamental and important part of the religious life of Dahomey; it is also the most difficult to explain. To the primitive negro mind – and as far as religion goes Dahomeyans can be included in this category – there is no such thing as chance or accident; everything is predestined and happens through personal intervention, either divine or human. But since the future – to use an inaccurate term but the only one in our language – is determinable it is necessary on every occasion to find out the will of the mystic powers concerning it. This is done by different tribes in a variety of ways; the most general is the consultation of omens and auguries, either from the behaviour of different animals, birds and objects, or the marks in sacrificial animals. There is no possibility of chance in this; the same force which causes the bird to fly from left to right (for instance) will cause a man to be successful in his undertaking; indeed, it may be said that from the moment that the bird has flown from left to right the man has already been successful although the undertaking still lies in what we consider the future. In the event of the man not being successful it will be because between the omen and its realisation he has committed, albeit unconsciously, some offence against the powers who had already granted him success.

In Dahomey the will of heaven or Fa is discovered by means of palm-olive kernels and pebbles; and the man who can interpret the message in the kernels is called a *bokonon*. The bokonon is the servant of Fa-in-the-abstract; his unique function is revealing Fa's will; beyond what is necessary to his business he performs no ceremonies, and claims no magic power as other fetishers do. At the same time he is the most influential of all men; nobody will do anything without consulting him, and he is the intermediary between laymen and the fetishers. It is he also who discovers what sacrifices are necessary to obtain future benefits or to avert present or threatened misfortune; since there is no possibility of accident his word is law. In the time of the kings the royal bokonon had extraordinary importance, for it was through the commands of Fa, delivered by the bokonon, that the king waged wars, made levies and so on.

As soon as a Dahomeyan reaches an age when he can afford the ceremony he has his fa made for him by a bokonon. This material fa consists of a rosary of palm nuts arranged after a fashion which the Fa will indicate; this represents in a symbolical way the man's potentialities, as it were his horoscope. When a man is at home this fa rosary must be kept in a special room and only brought out when the bokonon is consulted; when the man goes on a journey he take his rosary with him and he is taught how to consult it; but since his ability to interpret will be slight it is only in cases of extremity that he will not use the offices of a bokonon. The function of the bokonon is hereditary, passing from father to son.

I did not have my fa made, but we consulted Prince Aho's bokonon; and since the ceremonies involved are similar in both cases, but more elaborate in the former, a single description will suffice for both rites. The bokonon has a special hut for divination. He is seated cross-legged on a mat with all the implements of divination in front of him. These consist of a wooden tray (*té*) about fifteen inches by twelve with raised edges; in the centre of the long edge facing the bokonon is carved a human face. The bottom of the tray is covered with fine white sand. To the left is a bowl which holds the sixteen palm kernels when they are taken from the bag in which they are ordinarily kept; these are the essential fa. In front of the tray is a box containing Fa's wife – which looked like four half coconuts in earth – two magic iron bells (*tcheraga*), two small wooden female figures holding trays, and a number of jars, bottles, knobkerries with chicken feathers sticking to them and knives. On the right is another bowl containing a mixed selection of pebbles and shells. When the consultation commences the bokonon takes off all his metal ornaments and amulets. Then a woman acolyte brings in a covered calabash of holy water – water which has been blessed and kept in a fetishist convent for eight days; the holy water is uncovered and the bokonon sprinkles a few drops in front of Fa three times. Then each person present drinks a little holy water and sprinkles the ground with it three times; the palm kernels are also moistened with it. The bokonon then proceeds to invoke Fa by all his Strong Names, holding the sixteen nuts in his hand and offering them to Fa. This litany is repeated three times, after which the tray is struck with a piece of wood and the holy water is covered and removed. The consulter is then given a small bowl containing a cowrie and a palm nut; he whispers as quietly as he can his request to the nut which is then for a moment mixed with the fa nuts, so that it can communicate the message; it is then removed and put on one of the eyes of the face carved on the tray, the unfavourable cowrie being put on the other. The fa nuts are then taken by the bokonon and thrown from hand to hand; then a little sand from the tray is thrown on the ground, and holy water spilled on it. A woman is then called and given the nut and the cowrie; she rubs them together in her hands and then without looking holds one in each. After this the real divining begins; the bokonon takes the sixteen fa nuts in his hand and throws them from hand to hand three times; at the third time the number remaining in the emptier hand are inspected; unless the number is one or two the throw has been useless; if two have been left a short mark is made in the sand on the board, if one a long mark. This is repeated sixteen times; and the combination of sixteen long or short marks gives the first answer, every combination having a definite relative value. From the message received the bokonon tells the woman which hand to open; if this hand contains the cowrie the gods are unfavourable and the project must be dropped; if, however, it contains the palm nut the gods are potentially favourable; and the bokonon will then proceed by means of the fa nuts to reconstruct the question asked, and also, by means of the nuts and a certain selection of the symbolical stones and shells which are given to the woman to hold, to find out what must be done to ensure its successful outcome. A full consultation may take as long as three hours.

As far as we were concerned the Fa reconstructed my question fairly inaccurately, Benga's more accurately but vaguely – it was easier. I do not think the bokonon are on the whole conscious cheats; it seems to me more probable that they have a hypertrophied sense of hearing, such as is not uncommon with 'telepathic mediums', and possibly unconsciously overhear the whispered request to the lucky palm nut. All the Dahomeyans I spoke to were unanimous in declaring that the Fa inevitably stated the question exactly in all its details, which would not always be possible through working by guesswork and local gossip. In direct consultation with a fetish the divination is done by throwing the four quarters of a cola nut on the ground, and seeing which sides turn uppermost; it is necessary to have two round and two flat sides for the fetish's favour. In all magical procedure it is customary to tell your questions or desires to some inanimate object, which has either been impregnated with magical power, or else is mixed with other impregnated objects. Speech by itself has a magical significance, and the spoken word must be treated with care.

While the bokonon is discovering the question and the sacrifices to be made he will address the consulter, telling him parables and religious history, and giving the reason for each action to be performed, illustrating it with legends and wise saws. I was told firstly that when Maou had made the earth He had to find a fetish capable of bringing life on to it; after a number of peripateias Fa alone was found to be capable; therefore he must always be consulted. Fa has as many entities as he has worshippers, each with a distinguishing name; mine was called Fa Létémidgi. He then told me that I had many people jealous of me; I must therefore sacrifice a sheep, for no one can take his clothes away. I was also to make a grigri with a banana stick, Fa's leaves (a monocotyledon I couldn't identify), black and white thread, a magic bell and the skull of a monkey; when an enemy threatened me I was to inform the grigri and then hit the earth hard with it; by this means my enemy would fall. By somewhat similar devices I could guarantee myself against opposition, and sudden death. Finally I was told that for my journey to be successful (the question that I had asked) I was to dig a special hole in the ground, called *kondio*, sacrifice a goat and three chickens in it, say to the hole that I didn't wish to fall into any hole or trap and then fill it up again; in that way my journey would go off successfully.

Benga's fa was named Fa Boussolété. The granting of his request depended entirely on Europeans (this was true: he had asked if he would have a successful winter season), and therefore he must say every morning on awaking, 'I get up thanks to God and the king; it is God who has made kings; therefore God comes first.' His diet also should consist largely of fruit. The reason is as follows. A long time ago a man named Kpate had publicly maintained, in face of general indignation, that God was far greater than the king; to punish such *lèse-majesté* the unfortunate Kpate was tied to a coconut tree on the edge of the sea and left to starve. In his despair he prayed to Maou who thereupon directed to the shore a ship full of starving Europeans. These white men landed and untied Kpate, and asked him where they could get food. He again prayed to Maou who caused all the bushes near to blossom with every kind of fruit; he showed these to the Europeans who in gratitude loaded him with treasure. When the people saw Kpate returning to the town loaded with treasure they realised that he had been right and that God was the most powerful. In remembrance of this miracle all who depend on Europeans should imitate Kpate as far as they can.

The bokonon also told Benga that he had three rivals who were jealous of him. In order to render them impotent he must take a large calabash and in it put the sacrificed bodies of three chickens and a kid, and also a straw-coloured head called a *voko*; on top of this calabash he must put three pieces of wood, and the whole must then be put on the side of the road and completely destroyed by Benga, who would thereby destroy his rivals.

The bokonon's advice to us is a very good example of the way in which by far the greater number of grigris are prepared. They are essentially symbolical. It is part of the underlying idea of all negro magic that a part of a thing is equal to the whole – a man's nail clippings or skull are the man – and a thing which is like a second thing is to all intents and purposes the second thing – a wax image is like the man it is modelled after, therefore it is the man, and anything done to the image is done to the man. Very often the similarity is merely in the name – which is the thing. The use of grigris is very like that of armaments (strangely like in the faith they both evoke, the expense they cause and the help they give): they can be used for self-defence and to destroy one's enemies. The former is usually the excuse, the latter the real reason. The amount of home-made grigris the Dahomeyans construct can be gauged from the fact that one side of the big marketplace in Abomey (the market is held every fourth day) is filled with witches' stalls; for a very moderate price fillets of fenny snakes, newts' eyes, frogs' toes, wolves' teeth, witch's mummy, gall of goat, slips of yew silvered in the moon's eclipse, nose of Turk and Tartar's lips, as well as every sort of animal skull and pelt, dried reptiles, birds, feathers, wooden images and iron wingle-wangles can be purchased to suit every prescription and every pocket. We spent many a happy morning watching old crones turning over the bats' wings to find the one best suited to their purpose and then bargaining for it as if it had been a bunch of bananas; or listening to the stall keeper apologising to a young man for the absence of monkeys' testicles; there has been such a run on them, you know, this spring weather, but I will make a point of reserving you a pair next market day; meanwhile, we are making a special line in addled parrots' eggs, which our customers have found extremely effective: can't we tempt you to give them a trial? To the negro magic is just as much an ordinary part of life as eating; they do not feel the need for the constrained silence, the hushed tones, the serious expression that we bring to our religion.

A special part of grigri making is the fabrication of charms which will remove misfortune or illness; these have the special name of Vô. A Vô usually consists of an animal sacrifice and a part of the afflicted person (usually clothes or hair) which are placed in a (generally broken) calabash which is then deposited according to the instructions of Fa, usually in a place where three roads meet; the person whose shadow first falls on this Vô will take the evil contained in it; consequently Dahomeyans are extremely circumspect where they walk. If a person is very ill a bath of special herbs is made with two pieces of wood laid crosswise upon it; very early in the morning the invalid is carried to a place where three roads meet and is bathed in this water; white clothes and a white sacrifice are left behind.

The really potent 'supernatural' grigris are made only in the fetishist convents by certain priests; their composition is unknown except to initiates and they are given very sparingly.

The non-human side of Dahomeyan religion so far described is called Tovôdoun; complementing it is Akovôdoun, or worship of the dead. Except that formerly the dead king used to be given divine honours the Dahomeyans regard the dead in much the same light as other primitive negroes.

The only natural death – and that not always – is one which follows an outlet of blood. For the Dahomeyans blood is life (for the Ashanti the heart), and therefore if a person dies without losing blood it is obviously the work of some hostile sorcerer. In order to find out who has done a man to death the corpse is interrogated about a fortnight after death. This is generally done by a fetisher of the fetish Osonika, who counter-feits the dead man's voice; but in very serious cases, so I am told, resort is had to necromancy and the corpse itself is made to accuse its mur-derer. When the guilty man has been named, revenge or at least expiation must follow, or the dead man will be angered and will blast the home. For although the dead take up after transition exactly the same position in the spirit world as they have in this, they are infinitely more powerful for inflicting weal or woe on the survivors, for they can control the weather and the harvest. Once the dead man has been revenged he is kept in a good temper by constant offerings of food, animals, clothes and everything else he may need; these are given to him through an assan or altar which is placed on top of his buried body in or near the house. These assan are made of metal; they are fixed into the grave by one pointed end; near the top is a round plateau surrounded with spikes from which hang pieces of iron like candle snuffers; very often the end of the stake is fashioned into an emblem which will recall the dead man's last name or his fetish. The assan are given a little food daily; on the anniversary of the man's death a special sacrifice is made; and on one day of the year there is a special festival in honour of all those dead whose names have been forgotten, the ancestors of the tribe. Little by little the individuality of a dead man is lost and with it his personal power; gradually he sinks into the corporate personality of the tribe. This mass of all his dead is what ties the negro to his land; his own neighbourhood is friendly to him as no other land can be, for it is completely permeated with the spirit of his ancestors who cause the crops to grow and the beasts to multiply. Though crops may grow better and beasts be more plentiful elsewhere they will not seem so to him, for they are filled with an alien virtue and are blessed by foreigners. For a primitive negro to be forced to leave his own land is to be cut off from the intimate communion with his ancestors and to be left as less than a man; and should he die in a foreign land and not even a small portion of his body, if only a tuft of his hair, be buried in his own soil, then is he doubly dead. For the primitive negro himself his land and his ancestors are all facets of the same unity.

3. Public Rites

When a woman is pregnant she consults the Fa and the priest of her fetish and these two between them discover whether the coming child is to be a servant of the fetish or not. If the child is designated as a fetisher the parents cannot refuse, for otherwise it will be stillborn. The day after the child is born it is taken to the fetish convent and then for eight days after it is bathed in holy water. Until the child is eight or nine it lives with its parents; it then goes into a fetishist convent for two or three years, during which period it learns the dances, the ritual and the fetish language. This fetish language is a curious puzzle; all I was able to learn about it is that it is completely incomprehensible to any negro who has not been initiated;

it is possible that it is only a made-up jargon, but I consider it far more probable that it is a possibly distorted jargon version of an early negro language. If that is the case it obviously has a great philological importance, and may possibly bear the same relation to African languages as Sanskrit does to Indo-European. The difficulties in the way of its investigation by Europeans are, however, almost insurmountable; even if it were possible for a white man to be allowed to live in a fetishist convent the conditions therein are quite insupportable. The only hope of learning about it seems to be through the negroes, and that hope is very faint; for most educated Dahomeyans are, at any rate openly, extremely scornful of the natives' superstitions, even if they are not Christians. I could not hear of an intellectual who had learned the language.

After the period of initiation is over the children are restored to their parents, who have to ransom them, with considerable ceremony. At first the restored children have to have everything done for them – they have even to be washed and fed – and usually they have forgotten the vulgar language, but after a little time they resume a comparatively normal life, though they have to follow a complicated and arbitrary system of taboos and prohibitions affecting their diet and many ordinary actions; the breaking of these taboos is punished far more heavily in a fetisher than in a layman. The position of a fetisher in the community is similar to that of a party member in the USSR. They have preponderating influence and power and many prerogatives, but they have to be far more circumspect than the rest of the population, for all faults are very heavily and exemplarily punished. The fetishers have a 'purge' once a year by means of an ordeal; they all have to drink a certain preparation of which the effect will show whether they have broken any commandments. Extremely elaborate penances are imposed on the erring fetisher.

In their spare time fetishers live a completely ordinary life, according to the state in which they were born; except that the most advanced priests wear a white cotton skullcap there is nothing to distinguish them from the laity. The more advanced fetishers do not use amulets or grigris; as one of these explained to me, they help the duller mind to concentrate its thought and thereby the power of the fetish, but they are unnecessary to one who has learned to call down the fetish into himself, and are even a stumbling-block.

From time to time the fetisher will return to his convent for esoteric ceremonies or for a 'retreat'; some of these occur at fixed intervals; at other times the fetish will directly inspire his servants, wherever they may be, to return to the sacred place. The fetishers have also to take part in all the public rites which are rendered to their fetish in their vicinity; these are habitually sacrifices, each of which is followed by eight days' dancing by the fetishers. These sacrifices are performed in and near the fetish hut; in every village where a fetish is worshipped is a hut specially dedicated to the fetish and impregnated with its essence; these huts resemble ordinary dwelling-houses, except that the straw roof comes nearly down to the ground, and they are completely surrounded by a walled courtyard; inside they are divided into two parts, one of them empty, and the other, usually curtained off, containing the altar of the fetish. The empty part can be entered by any fetish worshipper who wishes to pray; but the altar can be approached only in the company of a priest. This altar is merely a mass of clay, mixed with the bones of sacrificed animals and various iron instruments; it can be seen only dimly in the faint light which penetrates into the fetish house. It is extremely blasphemous to attempt to make any image of a fetish, though in the convents the initiate are given verbal descriptions of the esoteric appearance of their fetish; these appearances are vaguely human and highly symbolical. The temples of Sagbata (smallpox) and Danh (snake – rainbow) have their outside walls covered with small painted spots and wavy lines respectively. The temples of Nesshoué (the river) are long and narrow; all the others are round.

By the courtesy of Prince Aho we were able to witness the complete ceremony of the sacrifice of a bull to Héviosso, the thunder fetish. The whole description is rather long, but since I do not think such a ceremony has ever been witnessed, much less described, by a European before, I hope I may be forgiven a certain prolixity. We were told that if a man had been sacrificed, as was occasionally done 'before the conquest', the ceremony would have been exactly the same.

The sacrifice was being offered by the chief of a village called

Fontepamé; the rites took place partly in the fetish house and partly in the open square in front of it. On the two sides of the square adjoining the fetish house were the blind walls of dwelling-places; the fourth side was open to the fields; there were a number of trees, particularly bananas, here, and under them several legba shrines. In the middle of the square, under a tree, the sacrificial animal, a black bull without a mark on it, was lying tethered on the ground. All the roads approaching the place had small gates with a lintel of palm leaves, to keep away strangers and evil spirits.

The opening ceremony was performed in the fetish house. The chief fetisher was crouching in front of the altar, the chief who was making the sacrifice and the other notables, including ourselves, under the eaves of the hut, while the other fetishers and villagers prostrated themselves in the courtyard. The two chief fetishers wore a white cotton cap, red and yellow sashes across their chest, and round their waist a pagne which fell to their feet. The lesser fetishers were similarly dressed, except that their head-dress and body-sashes were of purple cord; they had small red ear-rings, and several black and white bead necklaces, the number indicating their rank. They all carried *sossyabi* – dancing sticks about two feet long with a worked copper axe-head at one end, and the more important had fetish sticks – long sticks with a double iron point at the end. In the rites of Héviosso men are far more important than women; such women as did take part wore ordinary clothes; they had the same necklaces and ear-rings as the men, and they wore a single scarlet parrot's feather in a fillet on their forehead.

The ceremony was started by the chief fetisher chanting a sort of litany, nodding his head; the others repeated his words after him, clapping their hands in accompaniment; from the tone it was obviously a formal prayer. The priest then announced to the fetish that the chief had offered a bullock for the prosperity of the community and then poured on to the altar beer, water and cola nuts; the chief people present were also given small portions of these sanctified substances to drink or chew. Everybody then went into the public square and the fetishers took up their position on the extreme left and the drums on the extreme right. The fetishers had carved black stools to sit on, graded in height according to their rank, and the two chief priests had huge sacred umbrellas (*hlého*) to shelter them. These umbrellas have a flat top and a panelled fringe; they are made of white cotton and the panels have designs in black cloth appliquéd on them; one was decorated with ships under sail, the other with rams and sossyabi. When the fetishers were resting, their fetish sticks were placed in front of them point downwards. The bull was now more securely fastened, and two young men knelt on it to make certain that its head would point continuously due north. The chief fetisher went and crouched in front of the bull; from a bottle he took some beer and spat it over the bull's neck; he then chewed some cola and spat it out similarly; finally he poured some holy water over the bull. These three substances and their containers were the same as had been used in the dedication; they were very sacred and were taken back to the fetish house. A little later they were brought back covered in cloths by three young married women fetishers; during the whole of the ceremony, perhaps a couple of hours, they knelt in front of the bull, their heads nearly on the ground, the sacred vessels resting on their upturned palms. From time to time two other women fetishers came up to them; one crouched in front and took the sacred vessel from one of the officiants and held it in a similar position, while the other pressed and massaged the relieved woman's back and neck and pulled her hands and arms about till you would think they would be disjointed; the women made no sign at this apparently very painful treatment, for they were meant to be in trance and were manipulated like dolls.

After the chief fetisher had spat over the bull, thus dedicating it, he laid his fetish stick across the animal's back for a moment and then danced round the bull, prodding it with his stick. He then rejoined the other fetishers and a circular procession was formed, the two chief fetishers having their umbrellas held over them and twirled slowly; all carried their fetish sticks. As each fetisher arrived opposite the tomtoms he danced the thunder dance, a stamping almost stationary dance with the arms raised and the hands held upwards and outwards; the arms are jerked so that elbows meet behind the back. After a certain time the fetishers seated themselves again, placed the fetish sticks in front of their seats and after an interval started dancing again, this time carrying knives. They danced in pairs in front of the tomtoms, clashing knives in mock fights, the tempo gradually getting quicker and the general feeling wilder. When the movement had nearly reached the point of frenzy the chief fetisher waved a white cloth at the tomtom to stop it. All the fetishers returned to their seats and two empty calabashes were brought in and placed by the bull. Then in turn the fetishers went through the ritual of simulating the killing of the bull. They received from the chief fetishers a knife and a sossyabi, which the fetishers blessed by laying their hands on it; they offered the instruments to the wind which was then blowing, to the sunset and to the tomtoms, holding them out at arm's length; they then did a curious prowling dance round the bull, finally putting their left foot on its neck, and making a number of feint slashes, first with the sossyabi and then with the knife. Among the other fetishers who went through this solo ritual was a very young boy, whose numerous necklaces showed that he had already reached high rank and who performed his part perfectly; the local chief also did it, but he was obviously terrified and very muddled and had to be loudly prompted. The three women who had been crouching all this time in front of the bull were now led away; women supported them on each side and shaded their eyes with their hands; they tottered like somnambulists. Water and cola were again given to the bull, and then by groups of three the fetishers sat on its back and did a sort of jogging dance, while their feet were laved in holy water. The chief fetisher named the man who was to complete the sacrifice; he girded up his loins and took a long sharp knife and stood behind the bull, while the rest of the fetishers crouched in front, the youngest holding the empty calabashes and the rest their fetish sticks. The ropes holding the bull's mouth were then untied so that it could bellow, and very, very slowly the sacrificer slit the bull's throat and continued carving as slowly as possible till the head was completely severed. The gushing blood was collected into the empty calabashes and the fetish sticks were held under the stream. For the Dahomeyans the life of a person or animal resides in the blood; for a sacrifice to be acceptable and potent it is necessary for the blood to be taken from a still living animal, with the result that sacrificial animals are killed in a most inhuman way; the longer they live after the blood is taken the more acceptable the offering. When the mutilated but still-quivering carcass was bloodless the head and tail and the bowls of blood were taken into the fetish house; the body was dragged away and divided between the fetishers and the offerer. Everyone now went into the fetish house; the chief fetisher was communing at the altar and sacrificing a white kid; after a little while its wounded body was placed on a heap of the leaves of Fa on the ground outside the fetish house; beside it on a similar heap of leaves was the bull's head, bloody neck uppermost, with the severed tail upon it. The chief fetisher came out for a moment and took the severed head on his shoulder and danced to the tomtom to show the prize; he then replaced it again and returned to the altar. Everybody was quite still, crouching and praying that the sacrifice might be acceptable; the only movement was that of the entranced young women who were fanning the offerings slowly so that no flies should settle on them. The suspense had become acute, when suddenly and most dramatically a man appeared standing on the roof of the fetish house, gesticulating and shouting wildly. The chief fetisher below put his foot on the bloody neck, waved in each hand a magic bell and shouted too. All the audience gave the thunder shriek Ho Ho Ho. The fetish had been fed. The sacrifice was accepted. With clappings of their hands and with prayers the fetishers made the man come down from the roof. Pandemonium broke loose; the chief fetisher took the bloody head on his shoulder, the man on the roof the nearly dead kid, and they danced in the centre of a wild sarabande of fetishers, shouting and dancing the thunder dance with the wildest frenzy. The courtyard of the fetish house was too small to hold them; they burst out into the open square, still dancing wildly; from time to time one of the dancers would approach his lips to the raw neck of the bull or the wound of the kid, still on the fetisher's shoulders, and suck the warm flesh. A kid was hastily killed for the Legba, and the dancer who impersonated this devil took it on his shoulders and joined the anarchical dance; till at length the chief fetisher retired to the fetish house, followed by the other fetishers; while they were changing into their dancing clothes the tomtoms moved to the centre of the square, where the bull had been – such blood as had been spilled had been covered with loose earth. Shortly the dancing began. It would continue for eight days.

Each fetish has its own special costume for dancing and its own particular dances; although all the dances are founded on the swinging rhythmic movement of the shoulder, yet they are so ordered as to suggest the particular qualities of the fetish they honour. Every dance in each fetish's repertoire has its proper names and sequence; there is nothing haphazard about them. The fetishers have, too, a special method of greeting the laity and their own superiors; the devotees of the thunder fetish, for instance, greet their superiors by crouching and putting their joined hands between those of the fetisher, while they wave their bottoms from side to side; when they greet a layman they hold their hands down and make a thunder noise in their throat.

The Héviosso have three separate types of dance. For some reason which could not be explained the Legba, or phallic devil, is mingled with the cult and special dancers represent him. For a costume they wear a red hat covered with horns and grigris, many necklaces and anklets and a very full knee-length raffia skirt. In their hand they hold a very realistic, albeit exaggerated, wooden phallus with a mop of raffia at one end. With the aid of this they perform some extremely indecorous dances, copulating with the earth, through a little furrow they make with the phallus, the trees, the crops and the houses. In front of each important spectator they go through a realistic though rhythmic panto-mime of masturbation, extremely difficult, for the body is bent backwards from the knees; the simulated orgasm is accompanied by the most convulsive grimaces. When two legba are present at the same time, which is rare, their behaviour together is extremely scandalous. We once saw a very young boy perform gestures he could know only by hearsay extraordinarily well.

The dance of the Legba is always performed first, to avert evil spirits; for the same reason the legba dancer always prances in front of the other performers, waving his *olisbos* in the air. The most general dance is the *gobahun*, which is danced in pairs, very quick with vehement arm movements and sudden twists. Both men and women dance this; for both the principal item of dress is a full skirt reaching a little below the knees, in various materials but chiefly white; when the dancers turn suddenly it spreads out wide like a ballet skirt. The most dramatic of the thunder dances is the *adahoun*; it is danced by a very few young men naked to the waist except for a necklace of big red and blue beads, and wearing a short very full skirt about nine inches long, like a tiny tutu, tight-fitting velvet drawers reaching to the knee and a scarf knotted under the skirt so that its ends fall down like a tail. They dance with one or occasionally two sossyabi, holding it in the mouth or the left hand. Their dance is completely wild, for they represent the destructive element of thunder; with the *sossyabi* in their teeth – no mean feat, for it is very heavy – they rush in every direction with their hands held out and their head jerking backwards and forwards; they are completely bacchic and frenzied, and their big-pupilled eyes are fixed on infinity. They destroy whatever comes under their hand – plants, trees, roofs, even objects sacred to the fetish; they seize what they fancy, hats and clothes off the spectators, animals and even children, shouting when they have got booty and waving it in the air towards the tomtom with whom they later deposit it. So possessed are they that they roll on the ground, eat earth, turn somersaults and walk on the narrowest coping. The onlookers are in a state of pleasurable terror; the dancers are filled with the spirit of the thunder and must not be opposed in anything they are inspired to do; who can oppose a thunderbolt? They once took my topi, which alarmed me, for I had no other; but the kindly legba returned it when the dance was finished. This dance was oddly fascinating to watch, and we saw it several times.

On one occasion the dancers of Sagbata (the smallpox) came to pay a friendly visit to Héviosso. The devotees of Sagbata are mostly women; they are dressed in double crinolines, one longer than the other, both ending with deep fringes; across their breasts were innumerable neck-laces of cowries crossing on their back; more cowries surrounded their ankles; on their arms they had plain bracelets. The men were dressed very similarly, except that their skirts were only knee-length and they wore embroidered hats, whereas the women had head-cloths. On their first arrival they greeted the Héviosso dancers and then waited quietly at one side; suddenly one of the men shrieked wildly and fell forward on his face; the fetish had entered them and they commenced dancing. Their dances are short and febrile; a couple were very strange. One was like a Russian gopak danced backwards; another resembled flying, the sossyabi held parallel to the ground and the dance consisting of steps in the air between jumps, the feet touching the ground so little and so lightly that it was hardly perceptible. From time to time one of the fetishers would start singing whatever came into his head – boastings about the superiority of his magic, telling of a stolen bicycle, crying that his wife had deceived him, in fact all the symptoms of delirium.

While we were at Abomey we saw the public dances of many different fetishes, for the Dahomeyans are pious people and in the numerous villages many rites were held (of course in the town of Abomey they don't dance); we saw the Lissa (chameleon) dancers, where all the clothes are covered in crosses and the men wear hats of feathers, and hold double silver bells in their hands; the dance is very quick and continuous, one dancer starting just before the other leaves off. We saw the Danh (snake) dancers, where the women dance in single file with a harmless boa on their necks; and many others. But of all the most spectacular and beautiful were the dancers of Nesshoué, the river.

The Nesshoué are always in a very great company and elaborately dressed in many cloths of different but harmonious tones, avoiding all pure colours except blue and green. They wear chased silver daggers at their waists, and on their arms cunningly worked armlets and bracelets in solid silver; the men carry sossyabi with the axe-like blade in silver, the women horse-tails, also mounted on silver. Their dances are mostly slow and undulating, after the character of a river; they dance together so that their varied clothes look like a bed of living flowers, their silver ornaments sparkling like dew. Against the background of the blue sky and the palms, with occasional trees of a deeper green and scarlet fruit, the effect is of the greatest beauty. Sometimes they dance in lines and sometimes in single file, but always with the strictest rhythm and co-ordination. There is only one dance which is done individually. Perhaps the most lovely of all their dances is the Selili, or gleaning dance (the river makes the harvest): in a long line they hold their sossyabi and fans parallel with the ground, and with one leg stretched behind them they advance with a quick undulating movement, gradually gathering speed till they seem like a sea wave. I deeply regret that I have not the skill to reproduce even faintly the most beautiful spectacle I have ever seen; and a colourless photograph is as dead as the Grecian landscapes without light.

4. The Fetishist Convents

In the chapter above the chief public rites of fetish worship have been described; but they constitute only a small and relatively unimportant part of fetishist religion. The greater part of the rites are of an esoteric and mystic nature and take place in the fetish convents; strangers, of whatever colour or creed, are never allowed in these; and except at the annual festivals or through their relationship with one of the fetishers on special occasions the lay fetish worshippers are also rigorously excluded. 'Convent' is possibly a slightly misleading term, on account of the visions of nuns and Gothic cloisters it conjures up; but it is the term that the French-speaking Dahomeyans habitually use.

A convent consists of a collection of huts and courtyards surrounded by a living hedge. The huts differ from ordinary living-huts by having the roof much lower; moreover, the straw thatch descends to the ground and the only entrance and illumination is a tiny hole in the thatch just wide enough for a person to crawl through. The courtyards are relatively large, for the rites take place in them; the living hedge surrounding the group of buildings is planted with various sacred or magic trees (particularly the leaves of Fa) joined by the commonest surrounding vegetation. These convents are always situated in the bush, usually amidst trees; there is no marked path leading to them, and unless you know where they are or unless a drum is playing it is possible to pass a thicket daily without suspecting any building near.

Except for a few guardians the convents have no permanent population. Child fetishers spend three years in them, and all fetishers return to them from time to time; moreover, if a fetisher has committed a sin it is in the convents that he must expiate it. The number of convents in existence is probably not known by anybody, and a great deal which goes on in them is completely secret. Even if they are inspected by the local authorities, whether black or white, they have, most of them, neighbouring hideouts. Children could very easily be born in them without their existence being known.

The convents that we visited were chiefly those of Agassou (the panther); for it was through Prince Aho's intervention that we were able to do this, and as a member of the royal family the panther was his fetish. We did, however, pay short visits to the convents of Lissa (the chameleon, the mother of God) and Héviosso.

In one of the convents women fetishers were preparing for a special rite. The fetishist convent huts, like the temples, are divided into two sections, of which only the second is holy. In the convent I am describing this second portion was filled with women packed so closely that they had barely room to sit. In an area which was certainly less than a hundred square feet there were more than a dozen women. They were all dressed alike with a cap of purple net from which hung long strings threaded with cowries falling to the breast, so thick that they completely hid the face. Across the otherwise naked torso were slings of cowries and purple beads; they had ordinary skirts and anklets of cowries. They were all in very deep trance and completely motionless; all the actions of everyday life, feeding, washing and so on, had to be done for them. They were no longer themselves; they were filled with the power of the fetish. They could no longer speak; only by a certain ritual could the priest make them talk, and then it was no longer the woman but the fetish itself talking through its agent in its own language. In the present instance the women were to be in this state for three weeks, during which, except for ceremonies, they could not go out of the hut or see the light. The wonder-workers are in this state permanently; if a man is completely filled with the fetish he performs no ordinary actions and never sees the light, nor does he eat any solid food.

These wonder-workers are few and live in the most deserted places; their powers can be controlled because they can work only through the agency of a normally conscious priest.

To call these entranced women out of the hut an elaborate ceremonial is necessary. They can move only to the sound of a special tomtom; when this starts playing the chief fetish priest kneels by the entrance and shakes a rattle while he invokes the fetish with prayers; the other fetishers present prostrate themselves and repeat the prayers, rubbing their hands together. After some time the tomtoms become louder and the fetishers shriek; one of the women has shown her mask at the door. A cockerel is immediately fetched; its legs and wings are broken and its tongue pulled out; its beak is stuffed with special leaves and it is held by its legs; a drop of the blood is let fall on each of the woman's big toes; she comes out and with head downcast starts dancing feverishly, swinging her shoulders with a force which would tire an ordinary person in a few minutes. After the first several more are called out with the same ceremonial; not all that are in the hut, for that can only be left completely empty at the greatest ceremonies. The women dance in a vague circle, but like blind people; they have to be continually guided to prevent them knocking themselves against the buildings. Before they can return to the fetish hut they have to be purified; they are led on to a special mat where their hands and feet are laved in holy water, after which another chicken is mutilated in the same cruel fashion and a drop of blood is allowed to fall from its beak on their thumbs and big toes. They are led back to the hut with prayers and rattles; they enter it backwards, creeping on all fours. This is the essential basis of fetish worship; the body is used as a vessel to be filled with the divine force, no less holy because the owner of the body is unaware of what occurs.

In another convent two women were undergoing penance for sins they had committed; from the priest and Prince Aho I got a short description of their misdoings and the expiations required.

One of the women had gone to her cousin's funeral, against the express command of her fetish. On the following morning she fell into a trance from which she could not be awakened; she stayed in this alarming state for some time, only recovering lucidity for a few moments on the second day, during which she said, 'I have seen my fetish in my sleep; he orders me to go to him. I don't know where', after which she immediately returned to her trance. Considerably alarmed, the girl's parents consulted the bokonon; the Fa replied that the girl had sinned and the sin must be discovered, and he dictated what sacrifices were to be made for that purpose. The parents followed the prescription exactly, but were much alarmed when during the sacrifice a couple of vultures entered the girl's hut. After the first moment of panic, however, they considered that the vultures might be omens; they offered to the birds some *akassa* (coarse maize flour) which they ate; this was a sign that the fetish had accepted the sacrifice, which was further confirmed by the girl's awakening and confessing. To expiate this sin the Fa ordered the girl to go to the convent. For seven days she was confined to the fetish house, where she had to sleep on the bare earth; she was not allowed to wash and was given no food except akassa and water. At the end of the seven days the girl was publicly exorcised, and bathed in holy water. This had happened a few days before we visited the convent; the girl was now allowed to walk in the courtyard; she could eat cola and the flesh of white chickens after a drop of their blood had been allowed to fall on her tongue and her forehead. Every day she was laved three times in holy water. This was to continue for a week; on the sixth day the parents were to bring to the convent two white goats, two white chickens and two white pigeons, two measures each of flour and oil and seven parrot feathers. On the evening of the same day her head would be shaved and all her belongings taken from her; she would be given a white pagne to cover herself. On the seventh day all her relations would gather at the convent as well as a number of fetishers. All the sacrificial animals would be killed and the oil and flour made into a paste. The chief fetisher would be dressed entirely in white; he would first of all bless the paste and then return the sinner to her parents, after praying to the fetish to keep all its children from sin. He would then give a portion of the paste to the sinner and after her to all present, and would say to the girl, 'Now you are clean again and can eat with us.' After a general dance the girl would return home.

The second woman while travelling with her husband had eaten some antelope, a food taboo to her. She was immediately seized with a belly-ache and became completely and immovably constipated; her skin turned 'antelope colour'. The Fa said that she had eaten some forbidden meat and before the fetish she confessed. (It is possible that she had not known what she was eating.) Her constipation was cured by a decoction of seven sacred leaves, and she was then purified in the same manner as the other woman. The only difference was in the final ceremony. The parents had brought with them a white antelope and two white chickens. The priest on his side prepared three packets of sacred leaves. The first packet of leaves was mixed with the saliva and nail parings of the sinner and placed in the antelope's mouth. The antelope was then killed and the heart torn out; the priest touched the sinner's body with it and said, 'This woman has not given her heart to the antelope but to the fetish.' This action and formula, with the necessary variations, was repeated with the head and tail. The heart, tail and head with the leaves in its mouth were then placed in a jar; the outside of this jar and the body of the sinner were then covered with spots of red and white paint. The jar would be transferred to a spot named by the fetish (probably where three roads met), and shortly after the fetisher would place the second packet of leaves in some water which he would bless and with which the sinner would bathe. The third packet of leaves would be placed in the *zenvi* (the hole in front of the fetish altar in which offerings and impregnated objects are placed), and the two chickens so killed that all their blood would fall on the leaves. The bodies of the chickens would be buried in front of the altar. This woman was less severely punished than the other because it was possible that her sin had been unconscious; though that did not make it less heinous, or her less dangerous in her unclean state (sinners are a source of contamination), yet the penalty was less severe.

The women in the convent of Lissa (the chameleon) were very similar in behaviour and dress to those of Agassou. There was only one peculiarity: as they danced they changed colour quite noticeably, their skin going through every hue of brown from a dirty white to nearly black. Although there is physiologically nothing inexplicable in this, the effect of half a dozen women with the colour of their skins visibly altering all the time they danced was very extraordinary.

5. Signs and Wonders

A man called Epiphane had had a silver bracelet stolen. Instead of going to the police about his loss he called in a fetisher. The fetisher took up a position just off the main road a little way out of Abomey (where the bracelet had been stolen) and had a chicken brought to him. He held the chicken by the claws in his left hand above his head, so that the bird's beak was level with his mouth, and started talking to it quietly. He was telling it about the theft, repeating the same words over and over again. After some little time the chicken began to bleed from the mouth, a drop every few minutes. The fetisher went on talking quietly. This had been going on for more than half an hour when a man suddenly arrived desperately out of breath and with his pagne torn; he fell panting on the ground by the fetisher. The fetisher went on talking to the bird, which suddenly gave a sort of strangled squawk, at which the exhausted man confessed that he had stolen the bracelet and explained how he had taken it and where it was. The fetisher put the chicken on the ground; it started pecking rather uncertainly.

Prince Aho explained that this was the usual method of dealing with stolen property. When the chicken started to bleed the thief was forced to come to where the fetisher was, wherever he might be and whatever he was doing. Only certain fetishers knew how to do this. I wanted to see it repeated, but never had another opportunity.

Benga and I were made, as it were, honorary members of the Agassou (panther) fetish, on the ground that I was certainly and he probably harbouring the spirit of a dead fetisher. But before our initiation we were made to swear that we would neither write nor speak about anything we might see or experience, and we had to leave cameras, pencils and notebooks behind. For the greater part I was going rather regretfully to keep my word – regretfully, for a number of very curious things occurred. I realise that this sounds rather like Herodotus with the

Egyptian mysteries,* and I think we may both be in the same position; after all, we are both of us pretty good liars, and could make up perfectly satisfying marvels if we wanted to. Concerning three incidents, however, I am going to break my vow; they are none of them fundamental but all to my mind interesting.

The first occurred before we were admitted into the convent. A sacrifice was being made at which we could not be present, and we both stood outside the courtyard on the grass in the moonlight holding a piece of dried grass in our left hands (this grass played a considerable rôle later), probably looking ridiculous and feeling very silly and rather alarmed. Our sponsor and interpreter was with the priest. After a time he came out and said to me, 'You live in a white house on a hill surrounded by trees; you have a mother and two brothers who are walking under the trees' (a quite adequate description of my home and family; and it was very probable that on 25 June they would have been walking in the garden in the evening). Then he turned to Benga and said, 'You have no home. In the place you think of as home there are many people. Your two sisters are well, but your dead mother's husband was taken very ill two days ago; he will recover, however, before you see him again.' This was exact in every particular; on 23 June Benga's stepfather had had a severe attack, as we verified on our return to Dakar, and he was quite convalescent before we returned. We were more than a thousand miles from Dakar at the time, and had received no communications from there for the better part of a month.

After a night spent in the convent we were considered to be fetishers. Fairly early in the morning we went with the priest and the other fetishers into the open country, among maize fields. A chicken was killed – the number of animals which were killed that night, and I presume every night in Dahomey, is astounding – and the priest started to sing in a low voice. The rest of us stood about, smoking or chewing cola. After about half an hour a full-grown panther walked out of the maize and started

* Incidentally, I think a number of parallels can be traced between ancient and modern African religions.

moving among the people; it was quickly followed by another, and in a short time there were fifteen panthers among us. They arrived from every direction. We had been told most earnestly on no account to touch them, and not to be afraid of them, for they would only harm wicked men (i.e. sorcerers). I was scared so that I felt my legs shaking, but I was able to keep quiet. When the fetisher stopped singing they went away again. The first animal had eaten the chicken. This was the only time in Africa that I saw any of the fiercer mammals alive and in freedom. There were a number of villages within an hour's walk. It was about fifteen miles from Abomey.

It was a particularly fine and cloudless afternoon when we visited the convent of the worshippers of Héviosso, the thunder fetish. After the usual sacrifice three men went into a trance inside the hut, while we stood in what shade we could find in the courtyard. Suddenly against the blue sky there was a flash of lightning, followed shortly by a loud peal of thunder. The flashes and thunder got more frequent and louder, till they seemed simultaneous, and the thunder gave that peculiarly unpleasant crack which it does in the tropics when the storm is nearly directly overhead. Gradually the thunder and lightning got fainter and finally died in a rumble. It had been exactly like a quick tropical thunderstorm, except that there had been no rain and no clouds; the sun was shining all the time.

6. Magic

So far I have only discussed the fetishist religions of Dahomey. It is in many ways eccentric, almost unique among negro religions, not in its principles or ideas so much as in the fact that it is the private reserve of a small portion of the population. In the small and more primitive communities religion is everybody's business; although there are priests their knowledge and power differ only in degree, not in quality. It would be tedious to describe in detail the religions of small groups of negroes living in the forest and savannah of the Ivory Coast; although each tiny tribe has its own language and its own ritual there is far more similarity between them than there are differences.

Fetish

It may be taken as axiomatic that if we are sane all primitive negroes are raving mad. They are not childlike, or simple or ignorant; they are just mad, far madder than most of the inhabitants of our asylums. Richard Hughes has said somewhere that you can no more think like a baby than you can think like a bee; but both of those acts are comparatively simple compared with the difficulty of thinking like an adult negro in a community which has not been destroyed by outside influence.

This madness is not always very apparent, for superficially negroes seem to go about the ordinary business of life in a fairly normal way; but so do many maniacs; a woman who thinks she's Queen Victoria will cook and eat her dinner quite normally. It is only if you talk to her, and especially if you try to persuade her that she is not Queen Victoria, that you will find she is mad. The soundest and most convincing arguments make no impression on her; she *knows* she is the late Queen, and no amount of logic or persuasion will shake her; indeed, logic and argument have no strength against her belief; they only annoy her without in any way influencing the most important side of her life. Primitive negroes are in a precisely similar case.

Primitive negroes *know* that the world is entirely spiritual; what we treat as the physical universe, whether animate or inanimate, bound by certain laws and producing certain predictable effects, is to them nothing but clots of matter entirely neutral in themselves and only taking on the qualities of the spirit, whether human or inhuman, which inhabits them. For us it is axiomatic that if you drink a substance called poison it is bound to disagree with you sooner or later; but for the negro the poison has no specific qualities. If you are a sorcerer or if a spell has been put on you or on the substance, then the spirit will make your body unwell; but if you are a good man and have the proper magic a diet of this substance will nourish you. We would think it unwise to bathe in crocodile-infested water; the negro *knows* that crocodile bodies are completely neutral lumps of matter; if a crocodile should hurt a man it is because a sorcerer has sent his soul into that animal, temporarily displacing that portion of the all-the-crocodile-there-is fetish which ordinarily animates it and which is friendly to the negroes who have propitiated it. If a man is hurt by a falling bough or drowned in a river, we speak of an accident; such a term is entirely meaningless to a negro; either a sorcerer has entered the wood or the water, or else, which is graver still, the victim has angered the gods or the ancestors; since that may be the case the unfortunate must be shunned; though the 'accident' may not have killed him he is as good as dead.

The negro's madness does not end with this refusal to acknowledge a material and causal world. His idea of time is extremely peculiar; he certainly does not believe in a unidirectional and consistent time; the present, the past and the future are inextricably mingled. The reason for this is twofold: firstly, all events which we call 'future' are determined by omens which make them almost present; and, secondly, dreams have for them just as much 'reality' as waking life. In dreams the soul is free and is able to commune with the spirits and the dead who are invisible, though not impalpable, by day; most dream experiences are believed in as implicitly as physical ones; and I have considerable reason to believe that negroes are consistent Dunne-dreamers. Mr Dunne, it will be remembered, claims that everyone dreams the future as much as the past; and it is only our habit of thinking which prevents our realising this. Although my personal experiences have not been conclusive, despite one or two good prophecies, I put that down chiefly to the fact that I sleep heavily and wake very quickly and thoroughly, so that I seldom have the intervening period in which dreams can be recollected, and I am willing for the moment to take his fundamental premise for the truth (but certainly not the 'serial' superstructure he builds on it). It is my belief that negroes, without the inhibitions which our view of time and a causal universe impose on us, regularly dream the future as much as the past and as vividly, with the result that the ideas 'present', 'past' and 'future' have no meaning to them as they have to us.

The spirits which animate the negro universe are of three sorts: the living, the dead and those that have never had any body. The living and the dead behave very similarly; they are both divisible, so that a man's soul can be in several places simultaneously; the only difference is that a man's soul when he is awake is usually attached to his body. In dreams, whether natural or induced, it wanders about; the very clever and the very wicked (which are not always the same) can send bits of their souls into other objects, the magician for the good of himself and others, the sorcerer for evil, and to eat a victim's soul. The discorporate spirits – gods, fetishes, devils, forces, all equally misleading terms – are permanently present over the area where they are worshipped and felt, more especially in the places sanctified to them; by ritual or by getting into strange physical states these forces can temporarily be made to enter men's bodies or other inanimate objects; occasionally they will descend uninvited.

This peculiar view of the universe is permanent and allows of no additions or subtractions; religion is for us a thing apart, for the negroes their whole existence. Unless we wish to denigrate completely our own view of the universe we can only call people holding such utterly contradictory views mad.

For Europeans magic can be divided into two classes: that which gives a result and that which doesn't – a view which to the negro would seem completely blasphemous. By far the greater part to our eyes belongs to the latter class, pantomime and ritual and formula which appear to produce no effect, and which we should expect to produce none. But they do do some things which are very strange; I have recounted a few, and other travellers many more, particularly the early missionaries who thoroughly believed in the devil and all his works and were not horrified to the core (though they might be shocked) by the idea of the 'supernatural' as our modern broad-minded clergy are. In the age of knowledge (roughly 1840 to 1932) such matters were either given a natural explanation – either jugglery or 'mass suggestion'; which, if it had a meaning, would be truly magical – or left to sensation-mongers and neurotics.

I chose the date 1932 for two reasons. It is a reasonable date for people to have grown up who cannot remember the certainty which was so completely destroyed by the 1914–18 war (I can just remember that distant period); and it was the year in which Charles Fort published his book *Wild Talents*. This book has not been published in England, and so far as I know has not attracted much notice in America; but nevertheless it marks an epoch; it is the first book to treat witchcraft and magic seriously since the Middle Ages. I do not count the literature which sprang up round the various magical religions of the late nineteenth century – theosophy, Christian Science, yogi, devil worship, Master Therions and the like – for they are all founded on a mystical basis and make wonder-working the prerogative of the faithful only. Mr Fort leaves aside all the religious superstructures; as he says, 'I never write about marvels. The wonderful, or the never-before-heard-of, I leave to whimsical, or radical, fellows. All books written by me are of quite ordinary occurrences ... My interest is in magic, as the daily grind – the miracle as a job – sorceries as public utilities.'

Mr Fort* is a (presumably) middle-aged man who has spent a most industrious life reading all the newspapers published in English and French in the last century – from *The Times* to the *Madras Mail* and from the *Journal des Débats* to the *Bedford Mercury* and the *Brooklyn Eagle* – and has carefully extracted from them all accounts of 'inexplicable' happenings of every nature, meteorological, personal, zoological – and the occurrences which would not fit into the existing scientific system. He has filed and indexed all these cuttings and joined similar phenomena together, paralleling something peculiar which happened in New Zealand in 1872 with something of a similar nature in Brooklyn in 1903 and in the Alps in 1931 (he has a preference for things which happened in this century); he has published several books on his findings; the title of the first gives his general attitude; he called it the *Book of the Damned*, because the facts did not fit in with the existing scientific religion, and were therefore ignored as heresies. This book deals chiefly with peculiar meteorological events.

In *Wild Talents* he deals with peculiar things which have happened to or near people – poltergeists, mysterious fires, explosive coal, strange robberies like the disappearance of the Ascot Cup and the Dublin jewels and the first 'cat burglar', stigmatics and wounds which appear on other people 'made by an invisible assailant', group illnesses and deaths and woundings, people who could not be drowned, who could not be

---

* I have since learned, to my great regret, that Mr Fort died in June, 1932.

hanged, who could not be shut up – the sort of things that we so frequently read in small paragraphs in papers, and because we cannot parallel them dismiss as curious stories. But Mr Fort has collected so many stories that there seems to be a uniting principle behind them. This principle is what he calls *Wild Talents*; he believes, and shows good reason for believing, that certain people have an ability which is mainly unconscious, but is sometimes conscious, of affecting objects, whether their own or other people's bodies or inanimate substances, in a way which would normally require physical means, but which in the cases he quotes can be shown to be absent. He considers that these manifestations occur in connection with somebody with very strong feelings – usually fear or hate. He advances very tentatively the suggestion that a parallel can be found in the latest developments of 'ray' physics – the exploding of a bomb or the directing of an aeroplane from a distance and without contact. He stresses that most of these phenomena are unconscious and undirected – most poltergeist manifestations occur in the presence of frightened and unhappy little girls – but that in at any rate one case witchcraft has been set to work and admitted into respectable company. This is water-finding or dowsing – 'a miracle with a job'. Dowsers are magicians who have set their wild talent to work in an orderly fashion.

I have given this rather long account of Mr Fort's work, because it seems to me to give by far the most satisfactory explanation of negro, and all other, magic. Of course, there are a number of other phenomena which Mr Fort has not dealt with – clairvoyance, telepathy and so on, the specialities of the Society for Psychical Research, which are too subjective for his criteria, but which need to be taken into account.

Negroes can put themselves into very peculiar physical-mental states with extraordinary ease. They will go into trances, or throw fits at the slightest provocation. Even a negro beating a tomtom quickly becomes very strange; his pupils dilate and do not focus, he seems to become a rhythmic and unconscious automaton. For the primitive negro the whole universe is moved by spirit reacting on spirit, an idea in which they have such implicit faith that it can kill them, or make them impervious to pain; material or scientific ideas have no meaning for them. The relatively small number of distractions in tribal life permits of very great concentration. I believe that the wonder-working negroes have got their wild talents under some sort of control using their religion as a point of focus. There is nothing in the stories of negro magic that I have been told or read which cannot be paralleled by Mr Fort's cuttings from English newspapers. In South Kensington a stationer's stock started flying about and hitting people in the presence of his young apprentice; in Dahomey panthers arrived in a place where panthers are uncommon. In Willesden a house in Walm Lane exploded and in Islington lumps of coal exploded in the scuttle; in Dahomey something which sounded very like a thunderstorm happened to order. I should like to parallel Mr Fort's account of European ghouls and werewolves with the leopard men; but I know of these only from hearsay.

Of course at the moment science is far better than magic for controlling one's environment, even if every story and claim is allowed to be true. For one thing magic is so extremely specific and exclusive in its action. A man who can control panthers is quite helpless with elephants. The little girl who can make a grand piano dance on its hind legs has to carry her satchel to school. The story of the man who could not be shot with lead bullets and was finally killed with a silver one is well known, and if not true in fact is a very good illustration of the way magic works. But if these wild talents could be harnessed and employed under civilised conditions there is no limit to their possibilities. But it seems as though a miracle-working mind and a logically thinking mind are incompatible; the negroes are usually in a state of trance, and most of Mr Fort's and the SPR's wonder-workers are either children or peasants.

An account of negro religion would not be complete without some mention of the secret societies. Unfortunately I have no personal knowledge of them, and can only retail what has been told to me by other Europeans and negroes. Outside Africa the most notorious society is the Leopard Men of the Liberian frontier; it is said that the associates dress up in leopard skins and fasten iron talons on to their hands with which they claw the victim, usually chosen for motives of revenge, killing him in this way and then eating him. There was a leopard man among the prisoners at Man, but he wouldn't say anything.

It seems certain that the number and membership of secret societies is growing very rapidly in West Africa, probably owing to the break-up of tribal life, and the subsequent feeling of incompleteness which assails the individual negro. These societies are independent of tribal groups. They are nearly all of them anti-European and are mostly consciously evil. All negroes believe in sorcerers and these societies seek to develop unholy powers, in the hope that they will protect the owners better than the gods have done. 'Ritual cannibalism' plays a considerable part in their make-up. They are definitely rather sinister.

7. Missionaries

After having dealt with the original African religions it is only fitting to glance slightly at the religions we are imposing on the negroes in their place. I do not intend describing and analysing the various versions of Christianity which are preached in Africa – thought that might be both instructive and amusing – but merely the effect that these religions have on the negro.

One Sunday morning in a small town where I had nothing better to do I went and listened to the missionaries preaching. The Catholic priest said to his flock, 'The Protestants are the children of the devil (enfants du diable). The Protestants arose because a monk called Luther wanted to marry a nun; since the Holy Father forbade this, they broke away from the Church and dragged many after them to damnation. A heathen who has not heard the gospel preached may go to purgatory, but anyone buried in the Protestant cemetery goes straight to hell.'

At the other end of the town the Protestant missionary told his catechumens, 'The Catholics are not Christians at all: they are European fetishists. They believe in all sorts of grigris – bits of metal and necklaces and bread which they worship; they break the second commandment and worship graven images; instead of consulting the conscience which God gave them as a guide they put themselves in the hands of medicine-men.

They still allow their converts to dance. They do not even set a good example; Father X has taken a vow of chastity, and you all know that he has several children by a black woman living up at his house yonder.'

Except when they are scrapping among themselves (incidentally it would be interesting to know if it is true, as Protestants frequently told me, that Catholic missionaries working in the tropics do not take the vow of chastity) missionaries are on the whole hard-working, conscientious and kindly men. Several were very nice to me. I consider their influence in Africa is almost wholly deplorable. With possibly the best intentions they have made rogues out of honest men, self-seekers out of unselfish men, liars and perverts and neurotics out of men happily free from these defects. I think Catholicism is the more harmful socially, and Protestantism individually. I will try to amplify those statements.

I have already stated that the primitive negro does not think of himself as an individual, but as one of a group (family, clan, tribe); against such a background there is no place for individual selfishness; except for clothes there are no private possessions; men do not work for themselves, but for the group. In this society men cannot enrich themselves at the expense of others (chiefs and kings are only an apparent anomaly; they may be the titular possessors of the tribe's wealth, but they have to spend it on the tribe), nor can they gain advancement or salvation alone. Christianity's intense insistence on individualism naturally destroys this situation. Charity is a poor substitute for co-operation.

The very high standard of tribal morality is destroyed with the destruction of the taboos which upheld it. To give one example among thousands, the little kingdom of Dassa Zoumé may be quoted. It had a fetish called Koutoumbalu, whose symbol was a certain tree. This tree was naturally never used for any utilitarian purpose, but twigs of it placed over a hut or a plantation or a piece of goods would be an effective protection against robbery. The natives believed that the twig called the fetish to guard the object, and would not dare to violate the taboo (also the fetishers would be likely to revenge the outraged deity). They believed the greatest disaster would happen to anyone who laid sacrilegious hands on the tree. In order to demonstrate the folly of their superstitions to the negroes the missionaries built a chapel from the wood of this tree; luckier than Eve in similar circumstances, the missionaries were unharmed, and now no one can leave a cooking pot in Dassa Zoumé unguarded for five minutes. It is doubtful if the sanctions of Christianity, however fully believed in, can ever have the restraining power that the old taboos held. And the mere fact of presenting an alternative system and denouncing the older system as a tissue of lies has an inevitably demoralising effect both on the converts and the heathen. A particularly frank Catholic missionary was once asked what he considered had been the effect of his labours: 'If my church is robbed,' he replied, 'I shall be certain that it is one of my converts who has robbed me.' The negroes believe that absolution after confession is effective. The essentially selfish ethics of Christianity (What shall *I* do to be saved?) are inevitably antisocial. Incidentally, I think a case could be made out to show that the general decline of religious influence in 'civilised' countries is due, not to other attractions, but to the fact that individual ethics have advanced beyond religious *practice*, as they have to a great extent advanced beyond legal practice.

Missionaries do negroes another disservice by turning their very lively sense of sin from the antisocial acts on which it was directed (a broken taboo affects the whole tribe) to acts which were formerly harmless and natural. The chief of these acts are sexual, and all that a prurient mind can distort into a connection with sex. The greatest offenders on these lines are the Protestants, and I have seldom been more shocked than in conversation with Protestant missionaries. They have absolutely filthy minds. They cannot see anything in negro manifestations except illicit copulation. I was told twice quite seriously that girls were lured into the fetish huts to be outraged by the entire population (they didn't say what happened to the boys); dances are only an excuse for the orgies they inevitably end in; any negro meeting was an orgy. Because people think that unless they were held in by theological sanctions they would indulge in an endless bout of promiscuous delights, they have no excuse for attributing their unhealthy daydreaming to others.

More rot has been talked and written about negro sexuality than about almost any other subject, chiefly by Americans who wish to convince themselves that their enormous half-caste population has been produced entirely by rape. It is very questionable if puberty is earlier with them than with Europeans, and I certainly do not think that their sexual desires are stronger. They are, on the contrary, very much more difficult to stimulate than we are, and the pre-erotic states which can be so easily produced in us by contact, kissing, dancing, reading and spectacles, particularly films, can only be produced in the negro by far more violent measures which seem to us indecent. Dances which seem to us violently erotic are to the negro the equivalent of the Victorian sitting in the conservatory. Far from being oversexed they are by European and Asiatic standards frigid.

This does not mean that sex does not play a proper part in negro life. On the contrary, it is with eating their greatest pleasure, as it is with all simple men. And to a certain extent they have studied the technique of love as they have of cooking. But within the traditions of tribal life they are able to satisfy their appetites simply and calmly, without indecency and without fuss. Most of their dances have an erotic element in them, but so have most of ours, whatever balletomaniacs may say. Except in some of their marriage ceremonies – the Bobo husband takes his wife's virginity in view of the population – they are extremely modest. Polygamy is necessary under their economic system, and is essential for the rearing of healthy children.

The missionaries are changing all that. They have succeeded in making sex as overwhelmingly important and as filthy in the minds of their converts as it is in their own. With the obvious result that they either indulge their natural instincts and lie about it, or become neurotic and perverted. Anyone in the police department of the English colonies will tell you that the aggressors in the fairly numerous cases of rape, especially against small girls, are almost inevitably prominent churchgoers. In the Ivory Coast the missionaries put their young male converts to sleep in dormitories to avoid the occasion of sin, with surprisingly successful public-school results. They all turned pederasts (so one of the converts told me).

With unthinking cruelty the Protestants refuse to allow their converts to dance. This is done to avoid the heathen practices associated with dancing, and, of course, to avoid orgies. But for people who have no literature and no drama this means depriving them of their only mode of expression. All the negro's aesthetic and cathartic feelings are concentrated on the dance – music and sculpture only exist as adjuncts to it – and to prevent them performing or even watching dances is to be even more severe than the Puritans who at least left some books. English missionaries, under the widespread belief that the seeds of the Church were gathered on the playing fields of Eton, have introduced compulsory organised games and sports as a substitute. In one compound Christmas Day last year was spent in strenuous sack races and hurdles, to avoid dancing and orgies, and in the belief that physical fatigue drives away sexual desire; but although English public schools and the Army are run on this superstition, neither my personal experience nor that of people I have questioned confirms it.

The question of the forcing of clothes on savages has been so often dealt with that there is no need to insist on it; sweat and rain on unchanged but modest clothes are still producing tuberculosis and pneumonia according to plan.

On the positive and material side missionaries have very often improved the health of the negroes, taught them a good deal – not only the three R's, but also various domestic arts, hygiene and agriculture – and have on occasion protected them against the aggressions of the administration and traders. They have also more or less put a stop to the more inhuman features of negro religion, such as the killing of sorcerers and of babies born with the stigmata of sorcery (abnormal presentation at childbirth, children born with teeth, children whose teeth descend from the upper jaw first) and human sacrifice generally. In this way they have made good many gaps in the work of colonisers, but I do not think the material aid compensates for the moral ravages they have caused. However excellent Christianity may be in temperate climates, I think it is unsuitable for negroes. So for that matter do negroes; and there are very few converts who don't keep up the old practices on the quiet. It is an admirable training in subterfuge, which should do much to fit them for civilised society.

Negroes are converted for three reasons (of course, excluding Grace): fear, desire to learn, and bribery. In some regions, and particularly in the English colonies, missionaries have so much power that they can prevent a heathen from getting work, hospitality or a wife. That is a very potent argument for conversion. A more frequent reason is a desire to learn the white man's wisdom, particularly reading and writing; for the primitive negro this is part of the white man's magic, and cannot be acquired without embracing the gods which gave it to him. For even if they could learn it without conversion, and often the missionaries are the only teachers, they would be divorcing themselves from their tribe and their ancestors by learning an alien art, and if they did not join the Christians would be terribly alone. But by far the most general reason for joining is straightforward bribery. Every negro soldier in the war knew that the Catholics gave twenty-five francs to a convert at baptism, and the Protestants fifty francs, which makes seventy-five francs together; although it is harder to receive double fees in Africa the principle still holds good. Not only is the catechumen rewarded with money: he also gets many presents of clothes – the results of sewing parties enlivened with poisoned gossip at the vicarage – and quite a number of missionaries, especially if their creed is one of the less popular ones in the neighbour-hood, regularly pay their converts' taxes. This is pleasing to both parties, for a missionary is judged by his returns as much as an administrator. Whether the negroes understand the creeds they embrace and the catechisms they repeat is to say the least of it doubtful; but they have extraordinary memories and can learn whole books by heart. Besides, who save an unworldly missionary could expect a negro, whom most legislators consider incapable of planting a cocoa tree, to be able to grasp the Highest Truths Revealed to Mankind? Why, the very idea is absurd, and therefore worthy of belief, as Saint Augustine is supposed to have said.

8. Strange Pilgrimage

This story was told to me, and except in the broadest outlines I have not been able to confirm it, but it seems to me sufficiently interesting to repeat for what it is worth. It is about the little kingdom of Dassa Zoumé, some miles to the north of Abomey. Dassa is geographically very curious, for it is mostly a level plain from which rise extremely sudden and precipitous hills, so rocky that although they are not high they are very difficult to climb. These hills form a circle in the plain; the plain was captured by the Dahomeyans, but the original inhabitants led a precarious existence in the hills until the kingdom of Dahomey was destroyed. Dassa Zoumé is such a tiny kingdom that it is not able to look after many gods; the chief and practically the only one is called Boukou. Naturally his altar and his fetish house are in the hills; everything sacred has been left up in them, and the kings are still buried there. There are a number of officers in the service of Boukou, the chief being an old woman who never goes out of the fetish hut, a sacrificer and a drummer. If there is not enough rain or too much the drummer goes up the mountain to tell Boukou about it; and if a man is to be cursed the drummer goes up the mountain for seven mornings and seven evenings to curse him. The greater part of Boukou's worship contains no peculiarities; but he is unique in having his principal shrine and oracle a long way away from his worshippers. This shrine is in the mountains on the borders of Togoland, and about once every six years the king sends an embassy to it. But on no account must the king send more than twice in his reign.

The pilgrimage is prepared three years in advance. The king, his 'father by protocol' and the council of elders send secret gifts to the house of Boukou in the mountain. They are left there for two years. At the beginning of the third year the dances start, and three months before the date of setting off porters are looked for. It is very unpleasant to be chosen as porter, for it is impossible to refuse; and although it is forbidden to ask after anyone who goes on this sacred pilgrimage, it has been noticed that none of the porters ever returned. The reason for this is that Boukou hates wicked men; therefore those suspected of sorcery were chosen as porters, and Boukou's vengeance proved the suspicion correct. (This was changed at the last embassy when the missionaries told the administration what they had learned.) Besides the porters the cortège consists of the *Akbalé*, who is the leader of the journey, and six *Akokpa*, or staff-bearers. The embassy is away about nine months; it can travel only very slowly, for it has to spend a day in every village it passes, where it is entertained to a feast. After about four months the embassy arrives among wild mountains; in the midst of these mountains is the home of Boukou himself; this shrine is administered by 'the little people' or pygmies, who are not numerous. Conducted by one of the pygmies, the Akbalé and the oldest stave-carrier, who will succeed to the office, enter the home of Boukou. They lower their heads and close their eyes, for Boukou himself is present, and no one can look on his face and live. Using the little priest as an interpreter, the Akbalé presents his gifts and asks the questions which have been the motive of his journey; he hears the voice of Boukou give the answer and receives from his hands an unbroken coconut, which on his return will be found to contain seeds of all their crops; these will be planted with the ordinary seeds and will bless all the harvest. The embassy returns as slowly as it went, smaller in number but received with even greater rejoicings. When they return to Dassa Zoumé they rest the first day and deliver the oracle the day after.

One king was so perplexed that he decided against all rules to send an embassy for a third time in his reign. The Akbalé was very much against this break with tradition, but he was overborne by the king and the stave-bearers, and made the journey, though unwillingly. The day he returned the king sent him as a present a bottle of gin. Not feeling thirsty, or being suspicious, he did not drink it immediately but had it stood on one side; it very shortly after exploded, but no one was hurt, and so on the morrow the Akbalé was able to go in person to deliver the oracle to the king. But the king never heard it, for as he went forward to greet the returning embassy he was bitten by a small but extremely venomous snake.

English Interlude

IT WAS ONLY AFTER THE FOURTH TIME that we had decided to leave Abomey that we stuck to our decision. We had not intended to stop there more than a few days, for the chief object of our journey was to see as many dances as possible, and as much variety; and the longer we stopped in Dahomey the shorter time we would have for the Ivory Coast and French Guinea, where the most extraordinary professional dancers were to be found. But Abomey was oddly fascinating; it was really a land of mystery; the more we discovered about the people and their religion, the more puzzles appeared. The country and the people seemed strangely un-African; the abundance of palms and water, the gay hermaphroditic clothes, the very liquid language all combined to give an impression of the South Seas, which we didn't know, rather than of the Africa we did. The ceremonial which surrounded Prince Aho, our guide and friend, added to the fantasy of the place; when we wanted to see him we had first of all to apply at the porter's lodge; we were then conducted through courtyard after courtyard by different women, each door being unlocked and relocked for our passage, until we came to his reception hut, or on a few occasions to his living-room, with its wonderful collection of native-carved chairs and tables. Both the reception hut and the living-room had screens of mats, from behind which would appear various young women at the slightest command. All the women knelt before Aho; the men approached him on hands and knees, and when they got in front of him they would hit their head three times on the ground and then scoop handfuls of dust on to their hair. You could always tell when a man had been visiting Aho by the quantity of brick-red earth on his forehead and hair. No man ever stood up in his presence.

Aho himself was rather fantastic. He was very young – in the early thirties – and had held his important official position only for about four years, before which time he had been a quite unimportant citizen. His relation who had been chef de canton of Oumbégamé before him had died extraordinarily suddenly a few months before the French Colonial Exhibition, the Mecca of all African chieftains at the time, and Aho, but newly installed, went in his stead. He had excited a certain amount of consternation among the severer members of the cortège by his excessive devotion to magic and venery. These passions were constant with him; although he had been educated by the Catholics he had a complete faith in the claims of fetishism and a fervent belief in the potency of grigris; and in the four years in which he had been chef de canton he had married about sixty wives. He was extremely industrious, and had already acquired far more prestige than any other chef de canton in the neighbourhood; nearly all the French administrators knew of him. He was extraordinarily kind to us, and showed us everything we asked, sometimes it seemed against his will; he even provided us with extremely potent supernatural grigris to help our journey; and, indeed, until Benga commented on it, we did have extraordinary luck.

In the end we left at a few hours' notice. I decided that I had learned all that I could learn in a short visit about the fetish religion; to go farther I should have to learn the language (or languages) sufficiently well to be able to think in them – for speech is magic – which would take at least a couple of years. Negro languages are not difficult to learn for conversational purposes; but to use them as a negro does is extremely hard. To my mind, the real test of knowledge of a European language is the ability to appreciate its poetry; and the negro languages I know of work in a poetic way, for they are highly symbolical and full of association. Most negro languages are full of proverbs, usually consisting of a couple of words, which for the speaker and hearer expand into a full story. ('Words' is possibly misleading; there is no written negro language, and consequently the languages are holophrastic; although the languages can be analysed into single words [mostly monosyllabic] it is probable that the primitive negroes no more think in individual words than they think of individual persons; it is certain that the hymns and prayers which missionaries have painstakingly translated word for word into the local language are usually completely meaningless to the converts.) To understand negro wit, negro poetry and how much more negro magic and religion, it is necessary not only to know the literal meanings of words, but also all their associations; in short, you must acquire the negro background to your thoughts.

It is probably owing to this difficulty – and negro languages are numberless – that so very little anthropological work of any value has been done in Africa. Even those workers who can dispense with an interpreter can usually use the language only literally; and, indeed, the setting aside of a European habit of thought is extremely difficult. Few people have the time, the money and the inclination to live two or three years with a single tribe under uncomfortable conditions; and to my mind that is the shortest period possible for any really thorough work. Owing to the fact that I was spending the whole of my time with negroes – my contact with Europeans was slight and formal, and I read very little – I was able at any rate to realise that the difference in the ways of thinking was fundamental; although I do not for a moment claim that I learned to think like a negro, I nevertheless gathered enough to realise that most books of anthropology which present the negro's outlook on life as an eccentric version of what we consider to be the general outlook were merely constructing a 'logical' parody which had only slight connections with the original. If knowledge of the behaviour of primitive peoples – psychological as opposed to anthropo-metrical and linguistic anthropology – is desirable, a great deal of field work must be done immediately; the greater number of primitive societies have already been destroyed either by the introduction of alien influences or by dispersion; the few that are left relatively intact will so remain for only a very short time more.

We wanted to stop at Ouidah to see the snake temple and the 'revenant' dancers, so Prince Aho had given us an introduction to one of the chefs de canton there, while warning us that all the people of Ouidah were rogues. He was perfectly right.

The scenery on the road to Ouidah was most lovely; the vegetation was very thick and tangled and more flowery than any other stretch I saw in Africa. There were banks of wild cannas and caladiums; a number of the trees were covered with various orchids; there were two flowering creepers, one with trusses like a poinsettia, the other like a hydrangea. As we got nearer to the sea the palms dominated the landscape, until at the lagoon there was no other plant to be seen. All along this coast there is a salt lagoon separated from the sea by a narrow strip of sandy soil covered with palms; such a landscape is very romantic at first, but it quickly becomes excessively monotonous. The chauffeurs, but especially Alioune, were almost hysterical with joy at seeing the sea again; although a steamer would take ten days to reach Dakar they felt there was at last some direct connection between them and home. What was more, the car was now turned in the right direction; every day we would be nearer civilisation; under such a consolation the discomforts of savagery seemed less appalling.

Ouidah is a nasty little town, jerry built and ramshackle and very ugly. Till Dahomey was colonised it had considerable importance as a port, but all its business was taken by Cotonou; palm oil, which is almost its only produce, has fallen to a price where it does not pay to produce it; in 1928 the oil fetched four thousand francs a ton, and today three hundred, so that its business is destroyed. Europeans have been at Ouidah for nearly three centuries, and the inhabitants are thoroughly Europeanised; they are Christian, dishonest, boastful, class conscious (the classes are founded chiefly on wealth, but also on the distinction between literate and illiterate), ashamed of their origin, and drunkards. They are the only negroes I came in contact with who regularly prepared spectacles for Europeans; the small and shabby snake temple has two or three old servants and a few tame and harmless pythons: admission five francs, and a *pourboire* if you want to photograph the priestess with the serpents. This temple is immediately opposite one of the two large cathedrals; the snakes frequently pay visits to the altars of their rivals, but the courtesy is never returned. The Revenants, or ghost dancers, are even more of a ramp; it started as a cult of the dead, with dancers impersonating the ancestors (a very common custom) by completely covering their bodies with stuffs so that no skin could be seen; they would talk in hollow voices, and as a demonstration of the powers of spirits would perform 'miracles' by wriggling into peculiar and sketchy animal disguises – boas, crocodiles and so on. The family who made a speciality of this dance are now all Catholic; but they perform the, to them, completely meaningless pantomime for anyone who will pay. Since the eighteenth century travellers have written about the snake worshippers and ghost dancers of Ouidah – Bosman fills near a whole letter with the former – and the Dahomeyans are ready to dupe the Europeans whenever they want. Fetishism still continues under sufferance; three young people were doing their first public dances after leaving the convent of Sagbata while we were there, surrounded by a jeering crowd of supercilious negroes. They had pink scarves and a parrot's feather in their hair; but they were not allowed to do anything except dance; older people fed them and wiped their faces and hands.

The Portuguese, and I believe the English, still have a fort at Ouidah, standing in its own compound on neutral ground. The Portuguese fort was a quite characterless building. It was only the necessity of going to the police to expose and resist a particularly tiresome piece of chicane which kept us in Ouidah.

The next day we travelled along the lagoon, one of the most tedious drives I have ever made; we had to cross a ferry before arriving at Grand Popo, after which, for some inexplicable reason, we had to undergo a customs examination and unpack the car to show the engine numbers. Since we had crossed no frontier the reason for this performance is obscure. We stopped at Grand Popo for a few hours to see the family of Benga's friend Z, who should have accompanied us, and to try to get some news of him. We saw his family, but they had not heard from him for months. The family consisted of a half-brother, the manager of a branch of some European firm, very smart with a well-cut white suit and horn-rimmed spectacles, very very French and completely uninterested in the 'natives', and his old mother and father, who still lived as negroes in rather dilapidated huts and who were pathetically pleased to see us, almost in tears at getting some news of their lost son. There was something very pathetic about these old people, who had bettered their sons to such an extent that they had lost them; their children no longer spoke the same language, wore the same clothes or thought the same thoughts.

We stopped the night at Lomé to get the car greased and the oil changed. We had met J, one of the partners of the biggest garage at Lomé, on the road, and he had given us a line to his foreman. J was one of the very few Frenchmen I came in contact with who had really done well in the colonies. He was a real Parisian street-Arab, a native of one of the tougher quarters, very well able to look after himself physically, and as industrious and alert as they come. He had been a boxer and had done a certain amount of motor-repair work in Paris; in, I think, 1928 he had arrived at Lomé with about thirty francs in his pocket. He had started by doing odd jobs and had then first been employed and later taken into partnership by an Italian garage owner; he had expanded the business until all their rivals were driven out of the town; from straightforward garage work he had gone on to freight work; then he had started buying and selling the merchandise for his own profit; he had then started building work and construction, and had netted the most important government contracts. He intended shortly to return to France by air, chiefly, I think, because a deposit of a hundred thousand francs is demanded by the French government from anyone crossing the Sahara; he was owed that much money by the government, and it pleased his dramatic sense that a man who had arrived steerage should leave by the most expensive route. He was justifiably proud of his success and was happy to tell all the details; although he paid the negroes fairly badly (though above the average wage) he got on very well with them; he was scrupulously just in his dealings with them, he spoke their language, he worked harder than they did at the same kind of work, and he never employed the police. If he had fault to find with a man he fought him, and since he was very strong and a good boxer, invariably used to beat him; after which he either kept him on or turned him away according to the offence. The negroes admired this very much; they respected a man who could get his own way without recourse to any sort of authority; a man he punished could always defend himself to the best of his ability. He had had a number of his workers with him for years, many of them being ex-convicts; he was always ready to lend any negro money without interest on security if asked. During the riots at Lomé his was practically the only European house which was not touched.

He considered that his origin and upbringing were the chief reasons for his success. Most Frenchmen who come to the colonies are of petit-bourgeois origin, with a bourgeois ideology; they consider themselves superior to all workers, and think that by arriving in such an unpleasant climate they have already done sufficient to assure success; the only work they think they need do is to give orders. J as a proletarian understood the negro mentality far better than the other Europeans; and among proletarians prestige can come only from greater strength or capacity. Moreover, since he was not being paid a wage his profits depended on his own efforts. If he had to employ other Europeans as overseers he avoided Frenchmen as far as possible; he found Italians the most conscientious and the hardest workers. When we met him he was on his way north to build a couple of bridges under government contract; his tender had considerably undercut all others, but he nevertheless expected to make a hundred per cent profit on the work; moreover, he intended using the empty lorries for his other interests. He was slightly too self-satisfied to be a sympathetic character, but it was difficult not to admire him.

Lomé is a rather handsome town, planned on a generous scale with very wide streets, chiefly notable for its numberless churches of every denomination; these churches, the hotel proprietor said, are the only houses in town which are doing any sort of business. We spent the night in a hotel, the first night we had slept between sheets for several weeks; but this luxury was nullified by an open-air talkie just outside the windows. We left very early in the morning for Accra.

French and English colonies both pretend that the foreigners don't exist; it is almost impossible on either side to learn anything of what happens beyond the frontier, and there are practically no intercolonial roads, presumably for strategical reasons. Lomé and Accra are less than a hundred miles apart on the coast, but it is necessary to make a detour of nearly three hundred miles to get from one town to the other. We had to go north as far as Palimé before we could cross the frontiers.

Just before we reached the English frontier we had an extraordinary piece of luck. The Englishman in charge of the customs station had set out on some errand over the French border on a motor bicycle. A couple of miles beyond the frontier his bicycle had broken down and we met him and gave him a lift back to the base. Before we had arrived our relations were friendly, and it became difficult for him to subject me to the inquisition usually imposed on any European entering the Gold Coast. He also quieted the excessive zeal of his negro subordinates. The Gold Coast does not want Europeans, whether English or foreign, and everything is done to discourage their entry. Besides a rigorous customs examination, every European has to receive a special permit and make a deposit of sixty pounds; negroes pass as they please. Moreover, our car had a left-hand drive, which was illegal. The chief customs officer passed me through with a chit to the chief immigration officer at Accra. The customs-house shed seemed a regular arsenal; apparently there is considerable smuggling in liquor and firearms.

Until we reached the river Volta with its expensive steam ferry, there was little to show we had crossed the frontier; the country was wooded and mountainous, rather pretty, with almost continuous cocoa plantations. But once the river was crossed we seemed to be in another continent. The road was wide and asphalted, as good as any European road, and full of traffic, chiefly lorries and buses driven by negroes; the frequent villages consisted of houses instead of huts – true, the houses were chiefly made of mud and wattle and roofed with corrugated iron, but they had doors and windows to them; except in the biggest towns in French West Africa, I had seen no buildings comparable to them; they appeared far more sanitary than most Spanish villages. (Indeed, I never saw in Africa anything comparable to the poverty I had seen in Spain, where whole families lived in holes in the rocks or in burrows in the fields, the dwelling-place merely marked by a hump in the turf with a hole in it.) The people looked well nourished and very clean; they seemed friendly. At a second ferry I got into conversation with a negro elementary-school teacher; I found his English extraordinarily hard to understand, but I learned from him that there was no unpaid labour, that taxes were assessed according to the size of the dwelling, and in agricultural districts on cattle, and that all schooling was paid for – the lowest class paying a penny a week, the sum increasing with each rise in grade. I forgot to ask if there was a free medical service. I found far more difficulty in understanding and in being understood by English-speaking negroes than by those in the French colonies; they produce their voice very far back in the throat with a considerable slurring of consonants, and they speak with a quite un-English rhythm; until you can distinguish the words you cannot tell what language they are talking. They are inclined to speak pidgin or coast English when talking to Europeans, chiefly, I fancy, to annoy; when talking among themselves in English, which they frequently do, they speak fairly grammatically with a liberal sprinkling of biblical and prayer-book phrases. Pidgin English is probably the stupidist linguistic device ever invented; it has absolutely no point. It is no easier to learn than English ('chop' is just as difficult to pronounce as 'food', 'win' as 'find', 'pickin' as 'child', etc.), it sounds silly, it has little connection with negro languages and it is terribly ambiguous. Its only possible advantage – the moral one of making negroes seem childish, by talking to them childishly – is completely overbalanced by the endless muddles it leads to. One of the most difficult English idioms is the redundant negative in questions (i.e. Didn't you see him? No, I didn't) and the use of pidgin has made this always crucial point in interrogations needlessly complicated. If a negro is asked whether he has done something by two different questions he will deny it apparently contradictorily: Did you do it? No. (I did not do it.) Didn't you do it? Yes. (That is correct; I did not do it.) This apparently trivial point is the cause of endless muddles, lawsuits, apparent injustices and numberless memoranda. Nevertheless, pidgin is still used for the sake of tradition and prestige.

We arrived at Accra just after four, when the bureaux close, so we had to hunt for the chief immigration officer in the European ghetto. The Europeans at Accra are segregated some way out of the town in a garden suburb of bungalows. The Frenchman abroad tries to reproduce the illusion of provincial urban conditions, the Englishman the illusion of the country. The bungalows were dotted among lawns and trees quite haphazard, the only plan being to achieve the Englishman's great desire of being unable to see his neighbours. The result was fairly successful. The well-watered golf-course and tennis courts and the roofs peeping among the trees were quite reminiscent of the more select parts of Surbiton or Cheltenham. The only difference was that the houses were made of wood and stood on stilts.

The whole of English life in West Africa revolves very properly round the problem of Keeping Fit. It is, of course, axiomatic that you can only Keep Fit on pieces of ground specially devoted to that end; there is no virtue in movement over soil which is also employed for utilitarian purposes. The great god Fitness has five forms or fetishes under which He can be worshipped with little balls: the princely fetish is polo, and then in descending order of merit golf, tennis, cricket and football. The last is slightly plebeian. The peculiar rites attending the worship of these fetishes have been often described, and also the various ways in which the turf must be arranged and marked to consecrate it. In the face of great difficulties the worship has been transferred to West Africa, and I did not see any place in the Gold Coast where even one or two Englishmen were gathered together where there was not at any rate ground for tennis and clock golf. The work involved in keeping turf green under the tropical sun is tremendous; luckily unskilled labour is cheap. Worship is rendered more difficult by the fact that the sun is dangerous except for an hour or so after rising and before setting, both of which events take place at six o'clock. So to Keep Fit the siesta is abandoned; office hours are from eight to four with one hour for lunch; in the heat of the day, while Frenchmen lie on their beds and snooze and sweat, Englishmen plough doggedly on so that the last two hours of daylight shall be free for the real object of life.

Englishmen in the Gold Coast are divided into three castes or categories: first-class officials, second-class officials and traders. The position of the last category is somewhat amorphous, but between first-class officials and second-class officials there is a great gulf fixed. Second-class officials are Untouchable; they are not allowed into the first-class club house (the social centre of each concession); they are not Called On; their wives do not play bridge or exchange scandal with first-class officials' wives. There are very few Europeans in the Gold Coast, especially outside the few big towns, and women must have a very dull time there; their husbands always work, they are not allowed to keep young children with them, and it would be undignified to go shopping. It is difficult to indulge in physical vanity, for the pitiless sun restricts the choice of clothes, and makes white women look even more repulsive with make-up than without it – I never saw a European woman in West Africa who looked even moderately attractive; a very few of the keenest male devotees of Fitness managed to avoid the sallow blotchy complexion and the expression of irritable peevishness which a regular diet of quinine seems to induce – so that during the greater part of the day women have no other resource than scandal-mongering to pass the time. By being divided into two castes, according to their husbands' positions, they have all a large field of victims that they can observe and disparage without coming into contact with them, or risking the retailing of some spiteful remark to the woman discussed. It seems to me an admirable arrangement.

I finally tracked down the chief immigration officer, B, to his bunga-low, but since it was after office hours he refused to deal with me till the morrow. When, in reply to his question, I told him I thought of stopping at a hotel, he was appalled; he did not know if there was such a place, and if there were it would only be for Greeks and dagoes (Greeks replace Syrians in the Gold Coast). Gentlemen either stopped at the club or borrowed a bungalow (the customs officer had advised me to try for hospitality from the Principal of Achimota College); it was incredible that I should have arrived without having arranged to do one or the other. Despite my clothes, which were probably the shabbiest in Accra on the back of Englishman or negro, I had more or less the right sort of voice, and it seemed wrong to let me go among the dagoes; so rather half-heartedly B offered to put me up, explaining in the same sentence that he had only very restricted bachelor's quarters (after all, the fellow may not have any smarter kit in his trunks, and then how am I going to explain him?); I refused on the ground that I had a great deal to do, and any sort of hotel would do for the couple of nights I intended stopping in Accra;

relieved but still somewhat anxious, B sent his chauffeur with me to guide me to the Metropole.

The Metropole was in Accra, by the prison, except for its advertisements an unassuming little building; the proprietor was the fattest and the slowest Greek I have ever seen. I think there was only one proper bedroom, in which the proprietor was dozing when we arrived, but he had it got ready for me. He was so flabbergasted when I asked him for a room for Benga that for a little he couldn't get his breath; the situation was unparalleled, inconceivable. After a little while he had a sort of alcove off my room ready, and then accepted the situation as an inexplicable phenomenon, as did the other boarders. One of the servants whom I took as a guide, shocked to the core, pointed out a hotel 'for coloured people'; but I felt rather sensitive about going there.

Accra is a very large, sprawling, ugly, formless town inhabited by negroes. A few Europeans work in it (there was a surprising number of German storekeepers), but it is a negro town, and as such quite unlike any of the towns I had visited in the French colonies, which are European towns with negroes living in them on sufferance. Here they were at home. Accra resembled far less what I knew of Africa than what I imagined of Harlem, despite the difference of architecture. It was a town in full bourgeois development, with every grade between the mansion and the hovel. Negroes in smart cars with liveried chauffeur and footmen, dressed in the height of elegance with their womenfolk gowned as though they were going to Ascot, were held up by negro policemen to allow humbler housewives to cross the road. All the richer people were dressed with the greatest European elegance, but more of the working people than I had expected wore native dress, somewhat after the Dahomeyan fashion, but in rather ugly cloths with red predominating, instead of the lovely blue English cloths of Dahomey.

The inhabitants of Accra are the handsomest collection of people I have ever had the good fortune to see, both men and women. Until I was in Africa I had considered that the people in Southern Yugoslavia, particularly round Dubrovnik and Cetinje, were the most beautiful I had seen, followed by the people of Kiev and Tarragona, but I think that the people of Accra have the highest average of personal beauty. They are not very tall, but they are perfectly proportioned, their arms and shoulders being particularly lovely; their features are very regular and not markedly negroid; the men cut a parting in their hair and the women dress theirs in elaborate and complicated styles. Native clothes are far more becoming to them than European ones. They are extravagantly clean and their glossy skin shines like satin.

As far as I am concerned negroes are halfway between human beings and statues (in the Greek naturalistic tradition). With Europeans my appreciation of human beauty is falsified by my personal standards of desirability; if a person is not my type I can only approve without appreciating his qualities. With negroes the difference in surface – uniform colour, the absence of contrasting hair, the smooth texture of their skin which affects the eye like worked marble or bronze (my fingers were always surprised to find negro bodies warm and yielding) – makes them appear as much 'objects' as 'people', and my attitude is consequently far more detached, at any rate with strangers; after I have been talking to people for a little while I forget what colour they are.

The day we arrived a funeral concert was being held for a deceased chief in one of the squares; tomtoms were playing and people were singing, and occasionally a man or woman would do a few steps in front of the drums; but this was a very uncommon occurrence; as a whole the negroes of Accra have diverted all their energies from dancing to Christianity.

It would be an exaggeration, but not much of one, to say that every tenth building in Accra was some sort of church or chapel, with continuous services; you can no more escape the sound of hymn tunes in the Gold Coast than you can escape the military bugle in the French colonies. Not content with singing all day in the churches, they hold religious parades all night; three large processions passed the hotel during the first night; the Good Templars were all dressed in white, and were illuminated by acetylene lamps held on choirboys' heads; the Watch Tower movement were in European clothes and were extremely noisy; the one which passed at four o'clock in the morning I did not trouble to identify. Nearly all the churches are different forms of Protestant heresy (or should it be 'different forms of Protestantism'? I am not sufficiently a theologian to know what is the correct attitude of a member of the Church of England, a Plymouth Brother and a Peculiar Person towards each other) and they all seem to be exceedingly prosperous. The missionaries appear to have control of nearly all the education, and most of the bookshops.

The education is within its limits very good. The greater part of the inhabitants of the Gold Coast are literate, and can usually talk and write a sort of English; the pupils are dressed in a neat and useful uniform, trained to an elaborate system of hygiene, and, of course, play lots of organised games. But it is the higher education which is the most remarkable; Achimota College is, as far as my knowledge goes, unique in tropical Africa, and is to my mind the most astounding achievement of British colonial policy. It is a university, far better staffed and equipped than most European universities, entirely for the use of negroes. To have produced such an institution and to have educated negroes in three generations to be able to take full advantage of the extraordinary facilities offered, is a feat which it is impossible to praise too highly. Sir Gordon Guggisberg, to whose initiative I believe the university is due, has given a standing refutation to those imperialists and anthropologists who pretend the negro mentality incapable of acquiring European knowledge, and has thrown the interested lie back in their teeth. Indeed, the people who make this claim have now shifted their ground; it is only 'some negro races' which are incapable of improvement. Actually, given adequate nourishment and a proper environment, there appears to be no evidence to show that there exists any race with an innate incapacity for learning, provided that at infancy they learn the language in which they will have to study; if, as mostly happens in French West Africa, they learn a European language comparatively late in life it is only to be expected that they should be below European standards.*

* As a generalization I should say that negroes have a better memory and are more observant than Europeans, but have considerably weaker powers of

With small exceptions all the land in the Gold Coast belongs to the negroes, who are governed by English common law, modified by ordinances passed by the Governor and his council, of which about two-thirds are European. The negro chiefs or stool holders have considerable power under the guidance of administrators. There are very few Europeans in the Gold Coast, about two thousand in all. The Gold Coast proper (as opposed to Ashanti and the Northern Territories) was neither conquered nor ceded; in 1840 the people of the Gold Coast demanded to be taken under British protection, and to be governed by English common law, modified by native custom. This system is called a Crown Colony.

For a long time this arrangement worked extremely well. The colony had the luck to come under the direction of a succession of conscientious and courageous men (with a few exceptions), and the inhabitants became educated, civilised and rich, by European standards. As far as the ordinary needs of life are concerned the Gold Coast is self-supporting, and it has the very valuable export articles of gold, manganese, timber and cocoa. The precipitous drop in price of the last-mentioned article in the world market recently has considerably impoverished the negro planters and exporters, and they have consequently started cultivating more foodstuffs for home consumption. It is almost impossible for the Gold Coast to be really poor.

Now when a considerable proportion of the Gold Coast negroes are educated the system of government is not working so well, and the governors are becoming a bit scared. The negroes smart under a feeling of inferiority and discrimination; they are excessively race conscious – they are conscientiously reviving negro customs and dances in the spirit of English morris dancers: the *Gold Coast Independent* announces that 'the

---

induction and deduction. If a selection of European and negro infants were given identical education I should expect the negroes to excel in the 'humanities' – classics, history, law – and in applied medicine and as naturalists: the Europeans in mathematics, science and engineering. In abstract argument the educated negroes I met were as hazy as English politicians.

Africa Dances

Ohum Festival of Akyem Abuakwa will be celebrated on Tuesday, 3rd of July next, after which Yams will be brought to town for consumption' – and they feel that they have a right to a far greater amount of self-government, which they demand extremely loudly, both through the rather scurrilous native press and with occasional sporadic rioting. To quote another paper, 'the African has now reached the age of puberty and demands the right to assume, or put on, the *toga virilis*', 'God gave Africa to the negro, and he should be allowed to develop it for his own good.'

Even if the negroes have reached the age of puberty – and I think that about describes the situation, though it is worth noting that in ancient Rome the *toga virilis* was assumed, or put on, considerably later – the Colonial Office has no intention of abandoning the colony to the inhabitants if it can help it; but since to a great extent the negroes are in the right under English common law – which includes the Magna Charta – it has been necessary to repress these manifestations by a series of ordinances, of which the latest, the Sedition Act, is particularly oppressive and open to abuse. Our own Sedition Bill is bad enough, but at least it has to be proved to the magistrates that the possessor of a copy of, say, the Sermon on the Mount, or some of Mr Ramsay MacDonald's earlier speeches, has the intention of showing it to some member of His Majesty's forces; under the Gold Coast act the mere possession of literature judged seditious is a crime.

As a matter of fact the government is in an extraordinarily difficult position. My personal impression – obviously very superficial, for I was only in the Gold Coast a few days – is that the negro is not yet ready for self-government, owing to the very low standard of public or civic morality. I do not think this is due to any inherent fault in the negro character, but to the fact that they have taken what we have taught them much too literally. Most of what they have been taught is imbued with the spirit of the second half of the nineteenth century, when our own standards of public morality were extraordinarily low, as the slums and similar legacies witness.

Besides the antisocial or 'spiritual' morality of the missions, the negroes take the law far too seriously. I think it is correct to say that for the great majority of English people the law, at any rate civil law, is an antiquated, costly and cumbrous contrivance with which it is well to have as little as possible to do. Except for professional litigants the law is a last resort. I imagine that most of my compatriots are as ignorant as I am of the various property rights which eight centuries of legal verbiage have endowed us with. Unless very great inconvenience is threatened we do not try to oppose the plans of state or council which infringe on our rights; we usually submit passively, hoping that it is for the public weal.

The law is possibly the Gold Coast negro's greatest passion. It is the aim of nearly every young educated negro to become a lawyer, and there are few families in which at least one member is not qualified. In its practice they find an outlet for their natural eloquence, for their retentive memories, and for the ingenuity which they rate as highly as the admirers of Ulysses did. Almost every development of public works, such as road building, drainage, water supply, is held up by a long string of lawsuits. The negroes know what their rights are, or might be, and hold out for every penny of compensation they can get (all the land belongs to the negroes). This obstructionism is too typical of negro mentality today. We have taught them to think and act as individuals, instead of as clans or family groups as they did before we arrived; before they can be really fit to govern themselves they must be taught to think and act as a group again, but this time a group which will comprise the whole country. Race consciousness is not enough. Unfortunately we are ourselves very much in need of the same instruction; it would be a question of the lame teaching the bedridden how to run.

The negro officials are often venal. My car was frequently being held up by policemen in Accra because it had a left-hand drive. 'They want bribes,' the boy from the hotel, who was acting as my guide, explained. J, the contractor at Lomé, told me that whenever he had to go into the Gold Coast he used to take several bottles of whisky with him; a number of chiefs with the power of magistrates over their territories used to hold up cars on some minute offence, for which a fine was imposed to extract the ransom of a bottle of spirit. An extraordinary number of regulations surround the loading of vehicles – lorries and buses; the negroes are adept in evading the spirit of the law, while following the contradictions to the letter.

When they are not having lawsuits against the State the negroes are having lawsuits with one another. They somewhat resemble Italian peasants in the way in which they will squander all their savings over some minute point. They have three courts to which they can go: firstly, the native court, whose judgements are final unless an appeal is made; secondly, the district administrator, whose judgements can be reversed without appeal by the judges, who are the third court. This arrangement puts the administrators at a considerable disadvantage; their sentences have less finality than those of the local courts.

Although most of the inhabitants of the Gold Coast are nominally Christians, there are occasionally outbreaks of the older religions in their more bloodthirsty manifestations. At Accra in 1925 five young workmen had their hearts ripped out of them in the open street; the hearts were buried beside a recently deceased chief, so that their spirits should act as porters for him in the next world. In 1931 the Customs were renewed in Ashanti after a lapse of several years; the Customs cannot start without a newly severed human head; after lengthy investigation by the police the head, the body and finally the murderer were found.

The fact that one can judge Gold Coast negroes on the whole by European standards is a sufficient tribute to their extraordinary progress. The remarks I have made about their lack of civic morality could be applied with equal aptness to a number of European states; but the corruption, venality, intrigue and oppression which are such constant features in a number of the smaller Eastern European states seem to me definitely undesirable; and it is in such a direction that I think the Gold Coast would evolve if it were now left to itself.

In the meantime the position of the more conscientious English administrators is extraordinarily difficult. There is a very constant and palpable anti-white feeling; at Accra I had for the first time the experience of being hated by passers-by in the street – and there is a great deal of sporadic rioting and stone-throwing. The labour troubles, particularly strikes, are not specifically anti-white; they are on the whole justifiable protests against very bad pay and conditions; in the gold mines in particular, there have been disgraceful cases of workers being fired on quite unnecessarily, and of serious accidents due to faulty safety devices. The only means by which the Gold Coast can be conducted through this very difficult period (accompanied, as puberty so often is, by growing pains) is by the personality, integrity and disinterestedness of the men in charge. On the whole these qualities are recognised by the negroes, and are given wide publicity, just as is any falling from an extremely high standard by the very personal local papers. Unfortunately some of the people, and particularly the policemen, I came in contact with had an irresponsible schoolboy mentality which saw in every protest, however justified, Bolshevism, and who enjoyed the excitement of 'a good scrap'. But unless such hotheads can be controlled, we shall be saddled with a policy of violent suppression, which can end only by the destruction of a specimen of colonisation in which an Englishman, no matter how anti-imperialist in theory, cannot but take considerable pride. However self-seeking the policy at the back of such a development may have been, the results, chiefly owing to the efforts of individuals, have, up till now, been extraordinarily good. Captain Liddell Hart, writing about English policy in the Near East, has made some generalisations on foreign policy which seem to me to be equally apt in their application to colonial policy:

> The entanglement [concerning Turkey], might have its origin in the casuistry of policy, in that inability of nations to rise even to the relatively low standards of honest dealing that prevail among individuals. But its embarrassments would be due in large measure to the relatively high standard of honour attained by the individuals who were instruments of that policy ... In the light of those hundred years of history and their sequel, the use of our national gift for compromise may not seem altogether happy. Such delicate adjustment, to be truly effective, requires a Machiavelli – and the Englishman is not Machiavellian. He can never rid himself of moral scruples sufficiently to fill the part. Thus he is always and inevitably

handicapped in an amoral competition, whether in duplicity or blood-and-iron. Realisation of this inherent 'weakness' suggests that Britain might find it better to be more consistently moral. At any rate, the experiment has still to be tried.*

In the development of the Gold Coast we have for a long time been more or less consistently moral. That the morality is not of the highest is inevitable; black workers are not treated relatively worse than white. It would be more than a pity if with the work so near fruition we should turn Machiavellian.

Lest I should become unduly puffed up with nationalist pride – and I left the Gold Coast more of a 'patriot' than I had ever expected to be – Providence arranged that while I was planning this section the newspapers should contain accounts of the case of Mrs Selwyn, who was sentenced to twelve months' imprisonment in Kenya for having tortured a negro to death (this seems the only fit word to describe death resulting four days after a flogging with what the Crown doctor describes as 'an inhuman weapon when used on a human being'). But it is not so much the incident or the trifling punishment ('a fine example of impartial justice') which is shocking, as much as the system brought to light. Apparently if the man had not died Mrs Selwyn would still be free to flog and fine negroes with or without cause to her heart's content. If what I have seen of the French colonies justifies them being called the negro's purgatory and the Gold Coast the negro's paradise, all that I have heard of our East African colonies indicates that they are the negro's hell. It is probably the climate which is chiefly responsible for the original difference in policy. West Africa, until recently, was so lethal to Europeans that they abandoned the rights to land they could not live on; in East Africa they can live and multiply; therefore, 'the weaker go to the wall' with a good hearty push.

A great deal of my time at Accra was taken up in getting a number of permits from government offices scattered all over the sprawling town, and in shopping. Although the negroes appeared collectively hostile they

* *T. E. Lawrence*, pp. 68, 38.

were individually very friendly; a number of shop-assistants wanted me to enter into an exchange of letters with them. Their written English is almost as funny as the famous Baboo's; they mix metaphors and tenses with a breathtaking audacity; and sprinkle biblical and hymn quotations with the liberality of an Austrian cook with caraway seeds. The following quotations, taken from two articles on the same page of an issue of the *Gold Coast Spectator*, are mild compared with the really flowery efforts:

> British Colonial administration has slid into an evening of silence and anxiety. It is enveloped in pitch night, a breathless night of suspense for both the government and the governed. But the African is confident in his cause, and sincerely believes that the morning will not dawn upon the Crown Colony system without wholesome changes.

The second is from an article about education which begins:

> Palpitant and tense is the shrill voice of the public, wailing for the old standard of education which has given place to its shadowy self . . . The young girl from the school thinks only of finery and the means of obtaining it; while the mind of the seventh-standard lad is engrossed in roaming about the streets at night. On both there is no proper home influence. In both the first sign of cultural deficiency that stands out boldly before the observer is the jarring noise in conversation as if from the sighing bellows – a thing so foreign to the good breeding instinct. Meet them in society in general, and you will be shocked by the type of youth that the country is breeding. Demeanour, address and comportment betray them as people on whom culture has smiled but little. With some of the young men, one does not find the soft air of breeding with which diligent reading surrounds one. Some of the few that read only hunt for felicitous phrases to enrich their diction without being benefited by the beauties of the lessons before them. Others do not at all read. Of the latter class, one could say that they imagine that their education becomes complete with the seventh standard . . . By self-examination the person who aims high should assail his own ramparts of ignorance for self-improvement. Since

there are no established circles where the light of culture can trans-
mute the harsh natured into the Chesterfieldian in character, and
society is as vitiated as can be, individual units must be created . . .

It's a long quotation, but I think it's worth it. I am particularly pleased
with the 'good breeding instinct'. Moreover, it is extremely typical; the
real high spots would only excite incredulity. For lovers of the works of E.
Nesbit the poetry pages of the Gold Coast papers are a treasure field; the
muse of Noel Bastable has come into her own at last. I had intended
quoting the whole of a letter from a bookseller ending 'Cheerio! awaiting
for good news and life spent on the way and at Paris I remain Yrs beloved
friend . . . ' But on second thoughts perhaps it is rather unkind. After all,
the remark of Dr Johnson about the dancing dogs is really apposite.

The chauffeurs were very unhappy while they were at Accra. They felt
frightened and lost, they had great difficulty in making themselves understood, they found the money confusing (and, indeed, the bronze
'silver' coins are muddling), and provisions terribly dear; but worst of all
they felt themselves in a position of great inferiority with regard to the
other negroes, a new and unpleasant sensation for them; as Wolof and
Mohammedans they were accustomed to look down on negroes of other
races as uncultured barbarians, a pleasure they were here unable to enjoy.
I found out later that they had nearly starved themselves, partly through
shyness, but chiefly for fear that they would be given pork or lard to eat.
But when they got back to Dakar they told their friends the most
wonderful stories about England; their discomfort was forgotten, only
their admiration was left.

Benga acted like a Jew who had been given a short glimpse of the
promised land. He had heard great things of the Gold Coast, but what he
saw far surpassed what he had imagined. 'At last I have seen the poor
niggers in a place which they can call their own.' For him the negroes
are an accursed race, everywhere strangers and friendless, everywhere
oppressed, cheated, and despised. Even in their own country it was only
on sufferance that they lived their precarious and miserable lives. He was
also much impressed by the politeness of the English, when they didn't
ignore him; on the whole, for the Gold Coast Englishman, the negro is

just part of the landscape (none of the people with me needed passports, permits or any other papers), but when he is forced to take notice of him he is courteous in an impersonal way. One of the things which most impressed Benga was the absence of Europeans in shops and government offices; except for directors all the posts were filled by negroes. We had several letters of introduction to negro notabilities at Accra, but we did not use them; chiefly because it would entail stopping some days at the hotel with a resulting loss of time and money, and also I thought my position would be somewhat ambiguous: I should have to act as interpreter and it would be difficult to keep off the subjects of politics and religion, which I wished to avoid. Moreover, we were both much too shabby; under the influence of travel films I had not taken any clothes suitable for town wear, and the Gold Coast negroes have a more than English standard of male sartorial correctness.

The road from Accra to Sekondi is metalled for the whole distance; Fodé had not believed that such a road existed, and the car, surfeited by such luxury, developed a slight disorder which was skilfully repaired at a wayside garage. There was a good deal of traffic on the road, and the countryside seemed very populous and prosperous; between the villages were almost continuous cocoa plantations, covering the thinly wooded hills. The cocoa in fruit looks a very silly tree, for the big pods are attached by a string to the main trunk, and the leaves and branches seem quite lost and superfluous. The farther west we went the more the countryside and the population deteriorated; the cultivation became more haphazard, the people uglier, fewer and more diseased. At one place, I think at Cape Coast, there was a very pleasant seventeenth-century fort. Sekondi was like a smaller Accra; it is the head of a railway and has near it the stupendous artificial port of Takoradi. This was by far the most impressive piece of engineering I saw in West Africa, but I believe that it has not justified its construction, owing to the slump in and alternative sources of cocoa and manganese – the chief goods it was intended to deal with. At Sekondi we were told that the road to Axim was closed on account of rains, but on further inquiry we learned that it had been declared open three hours earlier, after having been closed for a week.

Axim is a small port, somewhat of a backwater. The tiny English concession consisted of four bungalows on a wooded hill a little way out of the town. I had the luck to find a kind PWD official (second class) who not only got me installed in one of the handsome bungalows, but also fed and entertained me. I also learned from him that I had been given completely incorrect information at Accra; there was no road at all beyond Axim; the French frontier could be reached only by motoring along the beach at low tide, and from there it was necessary to put the car on a tug to get it from the lagoon to the mainland. This was rather more than I bargained for, but I did not feel like retracing my footsteps, and on the PWD man's advice I engaged a local chauffeur to drive the car along the treacherous beach, beset with quicksands and fallen logs.

Axim had been recently disestablished as an administrative centre, but the young district commissioner was stopping there for a couple of days. It was a great pleasure and relief to me to meet someone who spoke the same language as I did, even though it was with a very marked foreign-office accent. In contact with the French administrators I had become very superior and class conscious; the great majority were ignorant, incurious and ill-mannered. It was a pleasant surprise to meet someone who was interested in the same subjects as I was (chiefly anthropology), and who could discuss them intelligently; we even had acquaintances in common. It was easy to foresee that prolonged residence amongst colonials would turn me into an arrant snob.

The district commissioner, W, was very envious of the French; he thought they were better colonisers than we were(!), and was jealous of the freedom of action that they possessed, while he was restricted by regulations at every turn. The district of Axim was particularly difficult to deal with, for there were seven small kingdoms, each with its own chief, customs and language. In an effort to create a larger unit to work with, W was trying to press the claims of one of the chiefs against the rest; this chief arrived on a visit accompanied by his court, bringing a couple of old Dutch documents which I translated rather inadequately. The chief was most imposing, a huge man with a blue fillet round his head, wearing a long robe of golden-yellow velvet and a green cloak; he had a gold-headed ebony cane and many gold rings and ivory bracelets; his court were dressed more simply, in the native style. He and W treated one another with the greatest courtesy.

The chief reason for the administrators' difficulties in the Gold Coast is our glorious legislature. The law is taken seriously by the whole population, and its innumerable loopholes, tricks and crookednesses are exposed and exploited. In a way it is a pity that the English are not equally legally minded, for then the government would be forced to codify, bring up to date and translate into English that imposing monument of obsolete tradition, chicane and obscurantism. (Or do I fall into the Gold Coast negro's illusion in expecting the government to do everything – or anything?)

Although the extra chauffeur made us horribly crowded, the drive along the beach was rather fun. Even at low tide there is very little sand uncovered near the equator, and we were mostly in the wash of the waves. The chauffeur was extremely competent, and skidded between the quicksands and the fallen logs at over sixty miles an hour. It was one of the very few occasions when I have found speed exhilarating, chiefly, I suppose, because travelling over the sand did away with most of the sensation of friction of which I am always conscious on roads. There were five rivers to cross, three of them with ferries manned by highway robbers, who, had not Alioune been very vigilant, would have been ordinary robbers too; they very nearly got my notecase out of my breeches pocket. There was also a hold-up – a barrier across the beach, so that the car had to be hauled over the dunes by a waiting gang who extracted ransom for the work. When we reached the frontier, Half Assinie, the hired chauffeur wanted to leave the car: he said he was very frightened of the French. But since there was still nearly twenty miles of beach driving, I bribed him to stop; a French frontier policeman held on with his eyebrows and toenails, and the heavily overloaded car staggered into Assinie. The second we got on to solid ground the hired chauffeur asked to be paid and disappeared.

We arrived at Assinie just after Sunday lunch, and everybody was far too somnolent to look after us. Beyond saying, 'You haven't anything dutiable, have you?' the customs official ignored me; W had given me a chit to the administrator, a very uncut Basque diamond, quite happily tipsy, who took me under his wing and ran with me up and down the tiny strip of earth between the sea and the lagoon which constitutes the town of Assinie, to call on all the traders to find out if there was any possibility of getting a tug without wiring to Aboisso, which would mean a delay of two or three days. By an extraordinary stroke of luck a tug which ought to have left the day before had been delayed and was leaving on the morrow at dawn; there was room for us and our car on it. When this was settled the administrator took me to see his great passion, his vegetable garden, installed next to the prison so that it should lack no attention. The result was very creditable; the vegetables looked as if they had been raised by intensive culture in the South of France. (Nearly all isolated French administrators concentrate on vegetable gardens.) My admiration was rewarded with some lettuces and radishes. It was then necessary for me to find somewhere to spend the night; Assinie is important as an outlet for the coffee and timber in the interior, but it is a minute strip of land, often washed over by the high seas, and there are very few buildings on it. Benga had found a schoolfellow (as he did frequently in the Ivory Coast) with whom he and the chauffeurs could spend the night, but his house was small, and however much I might have wanted to join them I should never have dared suggest it to the paternal administrator. The difficulty was solved by planting me on to an English trader resident there, a representative of one of the big exporting companies. Like most of the French officials living near the coast, the administrator was pleasant and kindly; although he was brusque with the negroes he appeared to know most of them and to be liked by them.

My involuntary host was a young man who had recently left Cambridge and had been sent out to this very isolated post. He was in a very neurotic state. Almost his first remark to me after we were left alone together was, 'I expect you've noticed that I'm a Jew.' Since his name was perfectly normal and his hair and complexion fair, I had done nothing of the sort. Unless people are called Levi and have black curly hair and a huge curved nose, I never do consider whether they are Jews or not; the

Jews are (despite their boasts) on the whole so very hybrid that it seems to me to be of little interest if one line of their ancestry has followed a peculiar form of Unitarianism and is possibly remotely descended from ancestors in the Near East. It is only when they have lived in an exclusively Jewish environment that they appear to me to show any special group characteristics. But K wouldn't leave the subject alone, and he soon succeeded in making me very cross by saying there was a good deal to be said for Hitler's actions: 'Some of the Polish Jews are simply dreadful; now my family has been settled in England for . . . ' I am quite inconsistent on this subject; on the whole, differences in race seem to me far less important than differences in class and environment, not to mention personality; but if people do stress this characteristic they should at least be wholehearted about it; you cannot insist on your Englishness or Jewishness, without accepting all that is done by the people who make up the group you attach yourself to; to separate your group, as my host did, into good and bad and only identify yourself with the first half seems to me as illogical and as stupid as the magistrates who dub certain forms of crime committed by Englishmen 'un-English'. And I should have thought from the merely pragmatical point of view, seeing the way the East wind is blowing, it would be politic for Jews to aim at as much solidarity as possible, and not vainly hope that many will be called to the concentration camps and they be chosen as bastards.

K put all his misfortunes down to his racial origins; although he had won a good education by a series of scholarships he had been unable to get a job in England, owing, as he thought, to racial prejudice; and he had got his present position only because the head of the firm was a Jew. He had not expected to be sent out to such a post and, although I dare say he managed competently, an academic education must have been a considerable handicap. He was unhappy and lonely; he did not get on with the Frenchmen in the district, whom he considered lacking in appreciation for the finer things of life (Galsworthy and Margaret Kennedy) and grossly immoral; his consolations were his intellectual superiority and his sexual purity. He slightly sprained his ankle in the course of the evening, and became peevish and anxious; I should predict a complete breakdown fairly soon if he doesn't find a more congenial environment. His race consciousness prevented him having any sort of contact with the negroes.

After a very uncomfortable night I was glad to be at the quay at dawn. The quay consisted of a gangway of rotten planks, and the tug was a tiny primitive wood-burning launch with a trailer which would hold the car. We were considerably delayed by Fodé disobediently trying to drive the car on to the raft; he didn't know which was the sound plank and consequently the wheels went through, and it took the united village about an hour to get it straight again. While this operation was being performed fishers from the lagoon returned with crocodiles' legs for soup; it was all the crocodile we ever saw. When we finally got on board we learned that instead of the couple of hours' trip across the lagoon that we had expected we had to go nearly forty miles up the Bia, before we would come to a landing-place and a road. Before we were halfway across the lagoon the hood of the car caught fire; Fodé had been told by the white skipper to keep the hood damped, on account of the frequent sparks, but he was still sulking over his previous folly and had not done so. Only a small hole was burned.

The day's journey up the river was one of the most enchanting of my life. After the lagoon was passed the river was narrow, and the boat moved very slowly and quietly past the banks teeming with the most varied vegetation, occasionally broken by tiny groups of huts on stilts; very rarely we overtook a fisherman in his hollowed pirogue. The weather was fine but with massy white cumulus clouds in the sky, so that the glare was lessened, and the blue of water and sky and the varied greens of the vegetation took on more distinct and vivid tints. The river was continually undulating, so that the perspectives and directions constantly varied; the gigantic trees which rose above the impenetrable undergrowth gave accent and form to what might otherwise have been too amorphous. There was something strange and inhuman, almost dreamlike, in the journey; there was so little sound, so much variety in monotony. It was my first introduction to the primeval forest and jungle, and it would be difficult to desire a better one. Perhaps because it passed before me without my having any consciousness of motion, it seemed to possess a quality which I have not found in any other landscape; it was not so much that it was more beautiful as that it was different. It annihilated time.

After I had long given up expecting or desiring a change we arrived at Aboisso, our destination. We got down fairly easily, but the car had to be driven down yielding planks of mahogany, an anxious business, for there was a drop of about four yards between the deck of the raft and the bank. A plank broke in the middle, but save for a heart-sinking wobble no harm came of it. Benga had immediately found a friend among the crowd. I was still undecided what to do, when the head of the trading establishment came and invited me to stop with him. Even as I was accepting thankfully, I noticed the surprise and whispering in the crowd; apparently such an action on the part of this man F was entirely unparalleled in the thirty years of his residence there. He was extremely nice to me, but it was obvious that the negroes and his two young French subordinates were very afraid of him. He treated me royally, giving me much too much to drink, and speaking most interestingly about his thirty years' experience in the colony. He had been there almost since the beginning of the conquest; I told him sincerely that it was a pity not to set down his experiences, which, if only for continuity, must be unique. He came from Nîmes and was a fervent Protestant (it was perhaps because my nationality made me a probable co-religionist that he had given me hospitality): he hated Catholics and disliked the administration. Dinner was rather an unpleasant ordeal; the food was good but the atmosphere very chilly; the two young Frenchmen sat with their eyes fixed on their plates, answered briefly when they were spoken to, and bolted to their own quarters the second the last mouthful was swallowed, to drink their coffee in solitude. This was their daily custom.

In the morning I discovered that the yellow-fever quarantine had been reimposed, as two Europeans had died 'suspiciously'. It needs elaborate diagnosis to discover yellow fever in a postmortem, with apparatus which practically no colonial doctors possess; so any European who dies suddenly is suspected of yellow fever. When there is a threat of an epidemic most elaborate precautions are imposed; no one is allowed outside after sunset, and during the day Europeans, Asiatics and mulattoes have to cover their faces with veils and swathe their hands and ankles. But these measures are not imposed on negroes, under the completely unfounded delusion that they are not susceptible to the disease; although it is not so lethal to them they catch it just as readily, but they have their own treatment for it, continuous massage with certain herbs, which seems to answer very well. (I have heard a doctor commend this treatment as more efficacious than European nursing and deny that negroes ever catch the disease in the same sentence. I wonder how he thinks they learned to nurse it?)

The only precaution imposed in my case was the possession of a sanitary passport which had to be renewed every four days, and which I would send in to be stamped by the doctor, if there was one, in the place where we were stopping. Since the doctors seldom even glanced at me I don't quite know what good that was meant to do.

Armed with this amulet we set out for Grand Bassam, which was the capital of the Ivory Coast that week, as far as I remember. I know Abidjan was going to be a fortnight later, but perhaps it was Bingerville's turn at that moment. The situation is very puzzling; there are three towns about twenty miles apart on the edge of the lagoon; one of them is the capital, but it is sometimes vague which. Government offices play General Post. However, an enormous governor's palace has been built at Abidjan; so I expect it will now stay fixed. If the barrier were pierced it seems to the ignorant eye that the landlocked lagoon would make a wonderful harbour, but a great deal of money has been spent on the foundations of a second Takoradi. At the moment there is no port on the Ivory Coast where ships can come up to the quay for loading; a great disadvantage, for the Ivory Coast, from the point of view of export, is by far the richest French colony in West Africa.

The whole of this colony from the coast to more than a hundred miles inland was covered with the primeval forest when the French occupied it at the beginning of this century. It was very sparsely inhabited by negroes, who gained a precarious living from hunting and cannibalism; their diet was supplemented by wild bananas and other fruits; the cola nut grew wild in the forest and they used to trade its fruit with the Dioula against salt and other necessities. For travelling on the numerous rivers they made pirogues from the trunks of the very light-wooded kapok trees. I do not know if they traded for iron or found it, but the latter seems probable, for the surface soil is laterite and there are probably small outcrops of pig-iron. Anyhow, they possessed hatchets, iron-pointed spears, with which they still hunt, and bows and arrows. They had a considerable knowledge of vegetable poisons. Despite their inferior arms, numbers and physique – the great number of the forest natives are tiny and uglier than monkeys – the local conditions made the pacification of the forest a very long and arduous business, which is not yet completed, for several regions are still not demilitarised. At first only the natural resources of the country were exploited; timber was cut and transported under fairly inhuman conditions by private exploiters; the government claimed the monopoly of ivory and skins. After the war the places where the timber had been felled were cleaned and enlarged and coffee was planted with great success; encouraged by a protective duty in the French market, this has proved the most profitable French colonial enterprise, and increasingly bigger areas are being given over to this cultivation. Given a certain amount of water and shade coffee is very easy to grow; the ground needs to be kept fairly clear, and once the shrub has started yielding, that is after four years, the old wood wants to be cut out; the gathering of the berries is a tedious business which requires a lot of workers during the season, but since the fruit is produced on the new wood it does not need the care which cocoa gathering does. The coffee plant is an uninteresting-looking shrub, with dark leaves rather like a sweet chestnut, but the bigger trees in the plantations are usually left standing, and it is only by its uniformity that cultivated land differs in aspect from the wild undergrowth. Other crops have also been introduced with varying success – cocoa, bananas, rice, cola, cotton, and fruit – chiefly by the initiative of the administration. If Europeans could live in the climate the colony would soon become prosperous and populous, but except in a few cases it seems impossible for white men to live there for more than two to three years at a stretch, and even so they seem in a very bad state physically; with the result that people come for as short a time as possible, with the intention of taking as much out of the colony, and putting in as little, as they can. The temperature is not very high – between 80 and 90 Fahrenheit – but the atmosphere is nearly saturated, so that one is in a perpetual vapour bath. I personally found this far less trying than the dry heat of the North; it merely made me lazy, whereas the dry heat made me nervous and irritable; I sweat very well and do not much mind being perpetually moist. But I am apparently exceptional, and the general experience is against mine. If the Ivory Coast were to be developed on the same lines as the Gold Coast it would probably become the more prosperous colony of the two; but the present policy is to keep the negro for cheap untrained labour; even leaving aside the question whether this labour will not become extinct fairly soon, it seems doubtful if the Ivory Coast will ever become successfully a second Kenya. Unless, of course, the increasing deforestation fundamentally changes the climate.

Grand Bassam was in the throes of town-moving when we arrived there, and we found that most of our business would have to be done at Abidjan. The bank, however, was still at Grand Bassam, and the cashier there, after offering me a ridiculously bad exchange rate, gave me five hundred francs too much (really about two hundred and fifty francs more than I should have received). I did not get away with the loot, however, for the harassed man caught us up just as we were leaving Abidjan. Since I felt he was cheating me – five francs in the pound off the official rate was surely excessive – I had not thought it necessary to return and point out his mistake. This is the only occasion on which I have not pointed out such an error; I am frequently being given too much change.

While we were lunching at Grand Bassam the chauffeurs discovered a Dahomeyan woman, a distant relation of Z's, who was keeping a restaurant and hotel for natives. She was one of those almost saintly women whom the negroes produce fairly constantly. She had been left a widow with two young daughters; entirely by her own efforts she had reared and educated these girls until they had become qualified mid-wives – the highest position a negro girl can obtain in the French colonies. Once they were settled she returned to Dahomey every year, bringing back from each visit some poor or unhappy youngster, whom she reared or educated until they were married or had found a situation. She had given fifteen people a start in life in this manner, and was constantly on the lookout for others in need. She knew Z was doing badly at the time in Europe, and wanted to pay his passage home and set him up as the manager of one of her plantations; besides her hotel she had been granted two plots of land to cultivate, and she thought it was more than an elderly and lonely woman could manage properly. Such disinterested and unassuming goodness is rather disconcerting; with this woman, as with Benga's sister Marie, I was at a loss to show the respect and admiration I felt.

Abidjan is a very new town, well designed and pretty; it already contains four thousand Europeans, more than twice the number of the whole Gold Coast. We stopped there only for a short time to fill in the necessary forms and make the necessary purchases; the suspicious deaths had occurred there, and I was afraid that if we stopped the night our movements might be controlled after; also it would have meant going to a hotel. So we went on about thirty miles to a small place called Dabou; nobody ever stopped there and the broken-down rest-house was nearly smothered in flowering plants.

The next day we made a considerable detour to visit Abengourou in order to see the king Boa Koassi, to whom we had a letter of introduction. He was reputed to be fabulously rich.

The rainy season had now fully set in, but the Gods were extra-ordinarily kind to us. Floods either subsided just before we arrived, or rose just after we had left. Rain fell either before we set out or after we had arrived, and only on one afternoon did the weather make us alter our plans, and then only for a couple of hours. If we had known anything about the average climate we should never have tried to visit the Ivory Coast during July, when it is said to be quite impassable. The chief advantage of the rains was that the countryside was far greener and more flowery, and the temperature much lower.

Although I never regained the first rapture of the journey down the Bia, I found constant pleasure in the journey through the forest. The great trees were of impressive majesty, and the rare flowers were curious and beautiful. Most of them were quite unknown to me, but I was able to identify the spectacular *Gloriosa superba Rothschildii*, like a climbing lily whose blossoms change as they age from the palest yellow to brick red, so that a single stem will present a dozen different tones; and the numerous pools were filled with pink, white and blue *Nymphoea stellata*. Except for a few bulbous plants and dull epiphytic orchids nearly all the flowers were on creepers. It was only in the Ivory Coast that Africa came up to what I expected a tropical landscape to look like. There was also the expectation of seeing animals; and although we saw only infrequent monkeys and antelope, there was always the hope that we might see more of an elephant than its spoor.

So as not to frighten Boa Koassi we went straight to the administrator on arriving at Abengourou; the administrator was away for the day and we were kindly received by his assistant, who gave us an empty room in the courthouse to live in, and sent us to Boa Koassi with an interpreter. We were very disappointed when we saw him; he was a mean little man, poorly dressed, with a disproportionately big head, and yellow heavily lidded eyes; he looked like a very cunning and calculating small French pawnbroker. His living-room was uglily furnished in very expensive gilt 'antique' furniture. He must have been very rich, for he had imported a large saloon car, and when he dressed up he was covered with unworked or badly worked nuggets of gold, like small lumps of coal. Even his sandals were golden.

His territory adjoined the Gold Coast, and the customs and beliefs (including matriarchy) were very similar on both sides of the frontier. The French had tried to install him and use his influence, as the English had done with the stool holders (local chiefs), but although he was on very good terms with the authorities, who were constantly placing more people under his jurisdiction, and had even given him a seat on the native council, he was treated by his subjects with a disrespect and rudeness which was quite unparalleled; he was pushed about and knocked into far more than any commoner. Except for his household, which included a couple of dwarfs who were presumably buffoons, nobody saluted him or paid any attention to him. It was rather pathetic. He promised to organise a number of dances for us, but needed twenty-four hours' notice, as some of the people had to come from a distance. He would not talk about his religion at all, and it seemed as if the intervening day was going to be wasted.

In the event it was fully occupied. Benga met some Senegalese traders who knew his family, and through them we got a good deal of information; moreover, the administrator returned and invited me to lunch with him and the government inspector who had arrived in the district. The lunch was magnificent and the administrator charming, but the inspector was somewhat disconcerting. He was a very old man, near seventy I should guess, and extremely difficult to talk to. He didn't exactly murmur 'bread and butter, bread and butter' all the time, like the White Queen of whom he reminded me, but he kept on interjecting 'au contraire, au contraire', which was upsetting until I realised that it was entirely automatic and meaningless. He sometimes varied this with 'mais non' or 'très interessant', applied equally inappositely. He seemed to believe that I had hidden sources of information about European and colonial politics and kept posing me completely unanswerable problems. He called me young man and patted me all over in quite a nice paternal spirit; and from time to time he said, 'You must tell everybody how much the administration has done for agriculture'. He considered this so important that he sent two messages to the same effect within the next twenty-four hours, and came round three times himself to remind me. I think I must have made a good impression, or perhaps saved the administrator an unpleasant tête-à-tête, for we were treated with the utmost cordiality for the rest of our stay.

The greater part of the day was spent in conversation and interrogation, varied by palmistry and amulet making on my part,* and about nine in the evening we were preparing to go to bed when we heard the distant sounds of a tomtom. We set out to trace the sound down, as

---

* The chief results of these and similar conversations are embodied in Chapter 6 of Book Three.

we always did in similar cases, and eventually found at the other end of the village that a musical evening was being held in a courtyard to mark the end of a period of mourning. The people belonged to the Niamaklé tribe, and there was a certain amount of dancing by the young men. They are already very short and they dance crouching so that their bottoms nearly touch the ground, holding their pagne forward with both hands, and doing a very quick and complicated shimmy shuffle. The dancing was only spasmodic, the chief business being singing and drinking raffia, a not unpleasant but very intoxicating beverage. At first the people were frightened that I might be an official or policeman, but luckily one of the people I had made amulets for was present, and I was quickly accepted and made one of the party, and nearly drowned in raffia. The details of the evening are somewhat vague, but I have the general impression that a good time was had by all, and that I experienced one of the most enjoyable and successful parties I remember. It was rather late when we were carefully escorted back to our room.

By the time we were ready the next morning the dancers had assembled. The Nana Boa Koassi, chef supérieur de l'Indénié, king of the Agni, had done us proud, and had got together the dancers of five different tribes, each with its own orchestra.*

* It may be of some interest to know the population figures of the Gold Coast and British Nigeria. I am indebted for these figures to Mr Ronald Burghes.

GOLD COAST (area 91,690 square miles)

1901	1911	1921	1931
1,474,000	1,504,000	2,298,000	over 3,000,000

NIGERIA (area 373,078 square miles)

1901	1911	1921	1931
13,607,000	17,127,000	18,631,000	19,928,000

Africans Dance

Hyram's Dance

AFRICANS DANCE. They dance for joy, and they dance for grief; they dance for love and they dance for hate; they dance to bring prosperity and they dance to avert calamity; they dance for religion and they dance to pass the time. Far more exotic than their skin and their features is this characteristic of dancing; the West African negro is not so much the blackish man or the cannibal man or the primitive man as he is the man who expresses every emotion with rhythmical bodily movement.

Perhaps all that paragraph should be put into the past tense, or rather into the passing tense. Africans used to dance until their families and clans were destroyed, until the constantly gnawing anxiety about taxes and military service and distant work clouded their lives, until missionaries forbade dancing as heathenish, and administrators stopped dancing because it disturbed their sleep or prevented people working, until they lost the physical strength necessary for the dance. They still dance in small villages where there is no administrator, no missionary, no white man. They dance with a verve, a precision, an ingenuity which no other race can show; the smallest group has its own ballet, distinct in costume, movement and tempo from any other.

It is very difficult for Europeans to understand the place dancing takes in negro lives. Except for scattered survivals of the old 'witch' religion over Europe – in parts of Somerset they still sing and dance round fruit trees at midwinter to make them bear – dancing for us is essentially a sub-erotic pastime. It is a method for people of different sexes to get together in public. Even the ballet is for the most part an occasion to show off young ladies' legs – and more recently young gentlemen's torsos – in the most alluring manner possible, with all the assistance that music, costume and scenery can provide. The more

Africa Dances

'serious' ballets are pantomimes performed to music with an elaborate and generally graceful technique of expression; but they are essentially alien to the audience; people watch them to be 'improved' or entertained, and not because they have any intimate significance for them. And in recent years, except for the rather sterile classical ballets, the dancing has taken a second place; under Diaghilev the scenery and costumes were the really novel items – before the war the barbaric splendours of Bakst, and after the ingenious inventions of the Parisian painters; under Massine everything is being subordinated to the effort of making us properly grasp the more obvious structural elements of quasi-sacred symphonies.

For the negro the dancing has always held first place; the music, such as it is, and the decorative arts have all been evolved to supplement the dance; and except for sculpture in certain cases they are still subsidiary.

The basis of negro music is the drum, which is very probably a negro invention. The variety of drums is almost unlimited, going from the huge 'speaking' drum to the tiny tambour which is hung round the neck; every possible combination of sound which can be produced by striking a taut skin, a piece of wood or metal, with the hand, another piece of wood or metal, or any other instrument, has been developed and differentiated to a pitch which is far too subtle for European ears to grasp; an orchestra of, say, four different drums will for the negro have a variety of tone where we can only find monotony. It is almost impossible for a European to understand the speaking drums, which apparently imitate directly spoken speech. The function of the drums for dancing is to set and alter the rhythms; a great number, though by no means all, are syncopated; and for the negro each rhythm has an emotional appeal which we with our bloated ears cannot appreciate, any more than we could appreciate the violent effects which Plato claims for the Lydian and the Dorian modes.

The drums are sometimes supplemented and occasionally supplanted by an instrument like a xylophone (the balafron) which has a more or less whole-scale octave, or the cora, a six-stringed instrument somewhere between a guitar and a harp; to the European ear these instruments

244

are far more musical and pleasant, for African music is founded on an approximate octave, and has consequently none of the puzzling subtlety of Asiatic music. These are the only African instruments I came across capable of a variety of notes; the numerous metal and wooden percussive instruments and the hollowed horns and flutes are capable only of variation in volume, not tone. I did not find any stopped wind instruments.

Except for the syncopated rhythm there is no connection whatsoever, as far as I can see, between African and American negro music. The better sort of jazz depends chiefly for its appeal on subtleties of harmony and chords, and particularly on the effective use of wind instruments. Musically Duke Ellington is far nearer to Paris than the Congo. It has already been remarked that Russian music, particularly of the first half of the nineteenth century, appeals to negroes far more than jazz; one can far more easily imagine them dancing to *Les Noces* than to *Mood Indigo*. There was a certain resemblance between the Russian and the negro peasant; they lived in a similar landscape, their struggle for life and their outlook on the world were not dissimilar; and the religion of orthodox Russians, though not so overwhelming, played a very large part in their lives. They both possess the same patience and passivity; the actions of both are unpredictable by logical civilised people; and until the abolition of serfdom the Russians, it appears, had an equally slight feeling for individuality. In the negroes who have prospered under European influence the risk of a 'kulak' class can be clearly seen.

To much dancing singing forms an important accompaniment. The most general form is for one singer to improvise and for the chorus to take up the refrain; but in some tribes there are two choruses which challenge and answer one another. This is most common among the Sérère to the east of Senegal. It is the nearest approach that I ever saw to the drama. There are a number of traditional tunes, some of them very pleasant (I am told a number have been recorded); they have a very long and elastic melodic line, and are also founded on a whole-tone scale. I think chords are produced entirely by accident; and the only counter-point arises when one group of singers commences before the other has finished. Occasionally there is unaccompanied singing – songs of praise, serenades and the like; the effect is not unpleasant.

African dancers can be roughly divided into two groups: professional and amateur dancers. In the more primitive communities there are nearly always professional dancers, people who are supported by the community to do their dancing for them; these professional dancers are generally young men; girls are usually professional dancers only to the beginning of puberty. The presence of professional dancers does not prevent the rest of the community dancing; but on the whole they confine themselves to chorus work, or to relatively simple round dances. Warriors are nearly always professional dancers; for various religious reasons they cannot take part in the agricultural or domestic works of the community, and when they are not fighting they dance. Priests also are generally dancers.

Every tribe has special costumes for dancing, which are generally very different from everyday wear. Usually more of the body is covered; and the costume is essentially decorative and unpractical. Garters which rattle and emphasise the rhythm are common to almost all tribes, and cowries (formerly a sign of value if not 'money' in the European sense) are much employed. But the variation in the effective use of coloured seeds, shells, beads, feathers, leather plain and dyed, cloth, animal pelts, tree bark and leaves is so enormous that an elaborate tome could be constructed to catalogue the different costumes.

Masked dancers occupy a special category. All masked dances were originally exclusively religious functions, and the greater number still remain so. Today in many tribes women cannot look at masks without risking death, and I once created a panic by holding up a mask I had bought to try to explain what it was I wanted. When the masks came to the village for the cannibal's funeral (which will be described later), the women not only shut themselves in their huts, they also swathed their heads in cloths. But in most communities women are allowed to see them, though they cannot touch or wear them.

The late Professor William Ridgeway, the most inspiring teacher I ever had, wrote a long book entitled *The Dramas and Dramatic Dances of non-European races in special reference to the origin of Greek Tragedy*, in which, by the accumulation of an enormous amount of evidence, he seeks to prove that all masked dances – and the habit is worldwide – are representations of dead men, and the masked Greek tragedies are an elaboration of ancestor worship. As far as his argument applies to Greece I think it is convincing, but my experience in Africa does not bear him out at all; indeed, it completely contradicts him; the masks never represent dead men, but always spirits, or fetishes; dances representing dead men are done, but the dead man is always represented by a dancer entirely covered in cloth; not a scrap of skin is shown and the features are always left extremely vague; they are indicated at most by vague designs in shells or beads. I saw four groups of 'dead' dancers altogether, belonging to different tribes; they were all dressed in much the same way, and a couple had hollow whistles, which gave out a very ghostly hooting noise, attached to the inside of the cloth face-covering. Ghosts are always described as white.

The mask is the fetish. It is not sacred as an object, but because it is filled with the spirit of the fetish; and the man who wears it is no longer a member of the tribe, but the fetish walking. This is the reason for the fiction that nobody knows who wears the masks; in a small community, where every member is known and can be recognised by a dozen idiosyncrasies, it is logically an absurd statement; but since matter is essentially fluid under the influence of spirits, it can be said with truth that although A is absent, it is impossible to know who is under the mask, for the spirit may have transformed the body and soul of the A we know into any guise. For the same reason only special people can see a man unmask; his transformation from the vessel of the spirit to an everyday person must not be witnessed.

A valid distinction has been drawn between paleolithic and neolithic art; the former is as realistic as possible – a bison as like a real bison as can be – the second essentially communicative and symbolical, an approach to generalisation and picture-writing. Most negro art is, to my mind, in the neolithic stage. As far as their drawing is concerned I think it is indisputable; their intention is not to represent but to communicate; the distortions and simplifications are an approach to hieroglyphics; they want to suggest the idea of a snake, not to make one.

I think the same principle is at the back of their sculpture. Some of the most primitive races make realistic representations of people and animals which are extraordinarily lifelike and vivid, almost European in feeling; but the greater number of masks are unrealistic, and for a European mind mostly impossible to interpret. In common with most people today I find a great deal of negro sculpture extremely stimulating and satisfying aesthetically; the strange compositions, distortions and symmetry, and the use of materials revolutionised the European conception of painting and sculpture in the first decade of this century; but I am certain that for the negroes these qualities, with the possible exception of symmetry, were entirely accidental and irrelevant; their chief object was to communicate as vividly as possible. As for the 'abstract' art which was evolved from it – that academic cul-de-sac, which after three years of exciting scientific discoveries became a refuge for frightened but pretentious decorators with no idea beyond a pattern – and which was fathered on to the unfortunate negro, such an idea had never occurred to them. Even their purely decorative motifs have a usually fairly obvious communicative meaning; cloth and plaster are lined to look like wood, in much the same way as the first stone columns were shaped like trees; and although we cannot always interpret the decoration I believe there is always a meaning there, though in some traditional motifs the original meaning may not be known to the decorator.

Except for the adornment of certain ceremonial objects sculpture is generally connected with the mask and the dance. The few carved objects which cannot be worn are for the most part the guardians of masks in their resting-places. There are a few idols – mostly of coloured clay or plaster – which are objects of permanent worship, but I found them only in two places and in each they were specially for women. The small wooden and brass figures which a few tribes have were, I think, at any rate originally sacrifice substitutes, exactly similar in function to the figurines in Egyptian and Chinese tombs, though in this case dedicated to the spirits or else representations of ancestors. Although some negro tribes have rituals to commemorate outstanding events in their history (performances which corroborate Ridgeway's theory) it is, I think, very seldom indeed that the memory of a dead man as an individual survives him many years; although there is no way of proving what characters are represented in these sacred charades a comparison with other ritual leads to the strong presumption that it is the conquering spirit rather than the conquering man who is remembered – Jehovah rather than Joshua.

The sculpture of masks is limited by the fact that the finished object has to be able to be carried on the head for a considerable time. This affects the weight only slightly – most negroes are used to carrying sixty pounds and more on their head, and it is arguable that their extraordinarily graceful and dignified movement and carriage derives from this custom – but it puts certain limitations on the bulk. If the total mass is much larger than a human head, a balance of weight and stress is necessary to preserve its equilibrium. Some masks are literally yards high and broad, and the practical considerations generally produce a very satisfactory combination. It is worth noting that masks are nearly always worn over the forehead, and not over the face as with us; although the wearer bends his neck slightly under the weight, they are very seldom worn quite upright; and in Europe when masks are placed flat on a shelf or against a wall the perspective is usually distorted; they should be looked at about thirty degrees out of the perpendicular (or sixty out of the horizontal); at this angle many apparent distortions – long noses and small mouths, for instance – regain their proper proportions.

The simplest masks are small fairly realistic representations of animals and people. They are mostly used for comparatively comic dancing (though this does not make them less sacred: cf. the satyric drama). As the masks get larger they become less and less realistic; human faces are endowed with extra eyes and ears, on the same principle of superhuman powers as the many-membered Hindu gods. Then on to roughly human faces are grafted animal features – the nose of the dog, the eyes of the bird, the sense organs of animals which are further developed than man's. The next complication is the superimposed image, which

Africa Dances

Salvador Dali claims, I think incorrectly, as the prerogative of paranoiac vision – the blending of two or more distinct realities into a single whole. Sometimes the two images are represented realistically – a bird is carved on top of a face – but more often the different visions are 'fused'. The best, largest and oldest mask I brought back is a representation of the attributes of the whole of animal creation; superimposed on a very roughly human face are the horns of the antelope, the boar, the hippopotamus and the elephant; the mouth is that of a crocodile; on the forehead is a small toucan pecking a large chameleon. (This mask was very sacred and was seen in public only once a year; the method by which I acquired it was not very creditable either to me or to the vendor.) Most masks are simpler than this, and have only the characteristics of two or three creatures 'fused'. But some are so complicated that they are quite indecipherable: a snake looking in all directions comes out like a swastika; some other geometrical constructions, in particular the very high masks, still remain unexplained for me. But I am certain that there is an explanation for every one of them, though they may be only slightly representative of objects; they may be intended chiefly to convey the idea of speed or strength, or power, through an accentuation of these qualities in the object endowed with them; at Javara, for example, the vulture was represented by two enormous beaks about four feet long pointing back and front; they were joined by a vague Janus head surmounted by a little manikin; the important thing about the vulture was his strong beak and the spirit controlling him. If I had not had this explained to me I should probably have considered it an abstract construction, for the completely non-naturalistic colour decoration was extremely distracting.

All the negro sculpture I saw was coloured in a very arbitrary fashion. The negroes have a fairly good selection of vegetable and mineral dyes, but they do not seem to apply colours with any view to what they are trying to imitate. The Cambridge School of Anthropology seem to have proved satisfactorily that uncivilised people can discriminate colours as well as untrained Europeans, so that the explanation of racial colour-blindness is as inapt as the explanation of collective stupidity.

I think the ancient Greeks can give the clue to this problem (as I think the negroes can give several clues to the problems of ancient Greece – for example, the behaviour of the priestess at the oracle of Delphi resembles strangely that of the fetishers of Dahomey). As far as I know it has never been pointed out that ancient Greek possesses no words for colour, but only for intensity of light – *chloros*: pale (green or yellow), *phoinix*: bright (red or purple), *poikilos*: dappled (any combination of colours), *oinops*: dull (grey or tawny or slate-coloured), *huakinthos*: dark (navy blue or iron grey) – the list could be extended through all the colour adjectives. The point is that every attempt to give these words a colour meaning, as the dictionaries and translators do, breaks down on application, and the Greeks are either made out to be unobservant fools or to possess a terribly inexact language – neither of which suppositions is supported by the other evidence. The explanation is, I think, that the Greeks were not interested in colour, as such, but only in the intensity of light refracted. They must have looked at colour rather as a dog does (or a photographer) – experiments show that a dog will not distinguish between red and green of equal refraction, but will quickly become aware of differences in tone which are imperceptible to the human eye. This theory is borne out by the remains of colour on some of their statues – horses' manes are coloured blue and green, for example – and Petronius somewhere mentions a monochrome picture by Apelles – an improbable abstraction by such a realist (the birds were said to peck the grapes he painted) unless colour was supremely unimportant. Anyone who knows the Greek landscape, with its relative absence of colour and intensity of light, will realise that this supposition is not so far-fetched as it seems.

It is probable that the negroes have the same attitude to colour, but I have no means of knowing. Their languages on the whole employ comparisons rather than adjectives, so no evidence can be gained that way, and my eye has got so accustomed to colour that I cannot even attempt any other approach; indeed, I doubt if any Western European could. Colour is as much a part of our world as causality; it is almost impossible for us to rid ourselves of either prejudice.

Most masks have holes pierced round the edges which will hold a fringe of raffia falling to the waist and completely covering the face and body; the dancers usually also have heavy raffia skirts, and their arms and legs are covered with different wrappings, so that no skin shall be seen; so swathed, and encumbered by the masks, their dancing is heavily restricted; except in one or two cases they can do little more than a syncopated trot. The moon-masked Goli dance with small sticks, with which they hit the beast skins on their backs and the nearby audience; the Wobé and the Niabois, like nightmare caricatures of the Empress Eugénie, are so clumsy that they have to be led about. I saw a large number of different masked dancers, but on the whole it is their appearance, rather than what they do, that is remarkable and interesting.

In my notes I have descriptions of more than forty completely different dances I saw, excluding the fetish dances of Dahomey, and the few already incidentally described. We saw the greater number of these in or near the Ivory Coast in a little over a month, never going more than ten miles off a road. (This was owing to the difficulty of getting about. We weren't equipped for travelling on foot any distance, and the hammock is probably the most unpleasant method of travelling yet invented; you feel like Captain Spalding, or something out of Peter Arno, and you are more jolted even than by a camel.) Anyone who could travel across country should find almost infinite variety. But, alas, dancing is almost as impossible to describe in words as music; what may be enthralling to see may be more than tedious to read of. The only way in which an adequate record of these extraordinary spectacles can be preserved is with a sound camera, for naturally the music is an integral part, unless Benga can realise his ambition and find an impresario who will enable him to bring a negro ballet to Europe, a spectacle which would be as much a revelation as the Russian ballet twenty years ago; but besides the financial difficulties there are also the administrative ones; negroes who in French territory are allowed to die as they like are immediately surrounded by an almost impenetrable barrier of regulations and precautions as soon as there is a chance of their earning any money outside. Since there seems slight hope of the public seeing for themselves the dances either in reality or in reproduction, I am going to give a description of a few of the most typical and dramatic dances, and shall hope to be brief without being tedious. The majority of the dances I am going to describe either took place at night, or for some other reason couldn't be photographed; on the whole the photographs are sufficiently explanatory. It may be remarked that all dances are directed towards the drums, which represent as it were the altar or focal point.

1. *Stylisation of Human Sacrifice* (Dalabani, cercle de Bougouni). This dance took place in a little riverside village by moonlight. Additional light was given by piles of burning straw. The music consisted entirely of drums, starting very slowly and working up with a gradual crescendo to almost unbearable speed, rather like the second act of the *Sacre du Printemps*. It was the most rigidly formal dance I saw in Africa. The dance opened with a young boy holding a long stick to the end of which was attached a small white pennant; he went round the dancing space very slowly several times waving his flag in every direction and then retired. He returned, followed by two young men dressed in white shirts and drawers each carrying standing on his shoulders a little girl aged about six, dressed in a flaxen wig, red coat covered with cowries and glass and little bells and long blue trousers. These were followed by an old witch naked to the waist and dressed in a white pagne, and holding a sinisterly empty calabash in her hand which she waved towards the dancers all the time. Also during the whole dance the flag-bearer circled round the dancers. At first the little girls waved their arms and heads rhythmically, while the young men bore them round the circle, doing a complicated and syncopated step with their feet. But as the rhythm mounted the little girls lost the perpendicular position; they hung upside down and were thrown about as if they were dolls; they seemed jointless, but their hands and heads still marked the rhythm. At last the climax was reached; suddenly and very violently the little girls were thrown towards the tomtoms, held by their ankles at arm's length, and were then swung in circles till they almost touched the ground. Just before they actually touched it they were suddenly lifted, completely limp, and carried away over the young men's shoulders upside down. The witch followed, carefully holding her empty calabash as if it were overflowing; last of all

went the standard-bearer, still carrying his flag. The drumbeats died away.

So impressed were we with this dance that we had it repeated. Not a single movement was altered. The villagers said that all they knew about it was that it was sacred; but I think the little girls' almost military dress – the only colour in the scene – very suggestive.

Somewhat similar, and even more exciting, though aesthetically far less satisfying on account of the lack of form, are the dancers of Danané on the Liberian frontier, already described by W. Seabrook. The dancers consist of four little boys dressed in tiny loincloths and mitre-like head-dresses of feathers and leather, and almost completely naked and extremely muscular young men. The little boys stand on a mat, nodding their heads continuously, and occasionally doing some slight acrobatics on the ground – somersaults, cartwheels, walking on hands and feet bent backwards and so on; the children are extraordinarily supple. But the real dancing is the most extraordinary adagio I have ever seen. The men throw the children like balls, kick them on to their heads with a backward jerk of the foot, whirl them around by a single wrist or ankle, and generally perform the most extraordinary feats at what appears to be very great risk of life and limb. All the young men have knives; and the climax of the dance is when one man throws a child at exactly the same moment as another throws a knife, so that the knife passes between the child's legs, and seems as though it transpierces him. The two dancers stand about ten yards apart, and the jugglery appeared so realistic and dangerous that, though I had a camera, I never had sufficient presence of mind to release the spring; at each repetition my heart went into my mouth, for fear that this time it would be fatal. Sometimes one man held two knives, points upward, and the child was thrown on to them; the man moved his arms just sufficiently to catch the child in the crook of his elbows. Occasionally, I think, the illusion was produced by sleight of hand with the knives. For pure thrill I have never seen any music-hall turn to touch this performance; they should make a fortune in Europe, except that possibly the censors might think it bad for us, as they did with the Egyptian fakirs a few years ago.

In their way the old men who accompanied these dancers were just as extraordinary and even more fantastic. Their costume was the oddest assemblage of inappropriate articles I have ever imagined. They had feather head-dresses like the children, but decorated with fringes of bells; the rest of their body was covered with a foundation of cloth, to which were attached an endless variety of skulls, bones, skins, amulets, beads and vegetable matter. They bristled with knives and spears in animal-pelt sheaths; they had false moustaches and beards of straw which they held in their teeth, and their faces were arbitrarily painted red, white and yellow in peculiar patterns. They looked as if the Fratellini had dressed up as the wildest savages with more than their usual ingenuity; and they behaved very like that. They pulled the most grotesque grimaces and indulged in obviously very funny backchat; they sang and danced in grotesque manner, even parodying the dancers they accompanied; they indulged in a good deal of funny but indecorous pantomime. I never met anything which in any way resembled them elsewhere. I wonder if such grotesques are common the other side of the Liberian frontier – that mysterious hinterland?

2. *Fertility Dance* (Ouangaladougou, S.E. Ivory Coast). We got to Ouangaladougou only by mistake; we were given false directions about the route and found ourselves with night falling in the vague middle of nowhere; the inhabitants were very primitive, both men and women being naked except for a loincloth. Since we had no adequate map and a thunderstorm was threatening we decided to stop at the first conglomeration which offered any sort of shelter. This happened to be Ouangaladougou, and although the rest-barn was infested with live-stock it did provide us with, at any rate, a leaky roof. There was a scribe who was able to act as our interpreter, and the chief very kindly presented us with victuals, which consisted of honey complete with bees, and a couscous which was almost solid pepper. We learned that there was to be a big dance that night, because the first rains of the season were coming. (The storm actually broke before midnight.) It was only a few nights after the dance at Dalabani, and the moon was

still nearly full, but it was often obscured by clouds, and the illumination was fitful.

The dance took place on a very large piece of bare ground in front of the village, which may have been a prepared field; a large assortment of drums was grouped in the centre. The first group of dancers was about a score of young men, naked except for a most exiguous loincloth and garters; they held rattles in their hands. They started dancing fairly close to the tomtoms, making a small circle; each time a round was completed the steps, always elaborate and complicated, were varied. The rest of the population stood around in a larger circle, singing some sort of chant to which the dancers replied. Gradually these onlookers added themselves to the dancing ring, first the older men, then the older women, then young women, and finally little children who could barely toddle, but who could dance with perfect rhythm. Except for the original young men the dancers did not indulge in a variety of steps, but followed with a sort of syncopated shuffle, singing loudly. The score of dancers became more and more ecstatic, doing increasingly complicated steps, cartwheels, forward somersaults and so on. When there were no onlookers except us, and the circle of dancers was right on the boundary of the field, a number of strangely dressed old men ran into the centre. The light was too bad to be able to make out the details of their costumes, but they showed a very odd silhouette. They held cymbals in their hands and had different whistles in their mouths, and in turn they went through an exceedingly realistic and well observed pantomime of the copulation of various beasts and birds. Each man represented a different animal, and his whistle had a more or less appropriate note. These dances were extraordinarily impressive and serious; the old men mimed so well that they almost became goats, or cocks, or bulls before our eyes; the movements were so essential that the body which made them seemed unimportant. When all had finished they made a ring round the drums, and then four little girls, naked except for a necklace of red seeds and a tiny apron, broke through the ring of dancers, approximately from the four quarters of the compass. Very slowly and seriously they danced their way to the centre, keeping exact time with one another. They danced almost squatting on the ground, holding their tiny aprons in one hand, and scattering imaginary seeds with the other; they progressed with a sort of zigzag, a few steps to the right, then as many to the left. They arrived in front of the old men together and knelt on the ground; and each old man (?priest) blessed them in turn, laying both hands on their heads. Four of them then picked up the little girls and carried them off on their shoulders out of the ring. During all this time the big ring of dancers had been circling and singing, shouting loudly after each clap of thunder. As the storm got nearer they shouted louder and louder, until suddenly the first drops of rain fell; the dancers broke the ring and rushed to the tomtoms, and with the drummers at the head the whole group returned to the village in a mass.

I was too tired to go and see if there was any further ceremony elsewhere.

3. *Hunting Dance* (Yammossoukro, S. Ivory Coast). This was only a semi-sacred dance, and I forget why no photographs were taken; perhaps because it took place over too big an area. There were only three performers, two hunters armed with bows and arrows and knives, and an antelope. The antelope was danced by a boy about fifteen, with a small antelope mask (realistic except that it was painted purple) on his head with a piece of dappled material under it, which covered his face and body; a straw tail was attached to one end of it and he had the usual jangles on his legs. His knees were permanently bent and his body held forward, so that he was able to see the ground under the cloth which fell away from his face; but the mask was so placed that the antelope seemed to be looking upwards all the time. The hunters stuck a tuft of grass attached to a stake in the middle of an open piece of ground, and then crouched in cover among the bushes and people surrounding it. The antelope came forward very timidly, sniffing the air, and starting at every tiny sound and shadow; one of the hunters moved so that his knife made a sound, and the antelope scampered off out of sight. It came back very cautiously, scurrying from shadow to shadow, until it arrived again at the open place. Suddenly it saw the planted grass, stiffened and then made towards it; a few yards from it it was overcome with timidity and hurried

to cover. This scene was repeated several times; the grass looked so tempting, but there was something wrong with the smell, and the position was too exposed. At last greed got the better of caution and the antelope sidled up to the grass, acting as though it had no intention of touching it; suddenly, when it was opposite, it darted towards it, and at the same moment the two hunters pulled their bows. The antelope was badly wounded, but it was able to stagger a few paces away; then it suddenly collapsed on its side, moving its arms and legs meaninglessly, quivered and lay still. The hunters came out of their cover and cut off the straw tail with their knives.

The pantomime was most exquisitely observed and acted. It seemed spontaneous, but could hardly be so, for the rhythm of the drums and rumba rattles was carefully observed.

From the point of view of observation and mimicry the monkey dancers near Odienné were even more remarkable. They had sad-looking monkey masks of polished ebony lined with silver, and were covered in costumes of dark raffia and monkey's fur, leaving their hands and feet bare. They huddled on the ground, searched one another for fleas, scuffled – they were more like monkeys than monkeys ever are. For pure mimicry I have never seen anything like it; but it was not a dance. It had no form, no beginning or end; they were just monkeys. The musicians who accompanied them were extremely strange; they were bird men, Papagenos. They wore a very loose sort of cloak falling to the ground, entirely covered with big birds' feathers, brown, black and white, all pointing downwards, so that they seemed entirely covered in some unknown plumage; their heads were also covered in feathers and a cascade of feathers fell over their necks; over their face fell a waist-deep cloth mask, embroidered in an elaborate and rather Minoan design in cowries; two holes for the eyes were the only realistic features. Under this mask they played a doleful sort of shawm which emitted a fitful piping noise. They were the only musicians I ever saw in costume.

4. *Totem Dance* (Javara, Upper Volta). At Houndé we had been given some completely inaccurate information by an administrator who did not want to quit the company of some extremely flamboyant described-themselves-as-artistes and most of the day we had followed a wild-goose chase after the masked dancers for which the region was famous. At last I asked a very thin, nearly naked, negro in a small village where good dancers could be found; he directed us to Javara, about six miles off the road, where the people were of the tiny Nouna race; the Mossi don't use masks. Our informant had recently finished his military service, and had returned home to find that most of his friends had emigrated to the Gold Coast, and those that were left had taken the best wives and land. He embarrassed me by bursting into tears when I gave him a couple of francs; he explained that he sweated blood to get the money for the taxes and yet couldn't manage to collect ten francs; I gave him the other eight and left him dumb and staggering; I was afraid afterwards the sudden relief had been too much for him.

Javara is a large conglomeration in a bare space surrounded by thin acacia scrub. It consists of a number of groups of mud-built houses, each group belonging to one clan with a special animal totem. The houses are built somewhat in the Moorish fashion, with flat roofs which are used for household tasks and for sitting on in the evening; a few buildings had two storeys. There were an extraordinary number of red albinos among the Nouna. Opposite the central group of buildings was a large open space with a pit in the middle; all the paths of the village debouched on to this space, and it was from a roof in the centre group – the chief's clan – that we watched the dancing. The chief, Nibili, was a very pleasant person and extremely generous to us; the chauffeurs took his name as type of the most desirable kind of chief; the one at Tenkodogo was the worst.

The dancers were about a dozen masked men, one for each totem group, and a master of the masks. The orchestra consisted of a number of very thin narrow drums beaten with curved canes, and several flutelike instruments. Besides perfectly enormous and very lovely masks, highly stylised and coloured red, white and black, the masked dancers were dressed in loose raffia pyjamas coloured brown and black, very bulky;

attached to the mask was a mop of brown raffia, falling over the head and shoulders to the waist. The masked men carried two long pointed sticks, which they used somewhat after the manner of ski-sticks, making enormous jumps with them; these sticks had a band of metal jangles round the middle. The master of the masks was naked except for a tiny flesh-coloured loincloth; he continually smothered himself with dust so that he looked dazzlingly white.

Each masked dancer performed in turn; and while he danced all the onlookers belonging to that totem-clan reproduced his gestures with tiny unconscious movements. The stork or the crocodile (or whatever animal it might be) would come out from his quarter very proud and haughty, jumping about and waving his sticks; everybody near would be terrified and run away from him, except the orchestra and the master of the masks, who followed him and egged him on. As no one dared approach him the mask became more superb and wild, doing the strangest acrobatic feats and waving his head backwards and forwards; the master of the masks encouraged him with gesture and pantomime. At last his movements became so uncontrolled that he fell to the ground, literally dazed; the master of the masks would go through the appropriate pantomime of stalking and killing the animal and would take away his sticks, which he gave to the orchestra; all the little children of that totem would run at the fallen masker and pull tufts off his clothes, and then would lead him crestfallen back to his quarter.

This pantomime was gone through with every mask in turn until only the master of the masks was left. This man was a dancer of extraordinary ingenuity and technique; for the three hours during which the ceremony went on he danced continually, sometimes dramatically, and sometimes in a burlesque fashion, making wicked mockery of Mohammedans and Christians at their worship, of soldiers and hunters, of different animals. He had a great command of expressive gesture, and could communicate over a considerable distance the various moods or people he was miming. He had a command of stage technique raised to a pitch of virtuosity which I have never seen equalled by a professional dancer. I am quite at a loss to understand the underlying symbolism of the performance, which appears to run counter to all that has been recorded of totemism.*

5. *Virtuosity Dancers.* The dances described above were the only considerable ones I witnessed which had sufficient dramatic content, as it were a scenario, to make it possible to give even a halting account of the movement in them. By far the greater number of dances, and the most impressive, were 'abstract', 'classical', just dancing. It might be possible with a strictly technical vocabulary to give some description of them, but I do not think it would be worth while; it would be making a gay thing heavy, a simple thing abstruse, an enjoyment tedious. After all, I am not a professional critic.

And yet what astounding dancers some of them are! The little girls of Duékoué and Man, dressed in tiny skirts of coloured leather strips, and covered with necklaces and with feathers in their hair; they are gay and wild dancers, with an enormous repertoire of movement and expression, grotesque and exciting, little Josephine Bakers. Or the male athletes in the same region, extraordinarily muscular, and looking rather ridiculous in the same coquettish and sketchy costumes as the little girls, performing acrobatic feats which would bring an American or European audience to their feet – pirouettes, somersaults, backward jumps, forward *sauts perilleux*, the tourniquet – I do not know how many other named and unnamed miracles of movement. Or the Dô dancers of Yammossoukro, the dance which is so sacred that no woman can see it, where young men, naked under raffia skirts, dance with a tiny drum in their hands, accompanying themselves while they spring and jump as if gravity had no effect on them. Or the Baulé dancers, with their extraordinary splayed headdress of ostrich feathers and their grass skirts, who in troupes of eight perform in absolute unison a dance of such controlled savagery that the eye can barely follow the precise and extravagant movements. Or the Dioula women with their gaudy clothes and head-cloths who jump and

---

* Monsieur Leiris suggests that the dance represents a totemic sacrifice, which can be paralleled elsewhere.

spin like a top. Or – or – or – the list could be continued indefinitely. Africans dance. They dance wonderfully. The Singhalese, the Balinese, the Cambodians dance more subtly, more dramatically; but as far as I have seen their range is limited and their invention small compared with the negroes. Africans have only one art, but to what a pitch they have brought it! First and last, Africans dance.

Finale

I WAS TOLD THAT SEVERAL YEARS AGO an administrator and his wife stopped among the Goro for a few days, so that the administrator could settle up all the long-outstanding affairs of the neighbourhood. The tribe is thinly scattered over a large area of the forest, and the administrator had to travel considerable distances; since journeying through the forest is somewhat arduous, he left his good lady behind him on one occasion when he had to be away for some days, putting her into the charge of the village chiefs. They took their responsibility very seriously, and would frequently look into the rest-house to see how the lady was doing. What was their consternation when looking in one afternoon shortly after midday they saw the woman lying on a bed, breathing stertorously and heavily flushed! Realising that she was near death, they quite simply and unassumingly did their duty. Some days later the administrator returned, summoned the village chiefs and asked for his wife. Proud of the *savoir vivre* they had shown the spokesman replied, 'Master, your wife was dying, so we cut her up and sold her, so that there should be no waste. Here is all the money we got from her; we haven't kept a penny or eaten the tiniest finger; the knowledge that we have acted as our master would have wished is enough for us.'

I don't know if this story is true or not. It might well have been. The Goro are happy, honest, extremely conscientious people, very friendly and anxious to please – and cannibals. They are not cannibals for any particular reason: human flesh is just part of their diet. Nowadays the administration tries to control this habit, of which they disapprove strongly; but doings in the forest are difficult to observe, and it is generally only a quarrel which drives a man to be a tale-bearer. Even so there are a good number of convictions every year.

I have never been able to understand why so much pother is made about cannibalism; it is a somewhat barbarous custom, true, but less so than so many European ones; compared with the trades which inevitably produce in those engaged in them painful and lingering diseases it is merciful; and as for modern warfare – 'Look, Sambo, how wasteful white men are. They have killed hundreds of times more than they can possibly eat.'

And yet it quickens and horrifies Western imagination as hardly any other negro custom does. W. Seabrook, with his naïve diabolism, gloats for pages and pages over the subject, telling the shocked reader – oh, what a *wicked* man he is! – that human flesh looks and tastes like any other meat. The only point of any interest – his feelings while he was eating – he omits; they were probably chiefly self-satisfaction.

We stopped among the cannibals by accident. We had only meant to stay among them a couple of hours to see their shawl dance, and stopped the night because a funeral was to take place on the morrow. The rest-house looked as if it had not been inhabited since the fateful day many years ago, nor now that there is a good road would it need to be. The village is only a little way off the main road from Bouaflé to Daloa, a little over forty miles from each. I never found out the name of any of the group of villages; our two interpreters, a bright little boy and a professional soldier home for three months' leave, spoke far too indistinctly for me to be able to assemble the mouthful of syllables they tumbled out each time I asked them.

I didn't make the slightest effort to taste human flesh; the only point of interest to me was the question whether, knowing it for what it was, I should be able to swallow it without nausea. I think I could. I am naturally rather morbidly sensitive to unpleasant sights and experiences; in my life I have never been able to kill anything larger than a mouse, and that with difficulty, and I flinch from even a film of a motor accident. But if for any reason it is necessary for me to overcome my disgust reactions I can do so by an effort of will; by contracting my stomach muscles I somehow deaden all emotional reactions, and in that state I can look at and experience almost anything without admitting its significance; blood becomes merely a red viscous fluid, signs and sounds of pain just shapes and noises. This control was very useful to me in Dahomey, where I could never have noted the sacrifices otherwise; and among the Goro it was again very helpful. As for eating a piece of my neighbour, I should almost certainly find it easier than seeing him killed or carved; once when I was in Nauplia in Greece spending the evening with some fishermen a slightly cooked fish's head and one fork were produced; everybody ate a piece in turn, and finally I was presented with the eye, impaled on a single prong of the fork; I was able to get that down, and since then I have always considered that I could swallow anything. That was the bravest moment of my life.

The day before we arrived a hunter had been killed by a wounded she-buffalo – or rather a sorcerer had abandoned him to the beast – and the man had been brought home and was lying in state preparatory to being buried on the morrow. There was no question of eating either the man or the buffalo, for they had both been involved in an 'accident', and were therefore unclean and sources of contagion. Anyhow, I don't think the Goro eat their own tribesmen. The body was placed in an open hut in the centre of the village, a hut with very low eaves which nearly swept the ground; the corpse was lying naked on a heap of all his pagnes, and women were rubbing it with different herbs which were claimed to prevent corruption. But their faith was stronger than their senses; the body stank and the belly was swollen.

For the whole day and the whole night people came from the forest to pay their respects to the dead. They arrived wailing most lugubriously, and as they approached the hut of mourning they took some very rough leaves and rubbed their forearms and their foreheads until all the skin was gone and the flesh raw and bloody. When they arrived opposite the corpse they rubbed anew until the blood dropped freely on to the dead body; in this way the unity of the tribe was reaffirmed. The place looked and smelt like a charnel house; bloody leaves were everywhere, and every man had great raw places on his arms and temples. The near female relations had matted their hair with mud, and painted their faces and bodies grey with it; they never stopped moaning for a minute.

When night fell the constant wailing and the pervading smell of blood were rather unpleasant, but I managed to sleep comfortably; the others, however, didn't close an eye or put the light out; we learned later that had they been unaccompanied their anxiety might have been justified.

Just before dawn the wailing stopped and we were called. The masks were entering the village to receive the soul of the dead man, and the men from twelve villages were gathered to watch them, while the women cowered hiding in their huts. They came in from the forest in an endless procession, so bulky with raffia that they looked like houses walking; they carried bells in their hands to warn women and strangers of their dangerous presence. The masks were half human, half animal, 'fused'; the bird masks had long handles tipped with feathers; they crowded into the hut where the corpse was, almost overflowing it, and bent over the dead man; then in an open space they danced in turns, vaguely panto-miming the animals whose features they wore; when they turned suddenly their raffia flew out like an enormous wheel. When all had danced they returned to the fetish house in the forest and the women came out and started preparing the morning mash of plantains, which is their only vegetable food, wailing all the time. The din was increased by a troop of professional mourners who shrieked like cats; their bodies were daubed with mud and soot.

After the morning meal the burial was proceeded with. The body was wrapped in all its clothes and bound with cord, so that it made a pitifully small and rigid parcel, and was carried in slings by its male relatives to the shallow grave which had been dug in the path leading out of the village, a few yards from the last hut. The man's wives and mother were already standing by the grave, wailing and dancing in a sort of frenzy. The body was lowered and loosened from its bindings and laid on its right side. Then suddenly the first silence we had heard for twenty-four hours fell; the man's empty eating bowl was brought, turned upside down at the head of the grave and tapped three times. The hollow symbolical note was strangely moving. Then the bowl and his weapons – spears, a knife and a bow – were placed beside the dead man, and the near relations, holding a straw in their mouth, said farewell to the corpse through clenched teeth. (I do not know if the straw had any significance, or if it was merely a device to avoid swallowing the infected air.) When the last word had been said two of his brothers seated themselves on the pile of earth at the side of the grave with their backs to the body, and with a few pushes shovelled the earth back. Nothing would mark his grave. Then everybody returned to the marketplace and dancing began. The young men dancers put monkey-fur anklets round their feet and draped themselves in a square piece of cloth like a shawl; ordinarily they wear only loincloths. They dance with the shawl, twirling it as some Spanish women do, so that it describes arabesques in the air; the result is very pleasant to look at. They dance one at a time, and when one has finished two or three others will come forward to lead him back, wiping him with the edge of their cloths. These dances marked the end of the funeral proper; it would be some days before the priests would find out (probably by ordeal) who had doomed the man.

The dances were cut short rather quickly, for there was other business to attend to. An elephant had been killed at the same time as the hunter, and the flesh was to be divided up among all the households (the Goro are still fairly communistic), and the chief had to weigh the demands and rights of each person. The elephant had been speared from a tree, the usual method of killing big animals; it was a broken branch which had been the cause of the hunter's death. The meat was divided into enormous chunks, and the tusks put on one side; these must go to the administration; they could no longer make the wide ivory bracelets which the older men wore. I was offered an elephant's foot, which I believe is a great delicacy; I refused on the ground that I had no pot to cook it in, but really it was because it smelt far too corpse-like for my stomach, which was turning queasy by reaction; for several days the sweet unpleasant smell of putrefaction seemed to spring up under my nose. All I would accept were some elephant's hairs, and those I quickly lost.

The Goro were among the most friendly and cheerful people I came across. They weren't handsome, but the men at any rate weren't so abysmally ugly as the other forest folk, and they were taller and looked healthier. The women looked pretty awful, and the marriage price of two to three thousand francs (the Goro buy their wives and children) seemed unduly high. But where people go nearly naked women are always at a great disadvantage; it is only for such a short time – between puberty and the first child – that a woman's body is at its best; and in a race which marries early and doesn't know of massage and bandages or birth control this is sometimes a matter of months; and to the European eye the bruised and pendulous dugs and the loose belly are inevitably repugnant. Moreover, the firmer and more architectural male body gains by the way of life which spoils the female; the constant effort develops the muscles harmoniously, and except in a few races where the legs are disproportionately short the men are usually aesthetically satisfactory, if not distinguished. Only people blinded by sexual desire could claim that under 'natural conditions' women's beauty could even be compared with men's; but possibly under urban conditions the sedentary or specialised habits of men, and their comparative lack of attention to their bodies, might reverse the situation, were the population suddenly to be struck naked.

The Goro men file the front teeth of the upper jaw to points – I should have imagined an almost intolerably painful process; and both sexes dress the hair in the most arbitrary and fanciful fashions. They seem to look on the hairy head as a material for sculpture; they will shave all sorts of designs and patterns in it – stars and crescents, birds and fishes, and just meaningless patterns; or sometimes they will leave them in relief, while the rest of the head is shaved. Some had the back half of the head shaved; the hairs growing along the ridge had been allowed to lengthen and had been trained into a series of peaks like a halo; besides other conceits too various to mention. The few that had beards treated them in a similar decorative and unsuitable fashion.

Even had I wanted to stop longer among the Goro the others would not have let me, for they were frankly scared, so in the afternoon we set out for Daloa, to have the car greased and the oil changed. Daloa was a large and comfortable, but fairly uninteresting town, still beflagged from the recent visit of the Governor of the Ivory Coast. I was unfortunate in missing the Governor on several occasions by a few hours; everyone agreed that he would have been sympathetic with the objects of our journey, and would have given us assistance. Indeed, the highly placed officials I came in contact with always assumed a polite interest; but I met only one man, and he was a sub-administrator, who showed any knowledge of the people he was living among.

We went slowly from Daloa to Man, stopping at different places to see the dances and to try to buy masks. Unfortunately we had so little room in the car that we were able to take very little; from almost every point of view it would be better to travel with a small lorry. We wanted to arrive at Man for the fourteenth of July; on that date all the local dancers are assembled in the principal town of the district, and those of Man had an enormous reputation since they had visited the Colonial Exhibition.

Almost as soon as we arrived we wished we hadn't. The administrator P was a retired soldier, thin-lipped and with cold, blue eyes, disagreeably courteous; he talked to me like a barrister trying to trip up a witness, metaphorically beginning every sentence with 'I allege . . . ' After a lot of palaver he gave us one small room in the guest-house, and refused to supply us with water or have the latrines emptied; everywhere else this had been done automatically for us by the prisoners. The rest of the officials took their tone from the administrator, but whereas he had a certain control and harsh dignity, they were merely sneaks and bullies, guttersnipes who thought they were gods. We had arrived on the twelfth, as usually festivities last for the better part of a week, and we would probably have left the next day, without seeing any dancing, if it had not been for the great kindness of a young planter G B – no, Georges Bouys: he was so good to us that I should like to thank him by name: I will break my rule of only alluding to casual acquaintances by their initials. He was installed at the other end of the guest-house, with a considerable retinue of wives, servants and children; he helped us out of all our difficulties, and made us as comfortable as we had been anywhere.

Bouys was a creole, the first European baby to be born in French Guinea; his father was an administrator, and he had lived almost all his life in the colonies. He spoke several negro languages more than fluently;

for the negroes he was one of themselves, so well did he understand their mentality and customs. He had a coffee plantation at Kobédana, near Touba, which was beginning to prosper; he was full of a number of plans for making his fortune, most of them rather vague. A sensible government should have been able to make great use of his unparalleled knowledge of negroes and the confidence they had in him; as it was, he was merely slighted and thwarted.

Partly from him, but chiefly through my own observation, I became aware of the reign of terror at Man. If men didn't salute the passage of white men, and women remove their head-cloths, the guards 'tickle them up a bit'. Man is the richest and most populous district of the colony, but the inhabitants are in a pitiable state; few of them have any land, and they have to work on European plantations for fifty centimes a day (the head-tax is twelve francs a year). Men, women and little children have to work on the roads, which are indeed excellent; but it was not pleasant to see small boys aged about six put down big loads of earth while they raised their hands to their heads in a quavering caricature of a salute. Here they actually demand to be allowed to become soldiers – and are refused. So great is the fear of the Europeans that they have completely displaced the other bogies as a menace for quieting unruly children.

I had been formally forbidden to arrange any dances, even the little girls' – 'it would distract them from their work' – and although Bouys gave me some help the outlook was poor. He warned us that on the fourteenth the dances would probably not be up to much; for the negroes were too cowed and their spirit broken by fear and misery. He was right.

Alioune had been unwell for some days, with intermittent attacks of high fever; I had already taken him to a couple of doctors, who had given him sedatives – aspirin and so on – but they had been of little help. They believed, as I had, that negroes were not susceptible to malaria, from which he was actually suffering, as Dr R, to whom I took him, proved. The doctor was very affable and conversational; he had only been in the district for a couple of months and hated it; before he had been in Togoland, where, with an eye on the mandate, doctors were given considerable facilities and money grants; he had had a laboratory and ambulance, and had been able to make colonies for lepers and sufferers from sleeping sickness. Here, with even more illness, he had no facilities at all, not even a hut where invalids could be kept; except for his private microscope he had no apparatus of any sort; he had a totally inadequate selection of drugs and no money. The administrator gave him no help or encouragement. Sleeping sickness, the growing scourge of the neighbourhood, was barely allowed to exist officially.

This gangrene of human misery festered under a landscape of overwhelming beauty and variety. The country was mountainous, just on the edge of the forest; and impenetrable jungle, so thick that it seemed impossible for even an elephant to move in it, was interspersed with park-like plains. There were numerous rivers and waterfalls. Round Danané and the Liberian frontier the virgin forest seemed a fitting setting for the palace of Kubla Khan; the huts, painted with white clay and scrawled with arabesques, looked far more important and solid than they actually were. Except for the depredations of the leopard men and other manifestations of religion, these people had been very happy and prosperous; love was very 'free' with them, marriage meaning little more than the ownership of children.

On the evening of 13 July the official military celebrations commenced with a torchlight procession. Twenty negro soldiers carried reed torches in a hollow square surrounding the military band – drums, cymbals and bugles – which completely drowned the poor tomtoms; in front six people conscientiously rejoiced by numbers, failing to dance to the hybrid noise, and shouting Hurrah! every two minutes. The administrator's orderly led the way and marked the step; at a respectful distance followed his other servants, showing joy with regulated gestures. Four little boys followed the procession questioningly; all the rest of the population stayed indoors. The procession advanced to various points according to schedule, where the soldiers shouted and danced if they could see anyone observing them; otherwise they just waited till the bugle gave the signal to proceed. Every half-hour they stopped outside the residence, so that the sounds of rejoicing could gladden the administrator's kindly heart, and then went out to another quarter. I was very sorry that I had no apparatus to record or photograph this incredible parody.

With unparalleled meanness the national holiday was cut down to three hours in the afternoon; all the morning the forced labour went on, though there was a little rehearsal dancing at the far end of the town. At three o'clock in the afternoon the official celebrations commenced – a greasy pole, a bran tub, bicycle and horse races, superintended by the assistant administrator. In the midst of this the commandant appeared, accompanied by a couple of ladies. He was greeted by a deathly silence. All the negroes turned their backs, and while he walked the length of the marketplace and back not a sound could be heard from the thousands of negroes present. It was an effective protest, but extremely embarrassing.

After this all the Europeans and many of the negroes surrounded the Danané dancers, who were being sent down to Abidjan for the consecration of the new capital at the end of the month. Georges Bouys and I gave some money to the dancers, the usual practice, and shamed the administrator into sending his wife into the house to fetch some notes to give in his turn; he had obviously had no intention of doing so.

While this dance was going on the most unpleasant incident of the journey occurred. Benga and I had taken up places on opposite sides of the circle, to try to get different photos; and shortly after the dances had started the doctor, accompanied by the lesser administrative fry – the assistant administrator, the agriculturist, the special officer – pushed their way into the circle past Benga, shoving him aside somewhat roughly. They had all very obviously been drinking the fatherland's health much too copiously for the climate. Benga started to protest, and was cut short by the doctor saying, 'I shall push you out of my way like any other nigger', and when he continued to argue the special officer sent for the police. Luckily the administrator had seen all that was going on – I had not, for I was watching the dancers – and called Benga over to him, saying very kindly, 'You can get as good photographs here', and during the performance nodded and smiled at us both in an embarrassed and encouraging fashion. When the dances were finished Benga came over to me, still furious, and started explaining what had happened, gesticulating rather violently. The doctor came up and said pompously, 'Dear sir, please order your *servant* not to point at me and insult me in this fashion,' and held out his hand. He knew perfectly well what he was saying, and fully realised that Benga was my companion. I was in an awkward position, for I didn't want to be involved in the quarrel, and yet could obviously not avoid it. I ignored his proffered hand and replied that fortunately Benga was not my servant but my companion, and was capable of looking after himself: fortunately, for if he had been my servant he would also have been my representative, and his quarrel would have been mine. I think the incident might have ended there, if the small fry hadn't started insulting Benga; either they thought the quarrel their own, or they enjoyed bullying; but Benga had completely lost control and gave them back as good as he got. I had never realised his powers of vituperation. From insults the lesser fry proceeded to threats, and without my presence a great deal might have happened; but the doctor was sufficiently sober to realise the possible consequences, and took them all to the administrator. The poor man was in an embarrassing position; he had seen enough to know that the tales of Benga's murderous intentions, and what other complaints they made, were fantasies, and yet for the sake of prestige he couldn't altogether ignore them. After, I imagine, a fairly straight talk, he sent all the small fry back to their bungalows, keeping only the doctor with him, and then sent a soldier to fetch us to him. The whole population was watching, and the soldier whispered to Benga as he conducted us in, 'Bonne chance, frère.' The administrator opened the proceedings with a long and flowery 'entente cordiale' speech addressed to me, going over the history of the last few centuries of the nations; coming down to the present day, he said no tiny incident must disturb the fraternal love of two countries so allied by common ties, and put into the astonished doctor's mouth the explanation that he had only acted as anyone did in a crowd anywhere, without the slightest intention of offence. Benga was still very angry, and blustered a good deal before I could persuade him to make a sort of apology; I think he wanted to become a test case. But that didn't suit the administrator at all; he told the doctor that the apology was handsome, and made the two shake hands and go away together. Then he started talking to me, metaphorically tying his arms and legs into knots; the whole incident could not have failed to create a bad impression, and he changed from his previous chilly brusqueness to an amiability which must have hurt, offering me every facility and help which could possibly be imagined, putting cars, men and rest-houses in his division at my disposal; at the same time, he said, under ordinary circumstances, he would have put Benga into gaol, right or wrong; discipline must be maintained, and a negro must never defy a European publicly. The fact that he was a citizen, and with some influence in France and at Dakar, was of no importance; here he was a nigger, and would I kindly see that he was circumspect in future. But if we wanted to see dances, we had only to give the word and he would arrange them ... This discourse went on for some time, and I was really rather sorry for the man; but he was quite unable to give me the only thing I wanted, information as to whether there were any roads into French Guinea, and if so were they passable. He was as ignorant as all other administrators about anything outside his circle.

When I finally got away I found the doctor lying in wait for me. He took my arm and explained almost in tears that what had hurt him most was that I had refused to shake his hand, and after we had been so friendly the day before too; he was no negrophobe, far from it, he had had a negress for three years to whom he was devoted; but there was a difference in the races, wasn't there? No one could deny that, least of all an Englishman. And there was no ill-feeling now, was there? Would I take his hand as a sign that all was forgiven and forgotten? I would; but the maudlin outpouring continued for some time. We arrived opposite the crestfallen lesser fry and the doctor suddenly kissed me on both cheeks and asked after Alioune. 'Stuff him up with quinine, man; stuff him up with quinine,' he shouted. I buttered him up about medicine for a bit and then got away.

We were the heroes of the hour. The negroes crowded round Benga to see the member of their race who had discomfited their bullies. Such an event was unprecedented; they began to hope again. The person who suffered most was poor Bouys, who was upbraided for consorting with cads and bounders. He had stood by Benga nobly.

Our departure the next morning was delayed by another long speech from the administrator; if we were in any need of help, we had only to telegraph him and he would send to us at once. A fine newly killed leopard was brought in while we were talking, and I was offered half of it; but the proposal was not concrete enough for me to have to refuse. Game is said to be very plentiful round Man, leopards and elephants and pigmy hippos; leopards had even been killed in the rest-house, before the scrub surrounding it had been cleared away.

We bought petrol and supplies from the old Senegalese storekeeper, who had sponsored Seabrook when he was there; he told us some interesting stories.

We set out rather late over the bad mountainous road. When we got over the crest the landscape and temperature suddenly changed completely; in a quarter of an hour we passed from the moist forest to the dry and parched savannah. Practically no rain had fallen and the countryside was bare, and scorching hot.

This sudden change of temperature had disastrous results; in twenty miles three tyres burst; on the last occasion the whole wheel came off, but luckily we were in a level place and no damage was done. The tyres were already somewhat worn, and the sudden heat appeared to make them burst to pieces. It wasn't a question of single tears; both the outer cases and the inner tubes split into ribbons. The chauffeurs patched them with extraordinary dexterity, but we could only limp along; our intention of returning through Guinea, if there were any roads (we never found out), was obviously unrealisable; we should be lucky to arrive at a town where we could re-equip ourselves. The splendid roads of the forest had given place to ill-kept rutted tracks; the only pleasant feature of the landscape was the great variety of monkeys. At Touba we found that the official normally resident there was away; there was no store, no garage where we could have repairs done. We stopped there a little while to see the dancing, and then set off for Odienné. We had three more punctures, so that we hadn't a single whole tyre; we travelled practically on faith, string and adhesive tape. Long after nightfall we arrived at Odienné, and roused the administrator, who sent a guide to show us the splendid rest-house at the other end of the town. Our position was so hopeless, that it appeared quite funny; it seemed as though we should never be able to move again. While we were eating our biscuits and sardines I heard a tomtom; a youth who had sprung up from nowhere in particular volunteered to guide me to the dancing, and we set off through the town. He told me proudly that he was a Catholic, as were most of the inhabitants; there were very few pagans left.

The dancing, when we came to it, was very peculiar; in a barn lit by acetylene torches couples were slowly and solemnly jazzing in a circle to the music of a concertina and drums. Both men and women were present, but on the whole members of the same sex danced together. They were all in European dress and shod, and a number of the boys looked as if they had dipped their heads in flour. They squeaked at one another in French falsetto. I was flabbergasted; it was as if Berlin of the bad old days had undergone an even stranger transformation than the putting of such *mädchen* into uniform. I had just heard of Röhm's death, which probably suggested the comparison. After a little while I discovered I was very tired and went home. On the morrow my guide turned up with his face and neck snow white.

In the morning things seemed gloomier, if possible, than the night before; not only was there no garage, there was not even any petrol for sale. I ransacked my boxes for sticky substances, and produced some adhesive tape and Elastoplast; with the aid of these the chauffeurs set about making four usable tyres out of the remnants of the original six. Meanwhile I went to see the administrator, to try to get some information about roads (which, of course, he didn't possess) and to buy a case of petrol from him. He was an enormous man, fat and bearded, and seemed very kind and genial. He was sorry for my predicament, but couldn't help me at all; but hearing we were interested in dances he sent half a dozen troupes, which had gathered for the fourteenth, to the rest-house, so that we could see the extraordinary virtuosity of his district.

All the morning the chauffeurs patched the tyres, while we watched the dances and prepared a big meal, for we had only eaten scraps for thirty-six hours, and were quite uncertain when we should eat again. I happened to remark, in the presence of the old guardian who was helping us, that the administrator seemed a good sort; whereupon the old man – he must have been over sixty – clapped his hand over his mouth and ran away. Later on he explained why he had acted so. He had been told to report to the sergeant if anything was spoiled in the rest-house, and so, when a blind went out of order, he did as he was told. The sergeant claimed that it was none of his business, and in a fury led the old man before the administrator who, without listening to any explanation, ordered the old man to be beaten up, which was done so thoroughly that a couple of his teeth were knocked out. Apparently his attitude was you-let-me-alone-and-I'll-let-you-alone, for the dancing went on very late, and the people beside the rotten roads seemed friendly and not at all scared. He was in charge of one of the biggest and poorest districts in French West Africa; there was literally not a ha'penny to be got out of the place, and the tax of eight francs a head (on all people over two years old) can be paid only by the men seeking work elsewhere. If the taxes were not paid punctually the treatment was very harsh. It seems as though the administrator had given too much power to his negro assistants, for no one could have been nicer to me than he was.

In the early afternoon we set out in the hope of reaching Bougouni by nightfall, where we intended buying petrol. The change of climate had made me feel rather seedy, and I dozed off after sunset. We got to Bougouni about seven, and Fodé and Benga had the brilliant idea of going straight on to Bamako while the going was good, so as to save time and spare the tyres the heat of a second day. Benga pooh-poohed Alioune's remark that we hadn't enough petrol: our luck had held so far, it would hold out to the end. I slept soundly through one puncture, but woke up a little after one to find that Fodé had embogged us in a pothole at the side of the road. It took us more than an hour to get the car out, but with the aid of the pieces of corrugated iron, which till then we had carted about uselessly, and by scraping the mud away with our hands we finally succeeded and the car lolloped along for a little while longer, when the petrol ran out, about fifteen miles from Bamako. As far as I was concerned the chief inconvenience was the mosquitoes, but the others were frightened of wild beasts springing on us in the dark, for the batteries were nearly down. I didn't very much believe there was such a person as the hyena; after all, we'd never seen one. We were among bare fields and there was no wood to be found for a fire. The night passed quietly enough; nothing came to disturb the insects. We looked very grimy and stupid by the light of the dawn; a car might pass from which we could beg some petrol; on the other hand we might stop there, on and off, for days and days without anyone passing. Fodé and Benga, who were the immediate cause of our plight, set out to walk to Bamako, while Alioune and I waited by the car to watch it and hope for a passing lorry. About nine o'clock a battered old Ford chock-full of petrol arrived from Bamako; but the negro who was driving it had received his orders, and neither bribery nor pity would make him give up a pint of his master's gasoline. We waited a couple of hours, while the tyres sagged under us, and a little before midday a lorry came up and sold us a tin; moreover, the driver gave us some bread, for which we were almost more thankful. We drove off and went nearly ten miles before the tyres fell to pieces; while we were tying them together Benga and Fodé came along in a car. They had walked the fifteen miles without meeting a soul except the conscientious negro – the end of the journey on their bare feet, for their boots had fallen to pieces; they had been held up nearly an hour waiting for the ferry across the Niger. In the early afternoon we stumbled into the Hôtel du Niger, and let ourselves be cozened by the kind proprietor; we were dead beat.

The next morning I set about the heartbreaking task of trying to discover if any of the three roads to Dakar were open; I was sent from government office to government office; from trader to trader, getting contradictory but generally unfavourable information. At the last bureau I went to I came across the young administrator who had been so kind to me our first night at Kaffrine; he had been interested in the negroes, so he had been changed over to office work in a big town where he would see only Europeans. He remembered me and had the practical idea of phoning up the key points on the roads; he learned that one river had overflowed suddenly and carried away all its bridges, making every route impassable; I was distressed, for it meant an extra expense of fifty pounds, which I could ill afford, as well as waiting three days in Bamako for the weekly train. I chatted with the administrator for some time, and just as I was leaving he called out, 'Bon voyage. Now I suppose you'll go home and write another book of lies about Africa.'

I didn't then know if I should succumb to the temptation; after all, I had been to Russia in the earlies and had been strongminded enough not to publish a single word about it; but I then vowed that if I should fall, I would write, if not the whole truth, at least the truth and nothing but the truth. To the best of my knowledge I have kept my vow; I have not consciously written a single sentence which is not justified either by my memory (obviously subjective), my notes, or my often imperfect sources of information; I may be guilty of bad taste, ingratitude and exhibitionism; but to the best of my belief neither of misrepresentation nor romancing.

The story of my journey really ends here. I made the horribly long and tedious train journey alone, for Benga insisted on travelling third class for the sake of economy, and would not let me do so; the reaction had made me rather weak and the climate and unpalatable food absurdly thin. At Dakar I found over two months' correspondence, links with another world, waiting for me. The boat on which I had booked my passage had been cancelled, and since Benga had to stay some time in Dakar I decided to leave by the next boat sailing, the *Brazza*. Since I should be travelling alone I spent what money was left to me transferring from third to first class, in the hope that the extra comfort and better food would make me look less of a scarecrow before I regained my family. The cabins were extremely comfortable and the food good; but first-class life on board was so hedged about with pretensions and restrictions that the extra comfort was hardly won. For its size the *Brazza* must surely be the slowest boat on the Atlantic; it could just do eleven knots all out, and a night's contrary wind set it back thirty-six hours on its schedule. After the short stop at Madeira – that paradisiac version of Cheltenham, with its resident retired colonels and old maids, and its native population divided into the overlapping categories of touts, pimps and whores – I had plenty of light reading. Occasionally I was bullied into taking part in various gambling and/or futile deck 'sports', and I played a little atrocious bridge – anyhow, I think plafond the worst of the whist games – with various functionaries. Dr 'L-F. Céline' has so well described the atmosphere of a colonial boat in his *Voyage au Bout de la Nuit* that it would be useless to try to improve on him, and otiose to repeat him; I, too, was, as far as I know, the only passenger paying his fare, at any rate in the first class; nearly all the others were functionaries or military people returning home on leave. There were a few merchants, among others the president of the Société des Batignolles, who was returning from the successful opening of the Congo–Océan railway which his firm had built. The people were, on the whole, nice to me, but I felt uncomfortable; I had been out of contact with the European ruling classes for three months and I had forgotten how unpleasant they were – self-satisfied, stupid, purse-proud, rude, heartless and hypocritical. And almost unbearably ugly. It was some months before my eyes got used again to the absurdly fussy and compli-cated European clothes, and the sharp features and lank hair of their wearers; even today, though some people seem to me breathtakingly lovely, the majority are still offensive to my eyes.

The journey was enlivened by the boat ramming an Italian trawler off the coast of Spain, one foggy night; a few plates were taken off the bows, but otherwise no harm was done; all the rich people gathered on the deck in their lifebelts, clutching their jewel-boxes; the poor and lazy like myself stayed in their cabins. So that I should experience every thrill of which modern transport is capable, the engine of the train from Bordeaux to Paris caught fire; but there again it was only an alarm.

I thought a great deal about the negroes during the lazy days on the boat; on the whole I had enjoyed myself very much among them. Although mad they were most of them on a level on which I could meet them and sympathise with them. I can get on with very simple people or with very civilised ones; it is with the intermediate classes that my difficulties arise. What was their future likely to be? For at least a century they must almost certainly be under the guidance of foreigners, until they have learned a common language, a common purpose and civic morality. A free Africa is today an unrealisable dream, whatever changes the misfortunes of war may bring. The ideal guidance would obviously be international and disinterested, developing the negro until he can give the Western world the riches of his country, and receive from it the benefits that Western science could give him. But most probably short-sighted greed and folly will continue their present rake's progress, until in the greater part of Africa the negro will become extinct, as the Zulus are already said to have become; in one or two places, such as the Gold Coast and Nigeria, they may linger in reserves; but all the signs point to the African negro following the Red Indian as the vanishing race. It seems to me a pity.

Afterword to the first paperback edition

I T IS A CHASTENING and, in some ways, humiliating experience to re-read a book one has written ten years before. So much is crude, so much might be better written or better expressed, so many other things might have been said.

Some portions of this book, however, still seem to me to have validity. The account of the French colonial system as it existed in 1934 still seems to me essentially correct; and it is to be hoped that one of the good results of the renovation of France will be a renovation of this system.

I am still convinced that the greater part of Africa will have to be under alien tutelage for several years, until the wrecked tribal cultures, now destroyed for ever, can be replaced by larger and more modern societies. I am also convinced that if this tutelage is not to be entirely destructive it is essential that the civil servants, who must administer it, are so well rewarded in money and prestige that some of the most capable people of each generation may be attracted to an ingrate career. It is too late to argue the rights and wrongs of imperialism; the lives of most of the inhabitants of Africa and Asia have been irremediably disrupted, their earlier local stone-age or bronze-age economies enmeshed in the world economy of light metals and plastics, their values and their habitual ways destroyed, if by nothing else, by modern communications.

We are responsible for this destruction, and often for increased misery, poverty and disease; in too few instances have we made it possible for the natives to construct a new society which will fit into the world of air travel, or supplied them with the science which can rid their lives of the earlier menaces of pestilence and famine. Until this is done, it would be cowardly and hypocritical to abandon them, uprooted and unprepared, disorganised and untrained as they must inevitably be.

'Political independence' sounds well in speeches made thousands of miles away; but it is a mockery and a farce for peoples whose economy is chaotic, and is too often an excuse for continued economic exploitation without the expense and moral responsibility that actual government entails. At the same time colonial government produces vested interests, just as does any other profession; we should question, as interested statements, continuous claims of the political immaturity of non-European peoples. It should not tax human ingenuity too much to produce a timetable of the various stages of development for each area, and the gradual transfer of power. Colonies which did not keep abreast of their schedule would demand special and disinterested investigation.

The journey described in this book turned me into a more or less professional anthropologist, for it left me deeply conscious of my incapacity to understand much of what I had witnessed. There are many generalisations about primitives in these pages which I would now indignantly repudiate; I was far too much under the influence of Lévy-Bruhl and his concept of 'primitive mentality'. I think some anthropologists go too much the other way in ascribing to every African negro or South Sea Islander the realism of Bayswater or Birmingham; but in the greater part of their lives African Negroes are much more sensible than I have described them here.

Many people who have read this book have asked me what subsequently happened to Féral Benga. He returned to Paris without his ballet troupe in 1935, and continued dancing there and in New York and London till 1939. The war interrupted very hopeful negotiations with an impresario to gather the most noteworthy of the dancers we had seen. In 1939 he was mobilised with his age-group, spent the winter and spring on the Maginot Line, and survived the débacle of 1940 without being either wounded or taken prisoner. Such news as I have had of him since then has come indirectly. Under the German occupation he was not allowed to dance; he was earning such a living as he could, and at the last news I had in late 1941 he was about to marry a girl from Martinique. His father's sister had refused to sanction his marriage with her daughter. By Wolof tribal law this was the girl he was bound to marry; but, as a devout

Catholic, his aunt preferred the tenets of her Church, as she understood them, to the customs of her ancestors. This, in miniature, is an example of the way in which, at every level, European influence has transformed African life. We may wish to disown it, may be assured that the Africans would be happier had it never occurred. But we cannot turn time back. We cannot disown the past. By using our knowledge of the past, and our study of the present, we can hope to control the future; and in greater knowledge, greater self-consciousness, and greater consciousness of the immediate and remote results of our actions, lies our best hope that the future will be nearer our aspirations.

Washington, DC
GEOFFREY GORER
August, 1944

About the Author

Africa Dances, which was first published by Faber and Faber in 1935, was pivotal to the life and career of Geoffrey Gorer. Born in London in 1905, he was educated at Charterhouse and at Jesus College, broken by an interlude at the Sorbonne from 1922–3. He graduated from Cambridge in 1927 with a degree in classics and modern languages. Over the next six years Geoffrey directed his precocious talents into creative writing, producing a picaresque novel, a number of unperformed plays as well as an impressive body of correspondence with such leading literary figures as Edith Sitwell and W. H. Auden. His first published work, *The Revolutionary Ideas of the Marquis de Sade,* came out in 1934. In this same bouyant year he made a first visit to Morocco and returning via Paris, stopped off for a few days with his friend, Pavel Tchelitchew. As the Introductory chapter relates, a chance conversation with Tchelitchew's friend Féral Benga led directly to Gorer joining him on a three-month trip across West Africa, the basis of *Africa Dances.*

The book was a very considerable critical and financial success. As Cecil Roberts wrote in the *Daily Telegraph,* 'He has made one of the most singular journeys of modern times, and he has given us a book which opens a window on a world that most of us hardly realise exists . . . There are no reservations in this astonishing book. Sex, religion, politics, the negro conception of life contrasted with the white man's, the place of fetish and magic, wrestling, dancing and marriage . . . a book I could not put down from the first page to the last.' It was also one of the most searing criticisms of the bleak reality of French colonialism to have ever been published. Although Geoffrey Gorer, with the manners of his class, would later try to deprecate this work, he always acknowledged the great effect which it had on his career. The success of *Africa Dances* provided him with willing publishers and in quick succession he wrote *Bali and Angkor*, *Hot Strip Tease* and a satirical novel, *Nobody Talks Politics*.

Africa Dances also brought him to the attention of a number of leading anthropologists, in particular Margaret Mead of the American National Museum of Natural History, Ruth Benedict of Columbia University and John Dollard of Yale University, who began to take an active interest in his career. In 1935–6 they educated him in the methodology and theoretical background of their discipline. At the end of 1936 he landed in India, where another fan of *Africa Dances*, Major Morris of the Gurkha Rifles, used his influence with the Maharajah of Sikkim to enable Geoffrey Gorer to study a totally isolated Himalayan people, the Lepchas. Having acclimatised and studied their language he would live in the village of Zongu during March, April and May 1937 and turn the experience into one of the classic studies of anthropology, *Himalayan Village*. Unfortunately it was to be his last major field trip, for he contracted a rare tropical disease – sprue – as well as fracturing his backbone in a bad rock fall.

During the Second World War he worked for the British Embassy in Washington advising them on propaganda issues as well as studying behaviourism under Clark Hull at Yale. He combined both interests in his study of *Japanese Character Structure and Propaganda* (1941), which in the author's own words had 'a quite fantastic circulation and influence'. Later he collaborated on a book-length study of a schizophrenic youth, *Tom Malden*, and undertook further investigations of national character: *The Americans* (1948) followed by *The People of Russia* – produced in collaboration with a psychologist, John Rickman.

In 1950 he returned to England and bought a small seventeenth century manor house near Haywards Heath in Sussex, an elegant sanctum where he wrote three substantial studies of English culture (*Exploring English Culture* (1955), *Death, Grief and Mourning in Contemporary Britain* (1965) and *Sex and Marriage in England Today* (1971)) and a steady stream of reviews and articles. Always professional, liberal and humane, he could also be waspish and self-deprecating. He accused himself of 'sloth', which was probably no more than a code word for the private wealth which removed him from the need to aggressively earn an income from his writing or keep hold of a professional salaried post. In 1976, after his 70th birthday, he stopped writing books though he remained an active correspondent. He became evermore devoted to his garden and died in May 1985 at the age of eighty.

ELAND

61 Exmouth Market, London EC1R 4QL
Tel: 020 7833 0762   Fax: 020 7833 4434
Email: info@travelbooks.co.uk

Eland was started in 1982 to revive great travel books that had fallen
out of print. Although the list has diversified into biography and
fiction, it is united by a quest for the defining spirit of place. These
are books for travellers, readers who aspire to explore the world but
who are also content to travel in their mind. Eland books open out
our understanding of other cultures, interpret the unknown,
reveal different environments as well as celebrating the
humour and occasional horrors of travel.

All our books are printed on fine, pliable, cream-coloured paper.
Most are still gathered in sections by our printer and sewn as well
as glued, almost unheard of for a paperback book these days.
This gives larger margins in the gutter, as well as
making the books stronger.

We take immense trouble to select only the most readable books
and therefore many readers collect the entire series. If you
haven't liked an Eland title, please send it back to us saying
why you disliked it and we will refund the purchase price.

You will find a very brief description of all our books on the
following pages. Extracts from each and every one of them can be
read on our website, at www.travelbooks.co.uk. If you would
like a free copy of our detailed catalogue, please write
to us at the above address.

ELAND

'One of the best travel lists' WILLIAM DALRYMPLE

Memoirs of a Bengal Civilian
JOHN BEAMES
Sketches of nineteenth-century India painted with the richness of Dickens

A Visit to Don Otavio
SYBILLE BEDFORD
The hell of travel and the Eden of arrival in post-war Mexico

Journey into the Mind's Eye
LESLEY BLANCH
An obssessive love affair with Russia and one particular Russian

The Devil Drives
FAWN BRODIE
Biography of Sir Richard Burton, explorer, linguist and pornographer

Turkish Letters
OGIER DE BUSBEQ
Eyewitness history at its best – Istanbul during the reign of Suleyman the Magnificent

My Early Life
WINSTON CHURCHILL
From North-West Frontier to Boer War by the age of twenty-five

A Square of Sky
JANINA DAVID
A Jewish childhood in the Warsaw Ghetto and hiding from the Nazis

Chantemesle
ROBIN FEDDEN
A lyrical evocation of childhood in Normandy

Viva Mexico!
CHARLES FLANDREAU
A journey amongst the Mexican people

Travels with Myself and Another
MARTHA GELLHORN
Five journeys from hell by a great war correspondent

The Weather in Africa
MARTHA GELLHORN
Three novellas set among the white settlers of East Africa

Walled Gardens
ANNABEL GOFF
An Anglo-Irish childhood

Africa Dances
GEOFFREY GORER
The magic of indigenous culture and the banality of colonisation

Cinema Eden
JUAN GOYTISOLO
Essays from the Muslim Mediterranean

A State of Fear
ANDREW GRAHAM-YOOLL
A journalist witnesses Argentina's nightmare in the 1970s

Warriors
GERALD HANLEY
Life and death among the Somalis

Morocco That Was
WALTER HARRIS
All the cruelty, fascination and humour of a pre-modern kingdom

Far Away and Long Ago
W. H. HUDSON
A childhood in Argentina

Holding On
MERVYN JONES
One family and one street in London's East End: 1880–1960